MASTERING ARTISAN ITALIAN GELATO

Recipes and Techniques

Gary J. Mihalik

ArtisanItalianGelato.com

Copyright © 2023 by Gary J. Mihalik

All rights reserved. Published in the United States of America. No part of this book may be reproduced or transmitted in any form or by any means, graphic, electronic or mechanical, including photocopying, recording, taping or by any information storage or retrieval system, without permission in writing from the publisher.

This edition published by Highpoint Life Books
For information, write to info@highpointpubs.com.

First Edition

ISBN: 979-8-9862590-8-6

Library of Congress Cataloging-in-Publication Data

Mihalik
Mastering Artisan Italian Gelato: Recipes and Techniques

Summary: "Written for home cooks, gelato enthusiasts, caterers, chefs, and restauranteurs, this beautifully illustrated and definitive artisan gelato recipe and techniques guide provides in-depth coverage of both theory and practice, with 75 recipes." – Provided by publisher.

ISBN: 979-8-9862590-8-6 (Paperback)
1.Cooking 2. Desserts

Library of Congress Control Number: 2023904019

Cover and Interior Design by Sarah M. Clarehart
Front cover photo by Ryan Castillo.
Back cover photo and photos on pages x, 2, 16, 22, 40, 42, 47, 63, 71, 83, 88, 106, 108, 123, 136, 138, 142, 148, 154, 158, 162, and 174 by David A. Lee.
Photos on pages 55, 56, and 105 by the author.

To my maternal grandmother, a legendary cook, who was the subject of so many stories I heard about food and cooking during my childhood.

To my mother, a wonderful cook, who taught me how to cook by telephone when I went away to university.

To my husband, an amazing eater, who has always been supportive of my culinary pursuits and who has eaten the evidence of my experiments.

Contents

Preface vii

Introduction to Gelato xi

PART ONE: Before You Begin: Gelato Ingredients, Equipment, and Process 1

    Chapter 1: Gelato Ingredients 3

    Chapter 2: Basic Equipment for Gelato Production 17

    Chapter 3: The Process of Making Gelato 23

PART TWO: Making Gelato: The Recipes 41

    Chapter 4: Gelato Formulas and Recipes for Component Ingredients 43

        Almond Brittle Gelato (Gelato al Croccante di Mandorle) 46

        Almond Gelato (Gelato alla Mandorla) 47

        Amarena Cherry Gelato (Gelato all'Amarena) 48

        Amaretto Gelato (Gelato all'Amaretto) 49

        Apple Cinnamon Gelato (Gelato alla Mela e Cannella) 50

        Apricot Gelato (Gelato all'Albicocca) 51

        Banana Gelato (Gelato alla Banana) 52

        Banoffi Gelato (Gelato al Banoffi) 53

        Blackberry Gelato (Gelato alla Mora) 54

        Blueberry Gelato (Gelato al Mirtillo) 55

        Bourbon Old Fashioned Gelato (Gelato al Bourbon Old Fashioned) 56

        Brown Butter Pecan Gelato (Gelato al Burro Rosolato e Noci Pecan) 57

        Cannoli Gelato (Gelato ai Cannoli) 58

        Cantaloupe Gelato (Gelato al Melone) 59

        Carrot Cake Gelato (Gelato alla Torta di Carote) 60

        Cheesecake Gelato (Gelato alla Cheesecake) 61

        Cherry Gelato (Gelato alla Ciliegia) 62

        Chocolate Gelato #1 (Gelato al Cioccolato) 63

        Chocolate Gelato #2 (Gelato al Fondente) 64

        Chocolate Peanut Butter Gelato (Gelato al Cioccolato e Burro di Arachidi) 65

        Coconut Gelato (Gelato al Cocco) 66

        Coffee Gelato (Gelato al Caffè) 67

Dark Chocolate & Candied Orange Peel Gelato (Gelato al Cioccolato Extra-Fondente e Scorze d'Arancia Candite) 68
Deglet Noor Date Gelato (Gelato al Dattero di Deglet Noor) 69
Dulce de Leche Gelato (Gelato al Dulce de Leche) 70
Egg Cream Gelato (Gelato alla Crema Pasticcera) 71
Fig Gelato (Gelato ai Fichi Secchi) 72
Fiordilatte Gelato (Gelato al Fiordilatte) 73
Grape Gelato (Gelato all'Uva) 74
Guava Gelato (Gelato alla Guava) 75
Hazelnut Chocolate Gelato (Gelato al Gianduia) 76
Hazelnut Gelato (Gelato alla Nocciola) 77
Hibiscus Gelato (Gelato all'Ibisco) 78
Honey Gelato (Gelato al Miele) 79
Irish Coffee Gelato (Gelato al Caffè Irlandese) 80
Lavender Gelato (Gelato alla Lavanda) 81
Lemon Gelato (Gelato al Limone) 82
Licorice Gelato (Gelato alla Liquirizia) 84
Lime Gelato (Gelato al Lime) 85
Mango Gelato (Gelato al Mango) 86
Maple Pecan Gelato (Gelato all'Acero e Noci Pecan) 87
Maple Rum Raisin Gelato (Gelato all'Acero, Rum e Uvetta) 88
Mascarpone Gelato (Gelato al Mascarpone) 89
Medjool Date Gelato (Gelato al Dattero di Medjool) 90
Milk Chocolate Gelato (Gelato al Cioccolato al Latte) 91
Milk Chocolate Peanut Butter Ripple Gelato (Gelato al Cioccolato al Latte Variegato al Burro di Arachidi) 92
Mint Gelato (Gelato alla Menta) 93
Mixed Berry Gelato (Gelato ai Frutti di Bosco) 94
Mocha Gelato (Gelato al Moccacino) 95
Orange Cream Gelato (Gelato alla Crema di Arancia) 96
Peach Gelato (Gelato alla Pesca) 97
Peanut Butter and Jelly Gelato (Gelato al Burro di Arachidi e Marmellata) 98
Peanut Butter Gelato (Gelato al Burro di Arachidi) 99
Persimmon Gelato (Gelato ai Cachi) 100
Piña Colada Gelato (Gelato alla Piña Colada) 101
Pineapple Gelato (Gelato all'Ananas) 102
Pistachio Gelato (Gelato al Pistacchio) 103
Pomegranate Gelato (Gelato al Melograno) 104

Pumpkin Pie Gelato (Gelato alla Torta di Zucca) 105
Raspberry Gelato (Gelato al Lampone) 106
Rice Pudding Gelato (Gelato al Riso e Vaniglia) 107
Rum Raisin Gelato (Gelato al Malaga) 109
Saffron and Rosewater Gelato (Gelato allo Zafferano e Acqua di Rose) 110
Salted Peanut Gelato (Gelato alle Arachidi Salate) 111
Stracciatella Gelato (Gelato alla Stracciatella) 112
Strawberry Gelato (Gelato alla Fragola) 113
Tamarind Gelato (Gelato al Tamarindo) 114
Tiramisù Gelato (Gelato al Tiramisù) 115
Toasted Coconut Gelato (Gelato al Cocco Tostato) 117
Vanilla Gelato (Gelato alla Vaniglia) 118
Vietnamese Coffee Gelato (Gelato al Caffè Vietnamita) 119
Watermelon Gelato (Gelato all'Anguria) 120
White Chocolate Extra-Virgin Olive Oil Gelato
(Gelato al Cioccolato Bianco e Olio EVO) 121
Zabaione Gelato (Gelato allo Zabaione) 122
Zuppa Inglese Gelato (Gelato alla Zuppa Inglese) 123

Component Ingredients 124
Apple Puree 124
Brown Butter 124
Candied Orange Peel 125
Croccante 126
Espresso 126
Hibiscus Infusion 126
Peanut Butter Sauce 127
Raisins in Syrup 127
Strawberry Sauce 127
Toasted Coconut Milk 127
Toasted Nuts 128
Vietnamese Coffee 128

Chapter 5: Troubleshooting: What Happened to My Gelato? 131

PART THREE: Pro Tips: The Science of Gelato 137

Chapter 6: The Texture of Gelato 139

Chapter 7: Freezing Point Depression 143

Chapter 8: Emulsifiers and Stabilizers 149

Chapter 9: Sweetening Power 155

Chapter 10: Scoopability 159

Chapter 11: Creating Gelato Formulas 163

Chapter 12: Adjusting PAC and POD 175

APPENDICES 183

Appendix A: Gelato Worksheets 184

Appendix B: Ingredient Composition 188

Appendix C: PAC Table 193

Appendix D: POD Tables 194

Appendix E: Pasteurization Tables 195

Appendix F: Glossary 196

Appendix G: References and Resources 201

Index 203

Preface

I started making gelato several decades ago (the Gelato al Croccante formula in this book is the current version of the first gelato I ever made, and one that I made many times in those early years). I refined my gelato-making skills while studying in the master's program at the *Istituto Culinario Italiano* (the Italian Culinary Institute). The Institute is located in the town of Stalettì on the Ionian coast of Calabria.

After completing the master's program, I went back to the Institute a number of times and assisted in teaching courses. Primary among them was the week-long gelato course.

Students who take the gelato course come from all around the world. By the end of the week, they know how to make gelato, and more important, they know how to create a gelato formula using the Italian method. My experience teaching this course is reflected in this book.

Several years after completing the master's program, I spent a week working side by side with Mirko Tognetti, the owner and *gelatiere*[1] of Cremeria Opera in Lucca. Mirko is a founding member of *Compagnia Gelatieri: Narratori di Gelato* (Association of Gelato Makers: Narrators of Gelato), a group dedicated to furthering artisan Italian gelato. In 2015, two years after opening, Cremeria Opera was rated as one of the top gelato shops in Italy by *Gambero Rosso* magazine.

Of course, I have eaten gelato throughout Italy, which is a learning experience in itself!

Why I Wrote This Book

I decided to write this book because my searches to find a good reference book in English on artisan Italian gelato always came up lacking. While numerous books on gelato are published in English, I have never found one that provides the information needed to create artisan Italian gelato the way it is done in Italy.

Many books offer gelato recipes, but few of the recipes would be acceptable to a gelato master because they are not balanced. That is, they do not contain the correct proportion of components that Italian *gelatieri* insist on when creating gelato formulas. This is perhaps the biggest failing of any book that purports to provide recipes for gelato. While there is a lot of room for varying the proportions of ingredients in ice cream, the requirements for what makes a frozen dessert truly gelato are clearly defined.

By definition, artisan Italian gelato is never produced at industrial scale. While a gelatician might make gelato for multiple venues — for example, for one or more gelato shops,

---

[1] A *gelatiere* (plural *gelatieri*) is an "artist" who creates gelato formulas and makes gelato. A *gelataio* is a technician who makes gelato from existing formulas or simply someone who sells gelato.

restaurants, and catering events — the production of artisan Italian gelato is always a local process.

Goals of This Book

In this book, I aim to achieve five goals:

1. Provide balanced and tested gelato formulas that will withstand scrutiny by any gelato professional in Italy.
2. Teach the process for creating and balancing gelato formulas using the Italian method.
3. Introduce the basic science related to gelato, providing sufficient information to understand how to achieve perfect gelato.
4. Describe the process for small-scale artisan gelato production aimed at anyone who wants to make up to a few batches of gelato per day. This includes but is not limited to home cooks, gelato enthusiasts, caterers, chefs, and restauranteurs.
5. Describe the process for commercial-scale artisan gelato production aimed at individuals who want to make many, and typically larger, batches of gelato per day. This includes individuals who own (or want to own) a gelateria or prepare gelato for local distribution, such as to restaurants.

How This Book Is Organized

> The only countries that have not adopted the metric system are Myanmar, Liberia, and the United States. I work exclusively in the metric system for gelato. Among other reasons, it makes it easier to discuss gelato with other gelato makers, almost all of whom use metric. And, while I don't believe the American system of weights is a reasonable alternative to the metric system simply because it is more cumbersome, you could make a reasonable case that measuring temperature in Fahrenheit isn't more difficult than Celsius. For this reason, I include approximate Fahrenheit equivalents throughout this book.

Part One, *Before You Begin: Gelato Ingredients, Equipment, and Process,* provides an essential overview of common gelato ingredients, the equipment you need to produce flawless artisan Italian gelato, and a detailed description of the process for doing so. In this part, I address the essential equipment needed for both small-scale artisan production and commercial-scale artisan production. (By definition, artisan Italian gelato cannot be made at industrial scale.) Because many production steps are consistent from one gelato to another, this part contains the most detailed description of the gelato-making process. Each recipe contains a brief set of instructions, knowing that the detail for the entire production process is covered in Part One.

Part Two, *Making Gelato: The Recipes,* is the heart of the book. This part is mainly made up of Chapter 4, "Gelato Formulas and Recipes for Component Ingredients," which includes 75 artisan gelato formulas listed alphabetically according to their English names. The instructions for making each gelato address small-scale production, just the way I teach the process in Italy. Even commercial-scale gelato operations use small-scale production methods when developing new flavors of gelato. (All the information needed to "upscale" the process to commercial production can be found in Chapter 3, "The Process of Making Gelato.") The formulas and instructions provided in Chapters 3 and 4 will give you everything you need to make wonderful gelato. You can dip in anywhere and you will be making true artisan Italian gelato on your first attempt. Chapter 4 ends with instructions on making component ingredients that are needed for some of the *gelati*. (In Italian, gelati is the plural form of gelato.) For example, several gelati use espresso coffee. I have developed a way of getting the flavor from espresso beans without pulling dozens upon dozens of espresso shots. This part also contains Chapter 5, "Troubleshooting: What Happened to My Gelato?", which you can refer to in case one of your creations isn't perfect. There I cover the typical problems encountered in gelato production and provide guidance on avoiding the issues.

Part Three, *Pro Tips: The Science of Gelato,* dives deeper into the science of gelato, providing advanced information and guidance with the goal of making you a gelato master. Many readers of this book may never look at the science part, and that's okay. However, informed by the advanced information in this section, you will be able develop your own perfectly balanced gelato formulas! Of special importance are the sections on creating gelato formulas and adjusting the *potere anticongelante* (PAC), which translates to anti-freezing power in English, as explained in Chapter 7, "Freezing Point Depression," and the *potere dolcificante* (POD), which translates to sweetening power in English, as is covered in Chapter 9, "Sweetening Power."

At the end of the book, you will find several appendices containing resources and tables to assist you in developing your own gelato formulas. I recommend that you first familiarize yourself with the basics in Part One before following the recipes in Part Two. Then, after you've become a bit more experienced, you can dive in anywhere for beautiful and delicious results!

I know you're ready for a big, delicious artisan gelato payoff, and here's where you start. This book will enable you to make true artisan Italian gelato rivaling the best in Italy. It provides a solid foundation to understand the basic science behind gelato, how to create and balance gelato formulas, and how to produce gelato at artisan scale. Enjoy your artisan gelato journey!

Introduction to Gelato

I am frequently asked to describe the difference between gelato and ice cream.

I have struggled with finding an answer that truly captures the essence of the difference.

At a practical level, I use the word "gelato" for the Italian product and "ice cream" for the non-Italian product. An Italian-English dictionary would have you believe that ice cream is the English word for gelato, and gelato the Italian word for ice cream. The reality is not so simple. Gelato and ice cream are both frozen, dairy-based sweets, so using the terms interchangeably in casual translation is understandable. But this ignores the reality that Italians have expectations for gelato that Americans do not have for ice cream, and when non-Italian speakers use the word "gelato," they almost certainly mean the Italian product, which we all agree is truly different from ice cream.

When the word "gelato" appears in this book, it refers specifically to the Italian-style product and not simply as a translation of ice cream.

But what is the difference between gelato and ice cream?

Some answers I have heard are that gelato has less fat than ice cream or more sugar or less air. While often true, none of these statements holds up to scrutiny. Gelato can have more fat than mass-market "supermarket" ice cream, and it almost certainly has less air. However, the amount of air incorporated into super-premium ice cream is often similar to the amount of air in gelato, but super-premium ice cream typically has more fat than gelato. There is an overlap between the amount of sugar in gelato and in ice cream.

Gelato and ice cream are made from much the same ingredients, as long as we are not referring to industrial ice cream with additives that would never be found in artisan Italian gelato.

Compared to ice cream (as made in the United States and the United Kingdom), gelato is designed to be served at a warmer temperature, approximately –13°C, plus or minus about 1°C (approximately 9°F, plus or minus 2°F). At that temperature, gelato is intended to be smooth, creamy, dense, and somewhat soft. Because gelato is served at a warmer temperature than ice cream, the flavors are often more intense, as cold dulls the sense of taste. To the extent that gelato has less fat than ice cream (which, as I have noted, is often but not always true) flavors will be more intense still, as fat tends to "coat" the taste buds, thereby dulling flavors.

For me, the difference between gelato and ice cream is the sensory experience: the consistency, the texture, the temperature, the appearance, and the intensity of flavor. Creating this sensory experience is dependent on:

1. Using the right amounts of each ingredient in the gelato base (often referred to as "balancing" the gelato).
2. Using good technique in preparing the gelato base.
3. Churning the base quickly to minimize the size of ice crystals.
4. Incorporating only a modest amount of air into the mixture while churning, which usually involves churning at a slower rate than ice cream.
5. Serving the gelato at the ideal temperature.

This book covers everything you need to know to make outstanding gelato and to develop your own gelato formulas, whether you are a home cook, a gelato enthusiast, or a culinary professional. It also provides instructions on how to make 75 different flavors of gelato. If you follow these instructions, you will be able to make true artisan Italian gelato on your first attempt.

Just What Is Artisan Italian Gelato?

Let's start with a definition adopted in January 2012 by Gelatieri per il Gelato, which is a cultural association in Italy:

DEFINIZIONE DI GELATO ARTIGIANALE DI TRADIZIONE ITALIANA

L'alimento Gelato Artigianale di Tradizione Italiana è il risultato ottimale del congelamento e contemporanea agitazione di una miscela di materie prime genuine, naturali, preferibilmente fresche e di ingredienti alimentari di alta qualità, scelti, equilibrati e miscelati sapientemente dal gelatiere artigiano nel suo laboratorio di produzione secondo la propria originalità e creatività.

Il Gelatiere Artigiano è il professionista preparato che conosce le particolari tecniche atte ad equilibrare gli ingredienti per la realizzazione di un prodotto ottimale, conosce le proprietà organolettiche e funzionali sia degli ingredienti di base che di quelli riservati a caratterizzare il gelato, è consapevole della fragilità termica dei suoi prodotti e possiede le competenze necessarie relative alla gestione dei processi produttivi utilizzando macchinari ed attrezzature disponibili per la produzione, di conservazione e di vendita nel migliore dei modi e curando la qualità dei propri prodotti fino al momento del loro consumo.

Qualsiasi prodotto mantenga la struttura e la consistenza propria del gelato ad una temperatura superiore agli zero gradi centigradi non può essere considerato Gelato Artigianale di Tradizione Italiana.

Soltanto mediante la mantecazione a freddo tramite mescolamento e contemporaneo congelamento della miscela si raggiungono la caratteristica consistenza e la morbidezza del prodotto. In tale stato è destinato alla vendita ed al consumo.

> *Il Gelato Artigianale di Tradizione Italiana ha nel nostro paese la sua terra d'elezione dove l'Artigiano Gelatiere trova la sua realizzazione ideale, in particolar modo nell'utilizzo di ingredienti tipici del territorio.*[2]

There is no official translation of this definition. Here is an unofficial one:

DEFINITION OF ARTISAN GELATO IN THE ITALIAN TRADITION

Artisan Gelato in the Italian Tradition is the optimal result of the freezing and simultaneous stirring of a mixture of genuine, natural, preferably fresh, and high-quality raw materials, chosen, balanced, and expertly mixed by the artisan gelato maker in his production laboratory according to his own originality and creativity.

The Artisan Gelato Maker is the trained professional who knows the special techniques suitable to balance the ingredients for the creation of an optimal product, knows the organoleptic [sensory] and functional properties of both the basic ingredients and those reserved to characterize the gelato, is aware of the thermal fragility of his products, and possesses the necessary skills relating to the management of production processes using machinery and equipment available for production, storage and sale in the best possible way, taking care of the quality of his products until the moment of their consumption.

Any product that maintains the structure and consistency of gelato at a temperature above zero degrees centigrade cannot be considered Artisan Gelato in the Italian Tradition.

Only through stirring and simultaneous freezing of the mixture is the characteristic consistency and softness of the product achieved. In this state it is intended for sale and consumption.

Artisan Gelato in the Italian Tradition has in our country its land of choice where the Artisan Gelato Maker finds his ideal achievement, especially using typical local ingredients.

Each sentence of this definition describes important requirements for artisan Italian gelato. I will mention only a few portions for emphasis.

The first paragraph describes the use of "genuine, natural, preferably fresh, and high-quality raw materials." Following this requirement means that many substances, especially chemically produced *emulsifiers* (which modify the interaction of fat and water to improve texture), *stabilizers* (which thicken water thereby improving texture), colorants, and flavorings, are not permitted. There are, however, nonchemically produced products

---

[2] Gelatieri per il Gelato (2012), *Definizione di Gelato Artigianale di Tradizione Italiana.*

that emulsify, stabilize, color, and flavor gelato that would be permitted even under a strict interpretation of this requirement.

Balancing, referred to in the first and second paragraphs, is the foundation of creating gelato that creates the characteristic gelato experience of consistency, texture, temperature, appearance, and intensity of flavor. The Italian method of balancing a gelato formula is essential for creating artisan Italian gelato. Balancing gelato is what reliably differentiates gelato from ice cream. Balancing gelato is addressed in detail in this book.

The third paragraph reads: "Any product that maintains the structure and consistency of gelato at a temperature above zero degrees centigrade cannot be considered Artisan Gelato in the Italian Tradition." This really speaks to the prohibition on using chemical stabilizers. I would argue that referring to "zero degrees" is overly generous. The temperature should be considerably less. If you ever walk into a gelateria and see gelato piled in big mounds in the display case, it is almost certain that you are looking at highly stabilized gelato. The upper half of a display case is significantly warmer than the ideal serving temperature, which is maintained in the lower half of the display case. Any gelato that retains its shape — that is, it does not melt in the upper half of the display case — is most probably overly stabilized, likely involving chemically produced stabilizers.

A Note on Recipes versus Formulas

A recipe contains quantities of ingredients to produce a particular batch size. A formula contains percentages or ratios of ingredients. Professionally, gelato flavors are always developed using a formula model. Gelato software is set up to provide the quantity of each ingredient needed once the desired batch size is entered.

For ease of use, every gelato formula in this book provides the quantity of each ingredient needed to make a 1-kilogram batch of gelato.[3] Consistent with the professional method, each formula also provides the percentage for each ingredient. Upsizing or downsizing the batch size is just a matter of multiplication.

Gelato formulas are unlike baker's percentages. In baker's percentages, the percentage of every ingredient is calculated in comparison to flour. For example, if a bread recipe uses 1000 grams of flour and 500 grams of water, the percentage of water is 50%. If that recipe contains 50 grams of sugar, the sugar percentage is 5%. When using baker's percentages, the baker decides how much flour to use and the other ingredients are calculated as percentages of this amount.

In gelato formulas, the proportions of the ingredients are calculated as a percentage of the total batch size, not in comparison to one of the other ingredients.

---

[3] A kilogram (1000 grams) is equal to 35.3 ounces, which is just about 2.2 pounds. A pound is 454 grams, which is just under half a kilogram.

In Summary

Although made from similar ingredients, the experience of eating gelato is quite different from that of eating ice cream. Gelato is served at a warmer temperature, making it creamier and softer than ice cream. Gelato is often more flavorful than ice cream both because it is warmer than ice cream and because it is relatively low in fat, which can dull the sense of taste. As with many of their iconic foods, Italians are proud and protective of gelato. Several organizations are dedicated to preserving gelato traditions and furthering the craft of artisan Italian gelato.

PART ONE

Before You Begin: Gelato Ingredients, Equipment, and Process

Gelato Ingredients

To make excellent gelato you need to start with excellent ingredients. The most common ingredients used in making gelato are milk; cream; sugars such as sucrose (table sugar), dextrose, and fructose; powdered skim milk; stabilizers (thickeners) such as egg yolk, locust bean gum, and guar gum; salt; and flavoring ingredients such as chocolate and cocoa, fruit and fruit juices, and nut pastes.

Beyond these basic ingredients, gelato may also be made with other dairy ingredients such as cream cheese, mascarpone, and sour cream; various spirits; coffee; extracts and flavorings; and candied or preserved fruits, to name a few.

Following is a review of the common ingredients used in gelato production.

Dairy Products

Without dairy, you wouldn't have gelato. The quality of the dairy products you use is of paramount importance to the quality of the gelato you make. Among the most popular gelato flavors in Italy is *fiordilatte,* which literally translates to "flower of milk." The flavor in fiordilatte comes solely from milk and cream. Gelatieri in Italy, even the excellent ones turning out true artisan gelato, often use ultra-high temperature (UHT) shelf-stable milk. The point is, you don't need to source milk directly from a dairy farm to make great gelato. Buy good-quality dairy products and use them when they are fresh.

The following dairy products are frequently used in gelato production.

Milk

In general, fresh milk is the most abundant ingredient in gelato on a weight basis. Some of the gelato formulas in this book are more than 50% milk. Every recipe includes a pasteurization step, so using pasteurized milk is not necessary. Homogenization, on the other hand, is beneficial for the texture of gelato. This is because the very small fat droplets created by homogenization are better at aggregating to trap air than are larger fat droplets. For more information on this process, see Chapter 6, "The Texture of Gelato," and Chapter 8, "Emulsifiers and Stabilizers."

Regulating fat, sugar, and protein content is important for the texture of gelato. For this reason, I use commercially available milk with its standardized fat, sugar, and protein contents, though I have taught gelato-making to individuals who wanted to make gelato with milk from their own cows.

Milk provides important components to gelato: water, fat (in modest amounts), and nonfat milk solids (abbreviated MSNF for "milk solids non-fat"), which consist of protein and lactose and trace minerals.

I always start gelato recipe development with reduced-fat milk, nominally listed as 2%. In fact, 2% milk is approximately 1.6% fat. Because the fat content of gelato should be between 6% and 12%, you will always need to add another source of fat in addition to milk, even if you use whole milk. This fat often comes from cream, but sometimes it comes from nuts or other products, such as brown butter, which adds fat and also flavor. Using a milk that is low in fat means you can pack more of the flavorful fat into the gelato than would be possible if full-fat milk were used. When adding cream to the gelato, as is usually the case, the tiny bit more cream that is needed because of using reduced-fat milk is of no importance. Because I try not to stock multiple varieties of the same ingredient, I use reduced-fat milk exclusively.

Although it would be possible to make gelato with milk from animals other than cows, such as sheep, goats, or water buffalo, this is an exceedingly uncommon practice. All recipes in this book use cow's milk exclusively.

Cream

The main purpose of adding cream to gelato is to regulate fat content. Fat impacts mouth feel, traps air bubbles to make gelato soft, and contributes flavor both from the fat itself and because fat is a vehicle for many flavor molecules that do not dissolve well in water.

Cream also contributes water and MSNF to gelato, though proportionately less than milk on a weight-for-weight basis. Cream with 36% fat is the highest-fat cream available consistently in the United States, though not so in the United Kingdom, where higher-fat cream (double cream) is common. Because the main purpose of the cream is to add fat, choosing cream with a high fat content provides the biggest latitude for adjusting other ingredients because it adds the smallest volume per unit of fat to the gelato. The cream called for in this book is 36% fat.

Nonfat Powdered Milk

As with fat, milk does not contain enough MSNF to reach the percentage needed to make gelato. The most common source for the additional MSNF is powdered nonfat (skim) milk. Powdered nonfat milk is more than 95% MSNF. The remainder is water and a small amount of fat and minerals.

Except for gelato that contains eggs, the milk protein found in liquid and powdered milk is the predominant emulsifying agent for gelato.

Powdered milk is made by drying milk with heat or by spray drying. Spray drying is the preferred method, as it introduces less of a cooked taste to the milk than heated drying does.

Evaporated Milk

Evaporated milk is not commonly used in the production of artisan Italian gelato in Italy. It is used, though, in countries where access to high-quality dairy products is limited or inconsistent. If the cooked taste of evaporated milk is not of concern, using it would add approximately twice as much fat and nonfat milk solids per volume of milk as would whole milk.

Mascarpone, Cream Cheese, and Ricotta

Mascarpone and cream cheese can replace fat in gelato when their flavors are important to the character of the final product. For example, mascarpone can be used when making tiramisù gelato, and cream cheese can be used for a cheesecake gelato. Ricotta can be used when making a gelato flavor for which ricotta would be in the namesake product, for example, cannoli or cassata. Whole milk ricotta contains about 11% fat, so it would be a partial replacement for milk and cream.

Yogurt and Sour Cream

Yogurt and sour cream are used when the tangy flavor is appropriate for the gelato. I have used yogurt and sour cream at different times when making cheesecake gelato. Unlike mascarpone and cream cheese, however, yogurt and sour cream will curdle the gelato base if heated, so they are added to the cold, mature base just before churning.

> I stabilize most gelato with guar gum and locust bean gum. After heating the gelato base to 85°C (185°F) to fully hydrate the locust bean gum, I usually add cream and then pasteurize at 75°C (167°F) for 15 seconds. Some ingredients, like cream cheese and mascarpone, cannot be heated to 75°C. Low-temperature pasteurization, if the gelato does not contain eggs, is completed at 66°C (151°F) for 30 minutes.

Sugars and Sweeteners

In addition to controlling sweetness, sugars of all types are the major determinants of the serving temperature of gelato. Sugars enhance flavors and, as the main solid ingredient in most gelati, largely control texture.

Sucrose, common table sugar, is the predominant sweetener for gelato. Next in importance are dextrose and fructose. The main reasons for using dextrose and fructose are to get the sweetness and serving temperatures right. As explained in Chapter 7, "Freezing Point Depression," both of these sugars lower the serving temperature of gelato more than sucrose does. However, as explained in Chapter 9, "Sweetening Power," dextrose is not as sweet as sucrose, and fructose is much sweeter than sucrose. When used in combination, two or three sugars enable you to get the desired degree of sweetness and the correct serving temperature. This is often not possible when you use one sugar alone. I avoid the use of glucose syrup and trehalose in this book, but information on both is included in the following sections. All of these sweeteners can be purchased online if they are not available locally.

> Simple sugars like dextrose and fructose are almost twice as powerful as table sugar in lowering the serving temperature of gelato. When gelato includes ingredients that contain these simple sugars, such as dates, grapes, or honey, the quantity needs to be carefully calibrated to produce a gelato that has the correct serving temperature.

Sucrose

The predominant sweetener in gelato is sucrose, that is, table sugar. Made either from sugar cane or sugar beets, the final product is chemically identical. Sucrose is a disaccharide, which means it is composed of two sugar molecules joined together to form a single molecule. One of these molecules is fructose and the other is dextrose. If used alone, sucrose can crystallize when the gelato is frozen. For this reason, you usually will want to add a monosaccharide such as dextrose or fructose to inhibit crystallization.

Dextrose

Scientifically speaking, dextrose is one of two forms of glucose. The other form of glucose is l-glucose (for levorotatory glucose). The word "dextrose" is derived from a combination of the words "dextrorotatory glucose." Levorotatory and dextrorotatory refer to the direction in which the molecules rotate a beam of polarized light. The two forms of glucose are mirror images, but dextrose is the most common form biologically. In a medical context, if we refer to "blood glucose" we really mean "blood dextrose" because dextrose is the form of glucose that is found in humans and other animals. However, gelato makers use the word "glucose" differently (see the "Glucose" section that follows). When reading recipes, other than those in this book, be alert as to what the author means when he or she refers to glucose. Dextrose is a monosaccharide. It is less sweet than sucrose but has a more pronounced effect on lowering the serving temperature of gelato. Adding dextrose to gelato, usually in quantities that are less than 25% of the amount of sucrose in the mixture, reduces the chances of crystallization. Crystallized sugar feels gritty, adversely affecting the texture of the gelato.

Powdered dextrose is readily available by mail order. Be careful not to buy powdered glucose (see the explanation in the "Glucose" section that follows). Dextrose absorbs water. Powdered dextrose contains approximately 8% water. Adding 100 grams of dextrose to gelato means that you are really adding 8 grams of water and 92 grams of sugar.

Fructose

Fructose is another monosaccharide. It has the same effect on serving temperature and inhibiting crystallization of sucrose in frozen gelato that dextrose does, but it is much sweeter than sucrose. The decision to use fructose versus dextrose, then, largely comes down to the effect on sweetness, as each has an equivalent effect on serving temperature. Unlike dextrose, fructose does not contain water.

When a gelato needs to be sweeter and the amount of solids cannot be increased, replacing some of the sucrose with fructose is an option.

Glucose

Common use of the word "glucose" among gelato makers refers to a complex syrup made from the *hydrolysis* (breakdown) of cornstarch or a similar starch. The products of hydrolysis are the monosaccharides dextrose and fructose, the disaccharide maltose, and other even larger sugars called polysaccharides (as they contain more than two sugar molecules). The amounts of each of these components (dextrose, fructose, maltose, and polysaccharides) contained in the glucose syrup depends on manufacturing parameters.

Glucose syrup is often discussed in terms of its "dextrose equivalent" (DE). Glucose syrups typically range between 28 DE and 64 DE. The DE of a particular syrup must be provided by the manufacturer, as there is no practical way to determine it without specialized scientific equipment.

Dextrose, and all monosaccharides, are known as *reducing sugars*. In short, that means they are able to "donate" an electron in certain chemical reactions. The DE refers to the extent to which a given sample is able to donate electrons compared to pure dextrose. The DE of dextrose is 100, so a syrup that is 50 DE means it has 50% of the reducing power of dextrose, i.e., it is capable of donating half as many electrons as an equivalent weight of dextrose. The DE refers only to the solid part of the syrup. If the syrup is 20% water, a common value, that means the remaining solids — 80% of the syrup — have a DE of 50.

The DE should not be confused with either relative sweetness or anti-freezing power. The DE of both fructose and dextrose is 100, but fructose is much sweeter than dextrose. The DE of sucrose is 0, as it is not able to donate an electron due to its chemical structure, but it is also sweeter than dextrose. Anti-freezing power is related to molecular weight, or in a complex system like a syrup, average molecular weight of the various sugars and polysaccharides in the syrup. DE provides no information about average molecular weight, though the supplier of the syrup should be able to do so.

When gelato makers refer to glucose or glucose syrup, they are *not* typically referring to a substance comprised of the molecule "glucose." They are referring to a complex mix of sugars and polysaccharides that can produce inconsistent results from batch to batch or manufacturer to manufacturer even if the DE is the same.

Glucose syrup is viscous and challenging to handle. Glucose syrup can be dried and powdered. In this form it is much easier to work with than glucose syrup itself. Note, however, that powdered glucose syrup is *not* the same as powdered dextrose. They are not interchangeable. I try to avoid using glucose syrups in liquid or powdered form without a compelling reason. None of the recipes in this book call for glucose syrup.

Trehalose

Trehalose is a naturally occurring sugar synthesized primarily by bacteria and fungi. It is significantly less sweet than sucrose. Some gelato-makers use it for gelato that is not intended to be particularly sweet. Having said that, its use is uncommon and no gelato recipes in this book call for trehalose.

Honey and Maple Syrup

Honey and maple syrup are used predominantly as flavoring ingredients that also are sweeteners. The sugars in honey are predominantly the monosaccharides fructose and dextrose. The sugars in maple syrup are predominantly the disaccharide sucrose, with small amounts of the monosaccharides fructose and dextrose. Because there can be variability from one batch to another, if you are producing gelato in quantity, it is best to buy enough honey or maple syrup to carry you through many batches of gelato. After making a test run of gelato with a newly acquired batch of honey or syrup, modifications can be made to the formula, if needed, to adjust sweetness and serving temperature.

Water

Most of the water in gelato comes from milk, cream, and fruit. Some gelato formulas call for the addition of plain water to achieve balance or as the base for an infusion or decoction of flavor ingredients. If the tap water available to you is not tasty, use bottled drinking water.

Stabilizers and Emulsifiers

In making gelato, emulsifiers manage fat to improve texture, whereas stabilizers help manage ice and water. See Chapter 8, "Emulsifiers and Stabilizers," for more in-depth information on these ingredients. Milk proteins are excellent emulsifiers. In most gelato, nonfat powdered milk is the only emulsifier you will need.

Guar Gum

The guar bean has been used as food for centuries, predominantly in South Asia. Guar gum is derived by milling the large endosperm of the guar bean. Guar should be slightly off-white in color and have little noticeable aroma. Guar gum fully hydrates without being heated.

Locust Bean Gum

Locust bean gum is derived from seeds of the carob tree native to the Mediterranean region. It has been used as a thickener for almost 2,000 years. Good quality locust bean gum should be slightly off-white in color and have minimal aroma. Carob (locust bean) is sometimes used to make imitation chocolate and, if not processed carefully, locust bean gum can have a strong aroma and taste that can overpower the flavors in gelato. Locust bean gum should be heated to 85°C to ensure that it is fully hydrated.

Eggs

Although used as stabilizing and emulsifying agents historically, eggs are no longer common ingredients in gelato. Exceptions include northern Italian gelato traditions that still include eggs, especially in the city of Bologna where the rich egg-based gelato is referred to as crema. Eggs were not commonly used in gelato made in southern Italy where plant-based stabilizers predominate. In modern gelato-making, eggs are used when their flavor is important, such as when making a zabaione-flavored batch.

Lecithin

The major component of eggs that provides their emulsifying property is lecithin. Lecithin can be extracted from plants, notably soybeans and sunflower seeds. Though I do not typically add lecithin to my gelato base, theoretically it could be useful for gelato that tends toward the upper end of the range for fat content. If you want to experiment with lecithin, I suggest starting at the level of 0.05% to 0.1% of the total mixture. Using sunflower lecithin rather than soy lecithin will avoid issues in individuals who have soy allergies. Lecithin has a nutty aroma and is not appropriate to add to delicate gelato flavors like fiordilatte. Lecithin can clump so it may be necessary to pass it through a very fine sieve to avoid lumps that will not disperse when the lecithin is added to the gelato base.

> The solids found in some ingredients, figs for example, have strong stabilizing properties. If you include additional stabilizers in the mix, the base can become very thick. (For this reason, my fig gelato does not contain additional stabilizers.) The need to decrease or eliminate stabilizers can become evident once the base is cooled. Your decision, though, should not be determined solely on the thickness of the mature base. Always test to confirm that the texture of the gelato is appropriate without added stabilizers.

Other Stabilizers and Emulsifiers

Gelatin and cornstarch have a place in the history of gelato and in some regional styles but are not widely used nowadays. Because gelatin is typically produced from animals, it may present an issue for individuals who do not eat animal-based products. Stabilizers that are not typically used in artisan Italian gelato include: xanthan gum, carrageenans, sodium alginate, carboxymethyl cellulose, and pectin.

Cacao (or Cocoa) Products

It is difficult to overstate the significance of cacao products to gelato. Gelato flavored with chocolate, in one variety or another, perennially shows up in lists of the most popular gelato flavors. Cacao (cocoa) powder and solid (bar) chocolate are the two most common sources of chocolate flavor for gelato. What follows is an overview of the most common products derived from cacao.

Cacao Nibs

Cacao beans form inside the fruit of cacao trees. After being removed from the fruit, the beans are fermented, dried, and roasted. They are crushed to make cacao nibs. Nibs have a bittersweet chocolate flavor.

Cacao Liquor or Cacao Mass

Cacao liquor is the result of grinding roasted cacao nibs. It is approximately 50% cacao butter. Cacao liquor, also known as cacao mass, is 100% cacao. It does not contain any added ingredients.

Cacao Butter

The fat found in cacao nibs is cacao butter. It can be removed from cacao mass by pressing.

Cacao Powder

Cacao cake is the result of pressing much of the cacao butter from cacao liquor. When ground, cacao cake becomes cacao powder. Cacao powder typically comes with 10% to 12% fat or 22% to 24% fat, though the range can be from 8% to 36%. Cacao powder can be natural or Dutch processed. Dutch-process cacao is treated with an alkali to reduce its acidity, darken its color, and give it a smoother, more mellow flavor.

Solid Chocolate

Solid chocolate, except for pure cacao mass, is a mixture of cacao butter, cacao powder, and sugar. Emulsifiers, such as lecithin, are sometimes added. Sometimes cacao liquor is added to the mixture. Milk or milk solids are added to make milk chocolate. High-quality chocolate with a significant percentage of cacao solids is required to make good gelato. If a milk chocolate gelato is desired, all that needs to be done is to decrease the amount of chocolate in the base.

White Chocolate

White chocolate is made with cacao butter, sugar, and usually an emulsifier. It does not contain any cacao powder. The best quality white chocolate does not contain any fat other than cacao butter.

Nuts and Nut-Based Products

Nut-based products used in gelato-making fall into three broad categories:

- Nut pastes
- Nut butters
- Whole or chopped nuts

Italian-made nut pastes are essential ingredients for creating traditional nut gelati. The most popular flavors are pistachio, hazelnut, and almond. The best nut pastes are simply finely ground nuts with no added ingredients. What differentiates a nut paste from a nut butter is the fineness of the grind. Well-made Italian nut pastes have virtually no grittiness. The quality of the nuts is important too, for example, Bronte pistachios from Sicily or hazelnuts from Piedmont.

Nut butters, such as peanut butter and almond butter, make very good gelato, though the gelato will not be quite as smooth as gelato made with Italian nut pastes. Whole or chopped nuts can be mixed into gelato as it is being put into the tub, such as when making butter pecan gelato, or sprinkled on top after the gelato has been scooped into a serving container.

Fruits

Many gelato flavors are based on fruits and fruit juices. Fresh, in-season fruit generally makes the best gelato, but some flavors would not be possible if a gelato maker relied solely on fruits available locally. Frozen fruit or pure fruit purees are especially useful for making some tropical fruit flavored gelati (unless you live in the tropics) and for making gelato from fruit that does not grow (or grow well) locally. Fruit that is shipped a long distance rarely produces the best flavor, as it is often picked before it is ripe and then ripened artificially. When using frozen fruit or a frozen fruit puree, look for one that contains only fruit with no other ingredients. Although most fruits used in gelato are fresh, some fruits are used dry. Among these are raisins, figs, dates, and coconut. With dried fruits, freshness matters. Coconut can easily become rancid, and raisins, figs, and dates can become overly dry.

> Although the ideal for artisan Italian gelato is to use local, fresh, in-season ingredients for flavoring, this can be limiting. I believe that using frozen fruit purees, made only with ripe fruit that would not otherwise be available locally, maintains the spirit of artisan gelato and allows for an expanded range of flavors.

Coffee

Coffee features prominently among popular gelato flavors. Coffee brewed from freshly ground beans usually makes the best gelato. Sometimes, though, pre-ground coffee is the only practical option, such as when using a coffee-chicory blend as I do in my Vietnamese coffee gelato.

Alcoholic Beverages

Distilled liquors and fortified wines are used in limited amounts to flavor gelato. Alcohol significantly lowers the serving temperature of gelato because of its anti-freezing effect. This limits the amount of alcohol that can be added. In my experience, gelato made with a flavoring meant to mimic alcohol, such as rum flavoring, is never satisfactory. I would rather not make an alcohol-flavored gelato if I had to use a flavoring extract in place of the real thing. Because of the effect on serving temperature, gelato that contains alcohol cannot generally be kept in the same display case as other flavors of gelato.

Extracts and Flavorings

Artificial flavors are never acceptable in artisan Italian gelato. Read the label of any extract you plan on using for gelato. The ingredient list should be short and should not contain any artificial components. For example, almond extract should contain oil of bitter almonds, water, and alcohol (the vehicle for the flavor). It might also contain a bit of sugar.

Vanilla (Pods, Paste, Extract)

In addition to being used on its own when making vanilla gelato, vanilla is often added to gelato to improve overall flavor as is sometimes done in baking. Most vanilla paste has the same intensity of flavor as a single-strength vanilla extract. Vanilla paste, though, has seeds and, sometimes, finely ground beans, which enhance the visual effect. Vanilla beans are expensive but are superb flavoring agents. I often grind up the entire bean to provide flecks of vanilla throughout the gelato. When using vanilla paste and extract, I add it to the gelato base just before freezing.

Other Extracts

Some extracts, such as rosewater and orange flower water, are traditionally used to impart flavors that are otherwise difficult to produce from raw ingredients. Other extracts are helpful when a particular type of fruit does not have sufficient flavor to make a stunning gelato on its own. While I would never use extracts exclusively to flavor a gelato, except for those extracts that are traditionally used ingredients in their own right, I use them occasionally to improve flavor. Extracts should not contain any artificial flavor or color.

Herbs, Spices, and Flowers

Infusions of herbs, spices, and flowers can flavor gelato. Some, like lemongrass and mint, are best used fresh, whereas others, like hibiscus and lavender, are used in dry form. Dried spices and flowers have a limited shelf life.

Confectionary

This category includes flavoring agents preserved with sugar. Many of these products are added to the gelato as it is removed from the batch freezer rather than directly to the gelato base before it is frozen.

Amarena Cherries

Amarena cherries are a quintessentially Italian ingredient. Buy a known brand and read ingredient lists. Some are made with artificial flavors and colors. Some are not. If you are using the cherries as a "swipe in," the brands are largely interchangeable. If you are adding the syrup to the gelato base, there may be different effects on serving temperature due to variations in sugar composition from brand to brand. It is best to find a brand you prefer and stick with it.

Candied Citrus Peel (Canditi)

The candied citrus peel commonly sold in the United States for baking is a pale imitation of good-quality Italian canditi. If you cannot get good, imported Italian candied peel, it is best to make your own from the recipe in this book.

Jam and Fruit Preserves

The challenge with using commercially purchased jam and fruit preserves for gelato is that they are not really formulated to maintain an appropriate texture at the usual serving temperature for gelato. I usually opt to make preserved fruits specifically for gelato using a high proportion of dextrose to inhibit freezing at low temperature. This book includes several recipes for preserved fruits.

Baked Goods

Cakes, cookies, and pie crusts are used as inclusions or toppings for some flavors of gelato. Bits of cake are often soaked in a flavored syrup (with or without alcohol) before being mixed in. While you can always make your own baked goods, unless you need a specific item that is not commercially available, you can often buy high-quality commercially available products that work well in gelato. Look for an ingredient list that mirrors what you would use to make the item from scratch. I find that madeleines, when gently dried in the oven and then dipped in syrup, are good stand-ins for Italian pan di Spagna (sponge cake) in gelati such as zuppa inglese or tiramisù. Crumbled or crushed spiced cookies, such as Biscoff, are a good stand-in for graham cracker crust in pumpkin pie gelato.

Canned Products

The use of preserved products has a long history in gelato making. Amarena cherries in syrup and candied citrus peel are two examples. Canning is another type of preservation and even though it doesn't have as long a history in gelato-making, I think it fits into the parameters of artisan Italian gelato in some circumstances. When I consider using a canned product, I ask myself a few questions. Is the ingredient commonly used in cooking of a high standard or is it mostly used as a shortcut? Is the canned product preferable to, or at least as good as, non-canned alternatives? Does the canned product provide an advantage for gelato-making not provided by other alternatives?

Pumpkin

Cooking fresh pumpkin to make pie filling is rare. Getting the correct type of pumpkin can be a challenge. Then there's the issue of creating pumpkin puree from fresh pumpkin that has a consistent composition. Good-quality canned pumpkin is 100% pumpkin, so the ingredient list is ideal. Because the pumpkin needs to be cooked to make pumpkin puree, the canning process does not alter the flavor from what you might obtain by making your own. Commercially available pumpkin puree also has the advantage of being more standardized in terms of water content than cooked fresh pumpkin, leading to more consistent batches of gelato. I would also argue that canned pumpkin is the default standard for making American-style pumpkin pie.

Coconut Milk and Coconut Cream

I have been making my own coconut milk and coconut cream for 50 years, long before canned high-quality coconut milk was readily available in the United States. I say that as a preface to my recommendation that you use canned coconut milk and coconut cream. The advantage of high-quality canned coconut milk and cream is consistency of composition. The texture of your gelato will be the same, batch after batch, if you use the same brand of coconut milk and coconut cream. If you want to use the homemade product, I suggest you refrigerate it, and once the fat has risen to the top and hardened, remove it from the watery liquid. You will need to rebalance the gelato formula, but this should produce a consistent product from batch to batch.

Pineapple

Though I generally do not recommend using canned fruit for making gelato, pineapple is a rare exception. Pineapple contains enzymes that break down milk protein causing an off-flavor and curdling. I always use cooked pineapple for gelato as heat inactivates the enzyme. Canned pineapple has the dual advantage of being already cooked and of being made from ripe pineapple close to the source.

Basic Equipment for Gelato Production

Most of what you need for gelato production may be found in a well-equipped kitchen. One exception is the *batch freezer,* what some people call the "gelato machine." This appliance takes the liquid base and turns it into frozen gelato, all while agitating the mixture. (See the batch freezer description that follows for more detail.)

This chapter is divided into two sections. The first describes suggested equipment for small-scale artisan production, including, for example, a home gelato enthusiast, caterer, restauranter, or chef who wants to make no more than a few small batches of gelato per day. The second section is aimed at commercial artisan production, such as a gelateria or an individual who wants to make gelato for delivery to local businesses such as restaurants. The difference between the two largely relates to the size and capacity of the equipment.

Equipment for Small-Scale Artisan Production

For making gelato in batches of 1 to 3 kilograms, up to several batches per day, I recommend the following equipment.

- Digital scale capable of weighing up to 8 kilograms in increments of 1 gram.
- Digital scale capable of weighing up to 200 grams in increments of 0.01 grams.
- Lightweight containers with smooth interiors of various sizes for weighing ingredients.
- Highest-quality stainless-steel pots of 3- to 4-liter capacity, preferably with lids. The pots should be larger if you intend to make more than 3 kilograms of gelato base at a time.
- Stainless-steel balloon whisks sized for the pots noted previously.
- Silicone spatulas.
- A digital instant read thermometer in increments of 0.1°C (0.2°F).
- An immersion blender tall enough to process the base in the pots noted previously.
- An ice bath setup for quickly cooling the gelato base.
  - A large stainless-steel bowl filled with ice and water works just fine.
  - If making smaller batches of gelato, such as 1 kilogram, an ice bath may not be strictly necessary as putting the just-cooked base in a refrigerator should get the temperature out of the danger zone in the required amount of time.

- A refrigerator that will reliably hold a temperature of 4°C (39°F) or less.
- A gelato batch freezer (a "gelato machine"). The most important factor is how quickly the machine freezes the gelato. The longer it takes, the more likely the gelato is to have large ice crystals and be less smooth.
  - You can buy tabletop models without refrigeration that make very good gelato costing as little as $70 (for example, the Cuisinart ICE-21P1, which is the current version of the machine I started with over 20 years ago).
  - Machines for small-scale production with refrigeration typically top out at about $1,200 (the Lello Musso Pola 5030, for example).
  - If I were just starting my gelato journey, I would probably go one step up from the Cuisinart ICE-21P1 and get the Cuisinart ICE-70P1 for about $150.
  - For small-scale production by a chef making a few batches per day for a restaurant, I recommend a unit with refrigeration.
  - You can find a helpful article on choosing a batch freezer for small-scale production at dreamscoops.com (https://www.dreamscoops.com/best-ice-cream-gelato-maker).
- Stainless-steel containers for the finished gelato. These are either rectangular tubs (the most common) or cylindrical containers called carapine (carapina is singular; carapine is plural). If you have a dedicated gelato display case, you will need to get the tubs that fit that specific display case. If not, I find that 1/3-size hotel pans work well. Pans that are 2 ½ inches deep will hold a 2-kilogram batch of gelato.
- Blast freezer or deep freezer. Once the gelato comes out of the batch freezer, it needs to be hardened quickly by taking the temperature to –18°C (0°F) or lower, and the faster the better. This is where a blast freezer comes in handy. Without a blast freezer, a good deep freezer will work fine as long as you are not adding batch after batch of gelato in a short period of time. Deep freezers just do not have the power to quickly chill large amounts of food the way blast freezers do.
- To store gelato for more than a few days, you will need a deep freezer. Gelato can stay at –18°C (0°F) for up to 1 month with no appreciable loss of quality.
- A service freezer or display case that can maintain a temperature of –13°C plus or minus about 1°C (9°F plus or minus about 2°F), will enable you to bring tubs of gelato to serving temperature without loss of quality. Gelato can typically stay at this serving temperature for up to 3 days before it starts to show signs of deterioration.
  - While a small, dedicated gelato display case could cost upwards of $4,000, a small chest freezer can be purchased for about $150. These are not going to run constantly, just when you want to bring gelato to serving temperature and hold it there for a few days.

- Somewhat more expensive than a small chest freezer, but smaller and much more portable, are AC/DC–powered thermoelectric cooling chests, the type that are often used in boats, campers, and cars.
- A sous vide setup is helpful when the gelato base needs to be pasteurized at lower temperatures for longer periods, such as 66°C (151°F) or 69°C (156°F) for 30 minutes. An alternative is to keep the gelato on the cooktop and regulate the heat to keep the gelato base at the required temperature.

Equipment for Commercial Artisan Production

I recommend the following equipment for producing many kilograms of gelato per day. In addition, most of the equipment needed for small-scale production is recommended as it will be useful for developing new flavors of gelato at small scale.

- Digital scale capable of weighing up to 25 kilograms in increments of 1 gram.
- Digital scale capable of weighing up to 200 grams in increments of 0.01 grams.
- Lightweight containers with smooth interiors of various sizes up to 20 liters for weighing ingredients.
- Programmable commercial pasteurizer with a capacity of up to 60 liters (depending on the largest anticipated batch size). A pasteurizer that will chill the mixture after pasteurization is ideal, but a separate chilling unit is another option.
- Large stainless-steel balloon whisks.
- Silicone spatulas.
- A digital instant read thermometer in increments of 0.1°C (0.2°F).
- A commercial immersion blender that can mix up to 20 liters of product.
- A refrigerator that will reliably hold a temperature of 4°C (39°F) or less for storing milk and other perishable ingredients and for maturing gelato bases.
- A walk-in refrigerator if large amounts of perishable ingredients or gelato bases need to be refrigerated.
- A gelato batch freezer sized for the anticipated batch size. Horizontal batch freezers typically freeze gelato faster than vertical units but allow less intervention by the person making the gelato.
- Stainless-steel containers for the finished gelato. These are either rectangular tubs (the most common) or cylindrical containers called carapine (carapina is singular; carapine is plural). If you have a dedicated gelato display case, you will need to get the tubs that fit that specific display case. If not, I find that 1/3-size hotel pans work well. Pans that are 2 ½ inches deep will hold a 2-kilogram batch of gelato.

- Blast freezer. Once the gelato comes out of the batch freezer it needs to be hardened quickly by taking the temperature to −18°C (0°F) or lower, and the faster the better.

- A deep freezer to store gelato, or a walk-in deep freezer for even larger quantities of gelato. Gelato can stay at −18°C (0°F) for up to 1 month with no appreciable loss of quality.

- A gelato display case or, if the gelato does not need to be on display, a service freezer that can maintain a temperature of −13°C plus or minus about 1°C (9°F plus or minus about 2°F). Gelato can typically stay at this serving temperature for up to 3 days before it starts to show signs of deterioration.

CHAPTER 3
The Process of Making Gelato

The first part of this chapter covers the typical steps used in making gelato, what I call the *conceptual framework*. I describe these steps in detail. I include information to help you understand the reasons for each step and, in some cases, when to employ a particular process. Afterward are two sections with detailed instructions for actually making gelato: one for small-scale production and one for commercial production. Within these sections, I discuss the differences in making one type of gelato versus another. This includes, for example, how to pasteurize a gelato that contains eggs compared to one that does not or when to add different types of flavoring ingredients.

I've abbreviated the instructions included with each gelato formula in the next chapter. Once you've made a few batches of gelato you will rarely need more detailed instructions. In the beginning, however, this chapter should be used to supplement the instructions included with each formula.

The production of gelato may be broken down into nine basic steps[4]:

1. Weighing ingredients
2. Mixing ingredients
3. Cooking the base
4. Cooling the base
5. Maturing the base
6. Blending and adding last-minute ingredients
7. Adjusting salt
8. Freezing (sometimes called *gelling*)
9. Hardening

Weighing Ingredients

Gelato-making involves chemistry and, much like baking, requires precision. All ingredients are weighed, except for some that do not directly affect the balance of the gelato. Chief among these are ingredients that are swiped-in after the gelato is frozen. Producing these swipe-in ingredients usually involves the same amount of precision, but their precise quantity in the finished gelato is of less importance because they are not going to directly affect the texture of the final product.

For ingredient quantities of 100 grams (g) or more, you will need a scale accurate to 1 gram. This will allow you to weigh out these ingredients with an accuracy of plus or minus 1%. For ingredient quantities of less than 100 grams, you will need a scale accurate to 0.01

---

[4] If you count "straining" there are ten steps, but I rarely strain my gelato base so I do not consider this one of the standard steps in the production of gelato.

grams. This is especially important for stabilizers as inaccuracies can negatively affect the texture of the gelato.

Mixing Ingredients

The order in which ingredients are mixed is dependent on whether you are using a commercial pasteurizer or not. This is discussed more in "Small-Scale Artisan Gelato Production" and "Commercial-Scale Artisan Gelato Production" later in this chapter.

There is absolutely one constant across all methods. Because stabilizers can clump when added to liquid if not dispersed slowly and mixed well, they are always thoroughly combined with one of the other solids, usually a sugar, first. For me, this solid is always the dextrose or fructose. If the amount of dextrose or fructose is too little to ensure that the stabilizers will be thoroughly dispersed, I use a bit of the sucrose. When dispersing stabilizers in sugar, I prefer that there not be less than 20 grams of sugar. This enables me to slowly sprinkle the mixture into the gelato without concern about clumping from adding too much stabilizer at one time. If I am making a very large batch of gelato, I try to use an amount of sugar that is about 8 times the combined weight of the stabilizers. For gelati that don't have crystalline sugars (because the sweetness is provided by liquids such as maple syrup, dulce de leche, or honey, for example), I disperse the stabilizers in a portion of the powdered nonfat milk.

> Professional gelato formulas are always based on weight, not volume. Even liquids are weighed. Volume measures are notoriously variable. Using the metric system is much easier than using the American system, even when all ingredients are weighed. For example, if you're developing a formula for gelato and you want to start with 40% fruit, you know to add 400 grams of fruit if the batch weight is going to be 1000 grams. How much fruit would you add if the batch weight were 2 pounds? Sure, you can do the arithmetic, but it's definitely more cumbersome.

Cooking the Base

The base is cooked for two reasons. The first is to fully hydrate the stabilizers. Hydration is the process of allowing the stabilizer to absorb as much water as it can. Think about it as the difference between a dry sponge and one that has been soaking in water for a few minutes. The second reason is to pasteurize the dairy ingredients. Not all stabilizers require heat for full hydration, but locust bean gum, one of the two stabilizers I use consistently, does requires heat. Though there is some variability in the temperature needed to fully hydrate locust bean gum from different producers, 85°C (185°F) is usually cited as the maximum needed.

Pasteurizing

Strictly speaking, if all the dairy products you use in making gelato are pasteurized and your gelato does not contain eggs, you do not need to pasteurize gelato made for home consumption. When using eggs, you must pasteurize the mixture. If not using eggs you will certainly be using stabilizers, some of which, as noted earlier, require heat for full hydration. I think it is good technique to pasteurize gelato made for home consumption, even if it isn't necessary.

Batch pasteurization, which is always required when producing artisan Italian gelato commercially, can be accomplished with a variety of time and temperature combinations.[5] If you are producing gelato commercially, you will need to refer to the applicable ordinances as there is variability between different countries and even between states. I rely on three time and temperature combinations listed in the U.S. Food and Drug Administration's (FDA's) Pasteurized Milk Ordinance (PMO) when producing gelato for home use:

- 75°C (167°F) for 15 seconds
- 66°C (151°F) for 30 minutes
- 69°C (157°F) for 30 minutes

The first of these is a time-temperature combination used for high-temperature, short-time, continuous-flow pasteurization for mixes that have a fat content of 10% or more, total solids of 18% or more, or added sweeteners. Except for fat content, which is sometimes below 10%, all these conditions apply to gelato.

The second time-temperature combination is for the batch pasteurization of dairy without eggs. I use it when cream cheese or mascarpone is in the mix, as higher temperatures can cause these cheeses to separate.

The third time-temperature combination is for mixtures that include eggs. The recipe instructions describe the pasteurization process for each gelato.

If all ingredients that need to be pasteurized are included in the base when it is being heated to 85°C (185°F) to hydrate the stabilizers, the pasteurization step is complete. On the way to 85°C (185°F), the base will have spent more than the required 15 seconds at 75°C (167°F) or above.

As I am careful about being certain that the entire mixture is heated to the required temperature, I am comfortable using the continuous-flow parameters for batch pasteurization in a home environment, especially because pasteurization is not really required for home production. In addition, regulatory requirements from other countries provide different time-temperature combinations than those included in the PMO. However, for commercial production it is important that you follow applicable regulation when pasteurizing gelato.

As noted, for non–egg-based gelato, you could pasteurize the mixture and hydrate the stabilizers in a single step at 85°C (185°F), but I usually use a two-step process when making gelato in a non-commercial setting. I combine all the heat-stable ingredients (described more fully later in this chapter), except for the cream, and heat the mixture to 85°C (185°F) to hydrate the stabilizers. Then I add the cream and bring the mixture to 75°C (167°F) for 15 seconds to pasteurize it.

---

[5] Food and Drug Administration (2019).

The closer the temperature of the mixture gets to 90°C (194°F), the more you risk denaturation of milk proteins in a way that will negatively affect the texture. Heating to 85°C (185°F) to hydrate the stabilizers, then adding cold cream immediately, brings the temperature down and eliminates the risk of overshooting the 90°C (194°F) mark. The only time I do not follow this process is if not enough liquid is present in the mixture without including the cream at the beginning. When adding cream at the beginning of the process, I am very careful about heating the base to avoid exceeding the 85°C (185°F) threshold by more than a fraction of a degree.

When cream cheese or mascarpone is in the mixture, I heat it to 66°C (151°F) and hold the temperature for 30 minutes. For egg-based gelato, I pasteurize the mixture at 69°C (157°F) for 30 minutes. These are the parameters for batch pasteurization of eggnog given by the PMO.

Some egg-based gelato has enough egg to fully stabilize the mixture. In this instance, pasteurization at 69°C (157°F) for 30 minutes is adequate, as the mixture does not contain any other stabilizers that require high-temperature hydration. For egg-based gelati that have added stabilizers requiring heat to fully hydrate, a two-step process is necessary to avoid heating the eggs above 69°C (157°F). First, heat the mixture to 85°C (185°F) to hydrate the stabilizers and then cool it to 69°C (157°F) or below, which is usually done by adding the cream. At this lower temperature, you can add the eggs or egg yolks beaten with some of the sugar in the mixture. Second, heat the mixture to 69°C (157°F) and hold the temperature for 30 minutes.

> I usually use a two-step heating process for my gelato. The first step is heating the base to 85°C (185°F) to fully hydrate the locust bean gum that I typically use as a stabilizer. Thereafter, I add cold cream to quickly lower the temperature of the mixture to provide protection against overheating, as the milk proteins can become gritty at 90°C (194°F). Some gelato formulas do not have enough liquid for the first step without including the cream. If this is the case, I add the cream at the beginning, but I am extra careful about not overshooting 85°C (185°F).

Straining

A gelato base rarely needs to be strained. Occasionally, however, you may plan to strain the base in order to remove particulates, such as seeds or fiber from pureed fruit. The only other time to strain gelato is if there has been some sort of a misstep. Usually this occurs when stabilizers are added too quickly or not thoroughly dispersed through another crystalline solid, or when the liquid mixture is not whisked vigorously enough as the stabilizer mixture is being added. Each of these situations can create gummy bits of stabilizer that are not fully dispersed in the base.

If straining is necessary, it is best to do it before the base is cooled. It will be much more difficult to strain the viscous base once it is cold.

Cooling the Base

When cooling the base, it is important for the mixture to spend as little time as possible in the "danger zone" — the temperature range where bacterial growth is significant. The U.S. Food and Safety Inspection Service[6] defines this danger zone as 4°C (40°F) to 60°C (140°F). Food that remains in this

---

[6] Food Safety and Inspection Service (2017).

temperature range for more than 2 hours should not be consumed. The temperature and time parameters of the danger zone vary a bit from country to country, and even between different states. You will need to follow local regulation if you are producing gelato commercially, but the concept is the same. The hot base must be cooled quickly.

Unless you have a pasteurizer with refrigeration capabilities, you will need to cool the base in a separate step. An ice bath is an effective way of doing this. If you are producing a small batch (approximately 1 kilogram) of gelato for home use and have a really cold refrigerator, you can probably put the hot mixture into the refrigerator directly. Leaving the mixture uncovered as it cools will also speed the process. Just be sure to cover it once it is cold to prevent the absorption of off-odors from other foods. As the batch size increases, however, you will quickly reach a point where air chilling in the refrigerator cannot cool the mixture fast enough to get it out of the danger zone in the required time. In this instance, an ice bath is a reasonable option for quick chilling.

Maturing the Base

Maturation occurs after the gelato base is cooled and before it is frozen. Physical changes happen during maturation[7] that continue beyond the time it takes to cool the mixture to 4°C (40°F). For example, the fats in the base crystallize — they harden and, at a microscopic level, begin to protrude from the surface of the fat globules. Casein, a protein found in milk, coats the outside of the fat globules emulsifying the mixture. Casein is a very effective emulsifier. When another emulsifier is in the mix, such as lecithin from eggs, some of the casein is replaced by that emulsifier as the base matures. These other emulsifiers tend to be more hydrophilic than casein, allowing the fat crystals from different globules to make contact and form a network. The added emulsifier makes the fat slightly more prone to destabilization.[8] This destabilization and partial coalescence of the emulsion usually results in an improvement of the texture of gelato.

In addition, proteins, stabilizers, and possibly other components of the base continue to hydrate. The gel structure of the stabilizers continues to develop over time. These changes, along with the formation of a network of fats, lead to increased viscosity of the mixture.

The time for maturation varies based on the composition of the mixture and the specific stabilizers and emulsifiers used. The maximum maturation time needed if gelatin is in the mixture (which is rarely the case) is 24 hours. The maturation time could be as short as 4 hours for many vegetable gum stabilizers.[9]

Rather than maturing the base, some gelatieri use the thermal shock method, which is putting the hot, just-pasteurized gelato base directly into the batch freezer. Using this method, the base is neither cooled nor matured before it is frozen. It has been my expe-

---

[7] Clarke (2004), 127.
[8] Underbelly (2016a).
[9] Clarke (2004), 127.

rience that gelato made this way is not as creamy as gelato in which the base has been allowed to mature at 4°C or less for 12 to 24 hours.

Blending and Adding Last-Minute Ingredients

After maturing, the base will have separated unless it was matured in a commercial chiller that keeps the mixture in motion. If it has separated, thoroughly blend the mixture before placing it into the batch freezer. An immersion blender is useful for this. The base should be as cold as possible when you place it into the batch freezer, so do not do the blending step until you are ready to freeze the gelato!

This is also the time to add last-minute ingredients. Some of these ingredients go in before blending with the immersion blender and some go in afterward. Basically, anything that can stand to be put through a blender goes in first. This includes fruit juices, flavorings such as extracts or vanilla paste, and fruit purees. Ingredients that go in after blending are items like cooked rice (for Gelato al Riso) and flaked coconut, where having whole rice grains or bits of coconut in the gelato are essential to its profile.

You should not have any big particles in the gelato as they can damage the batch freezer. It is also likely that they will get caught when the gelato is extruded, which is the usual method for getting gelato out of a commercial batch freezer. Items that are about the size of a cooked grain of rice is the largest solid that should go into the batch freezer. Most gelati with chunky ingredients have these ingredients added as the gelato is being removed from the batch freezer and layered in the tub, not before.

Adjusting Salt

This might seem like an unusual step to list independently. After all, adjusting salt occurs while blending the gelato base. However, I feel this step is so critical to producing flavorful gelato that I want to draw attention to it. Most gelatieri do not add salt to gelato except for just a few flavors such as nut and chocolate. I add salt to every gelato, though nut, chocolate, and coffee gelati require considerably more salt than most other flavors. You will see salt in every gelato formula in this book. I can assure you that when I taste the gelato base, I always add more salt.

Salt will make the flavors pop and will make the gelato taste sweeter in many cases. Taste the gelato base after you have blended it, then add a bit of salt. For a 2-kilogram batch of gelato, add a pinch of salt. (A pinch is the amount that you can hold between your thumb and first two fingers. Do not be stingy!) Blend and taste again. It will probably take a second pinch.

Each time you add salt, you should be able to taste the flavor of the base change just a little. When it comes to nut, chocolate, and coffee gelati, you will probably need twice as much salt as for other flavors.

Freezing

Unless you are using the thermal shock method (freezing the just-pasteurized, hot gelato base), the mixture will be just a few degrees above freezing and not more than 4°C (39°F) at the end of maturation.

Gelato is frozen in a *batch freezer,* so called because it freezes batches of gelato. An old-fashioned hand-crank, ice-and-salt-cooled, ice-cream machine is also a batch freezer. The batch freezer cools and freezes the mixture and incorporates air, all while agitating the mixture. The constant movement helps to keep the size of the ice crystals small, producing smooth gelato. The constant motion also traps air, creating softness. Gelato typically contains about 20% to 30% air, called overrun. Some ice cream, on the other hand, contains up to 100% overrun.

The batch freezer is the one piece of equipment that most separates the home gelato maker from the professional. However, there are excellent tabletop gelato batch freezers that will make about 1 kilogram of gelato at a time. When I returned from culinary school in Italy, I started making gelato in a vintage tabletop batch freezer called "Il Gelataio" that I bought at a resale shop for $30. I have since graduated to a professional Italian-made batch freezer, but I can assure you that the gelato made in my $30 machine was excellent.

A batch freezer consists of a canister that is cooled by refrigeration. Some batch freezers designed for home use employ a canister that is thoroughly chilled in a freezer rather than having refrigeration incorporated into the design of the equipment. The coldest part is the wall of the canister.

Inside the canister is a *dasher* — the part of the machine that turns the mixture and scrapes the inside wall of the canister. In most batch freezers, the dasher rotates, but in some it is the canister that rotates. Home batch freezers, whether for ice cream or gelato, turn comparatively slowly. Professional batch freezers turn faster than home machines but, all else being equal, a professional gelato batch freezer will turn more slowly than a professional ice cream batch freezer and will have a dasher design that incorporates only modest amounts of air.

A batch freezer can have a vertical cylinder (like a top-loading washing machine) or a horizontal cylinder (like a front-loading washing machine). Continuous freezers are always horizontal and are only used in industrial ice cream and gelato production. Artisan Italian gelato at any scale of production is always gelled in a batch freezer.

The gelato base is cooled as it comes in contact with the wall of the canister. The dasher scrapes the inside wall of the canister and moves the colder mixture to the center. Ultimately, the mixture gets cold enough that it freezes when it comes in contact with the canister wall. The dasher scrapes these ice crystals into the center of the canister where they initially melt, but further cool the mixture. Ultimately, the mixture is cold enough that the ice crystals do not melt as they are scraped off the canister wall and into the center.

As the mixture begins to stiffen, the dasher adds air to it. The dasher also causes fat droplets in the mixture to hit each other. As the fat droplets collide, they can join together in a process called *partial coalescence*. Partial coalescence can be aided by the use of emulsifiers, such as lecithin. Emulsifiers replace some of the milk proteins on the surface of the fat globules. Milk proteins are stronger emulsifiers than lecithin. The addition of non–milk-protein emulsifiers makes a slightly less stable emulsion than would be the case if they were not used. This slightly less stable emulsion improves partial coalescence, which can improve the trapping of air.

The continuous motion of the dasher aids in breaking up the air pockets, which ultimately become tiny bubbles surrounded by the partially coalesced globules of fat that stabilize the air bubbles.

If there is too much partial coalescence, as could happen without enough protein in the mixture or with too much emulsifier, the fat droplets become large enough to be felt on the tongue, creating a greasy sensation. With too little partial coalescence, as could happen with too much protein or too little emulsifier, the fat globules may not be able to hold the air bubbles in place.

Of primary importance in a gelato batch freezer is how long it takes to freeze the mixture. Ultimately, this is dependent on the power of the refrigeration built into the batch freezer. My vintage tabletop Il Gelataio only held 1 kilogram, but it froze the gelato in less than 18 minutes — about the same amount of time my professional machine takes to freeze a 2-kilogram batch. The batch freezer I frequently use in Italy will freeze a 3- to 3.5-kilogram batch in about the same amount of time.

Some batch freezers extrude the gelato from an opening at the bottom of the cylinder. Others require you to remove the gelato from the top. Gelato is usually removed from the top when using a countertop machine and by extrusion when using a professional machine. My favorite batch freezer, though, is the Cattabriga Effe 6, a professional machine. It is a workhorse — water-cooled and operating on 230V electricity. With this batch freezer, the gelato is removed from the top, not extruded.

Hardening

Gelato is taken out of the batch freezer at approximately –4°C to –5°C (39°F to 41°F) and placed into a freezer to chill further. In a professional setting, gelato is hardened by putting the tub of gelato in a blast freezer. Like the name implies, a blast freezer is designed to quickly cool whatever is put in it. For home use, a deep freezer or the freezer compartment of a refrigerator is a reasonable alternative.

Gelato is not ready to be served when it comes out of the batch freezer. It is still too soft, meaning it still contains too much unfrozen water. When removed from the batch freezer, the gelato should be slightly firmer than soft-serve ice cream.

Horizontal batch freezers signal when the gelato is ready based on resistance to turning. With vertical batch freezers, your decision to remove the gelato should be based on its firmness. Pressing a rubber spatula into the gelato in the batch freezer should be met with some resistance.

At this point gelato possesses the maximum number of ice crystals that it will ever have. If you remove it from the batch freezer too early, it may become gritty during hardening in the blast or deep freezer you use for quick chilling, as the unfrozen water will not create new ice crystals but will only expand the size of existing ones. This is why it is so important that a batch freezer create the smallest possible ice crystals. Small ice crystals mean smooth gelato. Large ice crystals make gelato gritty.

If you leave the gelato in the batch freezer too long, its stiffness may cause the machine to seize and not turn. If this happens as you begin to extrude the gelato, turning the machine off, waiting a few seconds, and restarting it generally solves the problem. If you are removing gelato that is too hard from the top of the batch freezer, you will have a difficult time packing it into a tub.

Once you pack the gelato into a tub, you must quickly harden it, usually to –18°C (0°F) or below. Commercial blast freezers have the power to chill large amounts of product. When using a regular deep freezer, be careful not to overload it with too much warm product, as these types of freezers do not have the capacity to quickly cool down large quantities.

Once hardened, you can keep gelato frozen at –18°C (0°F) or below for up to 1 month with no noticeable loss of quality.

Serving

For serving, bring the gelato to serving temperature. Gelato is typically served around –13°C (9°F) plus or minus 1°C (2°F). This is done by placing the tub of gelato in a refrigerated unit set at serving temperature and allowing the temperature to equilibrate slowly. Typically, this means putting the gelato into a display case. Many display cases have the space to store a second set of gelato tubs below the tubs that are visible, so another tub of gelato is always ready to replace an empty one.

Alternatives to a display case include a small chest freezer or an electrostatic cooler, the kind that is used in cars and boats. Although these units will not serve to display the gelato, they will enable you to hold it at the correct serving temperature without a huge expenditure. Most electrostatic units operate on both DC power from a car or boat and AC power. An advantage is that you can cart ready-to-eat gelato to picnics and the homes of family and friends!

If these alternatives are not feasible, I recommend portioning the gelato directly from the freezer into individual servings and placing these in the refrigerator for about 10 to 15 minutes. The gelato will soften without serious melting.

Note that without portioning, the gelato will melt too much before the center softens sufficiently. (This process is a one-way street, however. Placing the softened gelato back into the freezer afterward will allow larger ice crystals to form, resulting in gritty gelato.) I do not recommend allowing the gelato to sit at room temperature or putting it in the microwave as a way to bring it to serving temperature.

Small-Scale Artisan Gelato Production

There is no one-size-fits-all production process for gelato, but the small-scale process that follows is what I teach aspiring gelatieri. It uses a minimum of specialized equipment. The process is perfectly suited to the home production of gelato and professional production when large quantities of gelato are not needed, such as for caterers, personal chefs, and even some restaurants with small gelato programs.

> When making gelato at small scale, I recommend compensating for the loss of water through evaporation. At commercial scale, this is not as much of an issue because of batch size and the use of specialized equipment. In some instances, I use flavoring ingredients, like vanilla or almond extract, in place of some of the water that I add to the gelato base just before freezing it to compensate for loss due to evaporation. Even though I do not "top up" my gelato base when making gelato at commercial scale, adding small amounts of flavoring ingredients just before freezing the gelato will not upset the balance.

Small-Scale Production of Non–Egg-Based Gelato

Follow these general steps for creating non–egg-based gelato on a small scale:

1. Though not essential, to minimize work, plan on maturing the gelato in the pot used for pasteurization. If you choose to transfer the cooked base to a different container, be sure to weigh the container first.
   - If using a gas burner to heat the gelato base, the pot you use should have thick sides as well as a thick bottom. Many pots have heavy bottoms but thin sides. Heat from a gas burner, not buffered by a thick-sided pot, can burn the contents.
   - The pot should be made of high-quality stainless steel that will not affect the taste of the gelato.

   Weigh the pot and record the weight.

2. Weigh out all ingredients.
   - Ingredients used in quantities greater than 100 grams can be weighed using a scale that measures in 1-gram increments.
   - Ingredients used in quantities less than 100 grams should be weighed using a scale that measures in 0.01-gram increments.

3. Thoroughly disperse stabilizers in the dextrose or fructose.
   - If the gelato base does not contain dextrose or fructose, use a portion of the sucrose. If it does not contain any of these sugars, use a portion of the powdered skim milk.
   - Stabilizers tend to clump when added to liquid unless they are thoroughly dispersed in a powdered solid and sprinkled in slowly with constant whisking.

4. In the pot, combine the milk, water (if any), sucrose, and other sweeteners (if any), such as honey, maple syrup, dulce de leche, and so forth.
   - If there is insufficient milk and water in the formula to mix with all the dry ingredients, add the cream at this time, then skip steps 9 and 10.
5. Begin to heat the milk.
6. At approximately 35°C (95°F), add the powdered skim milk and whisk to dissolve.
7. At approximately 40°C (104°F), slowly sprinkle in the mixture of dextrose (or fructose) and stabilizers while constantly whisking the milk.
   - Thorough, constant whisking is necessary to prevent clumping of the stabilizers.
8. Switch from a whisk to a rubber spatula once the stabilizers have been added, and constantly scrape the bottom and sides of the pan while taking the temperature to 85°C (185°F) using moderate heat.
   - As the stabilizers cause the mixture to thicken, it can stick to the bottom of the pan and burn unless you constantly scrape it with a spatula.
   - The intent of heating to 85°C (185°F) is to fully hydrate the stabilizers. Note that by the time the mixture reaches this temperature it will be pasteurized because it will have been at or above 75°C (167°F) for 15 seconds.
   - If you are making gelato commercially, check regulatory requirements for pasteurization temperatures and times.
9. Add the cream while continuing to scrape the bottom and sides with a rubber spatula.
10. If the mixture does not contain mascarpone or cream cheese, take the temperature to 75°C (167°F) and hold it for 15 seconds. (If the mixture contains mascarpone or cream cheese, skip to step 11.)
    - Depending on the proportion of cream in relation to gelato base, the temperature may be above 75°C (167°F) after incorporating the cream.
    - At 75°C (167°F), the mixture will be pasteurized in 15 seconds.[10] You do not need to heat the mixture to 85°C (185°F) again as the locust bean gum will have been fully hydrated during the previous step.
11. If using, add mascarpone and cream cheese immediately after the cream, at which time the temperature of the base should be 66°C (151°F) or below. If the mixture does not contain cream, allow the base to cool slightly before adding the mascarpone or cream cheese.
    - Once the cheese is added, gently heat the base to 66°C (151°F). A whisk will make it easier to incorporate the cheese. At temperatures above 66°C (151°F), these cheeses can separate.
    - Gelato with mascarpone or cream cheese should be pasteurized at 66° (151°F) for 30 minutes.[11]

---

[10] Food and Drug Administration (2019), 91–92.
[11] Food and Drug Administration (2019), 91–92.

- This can be done on the stove by adjusting the heat and monitoring the temperature.
- It is easier, however, to cover the pot and put it a water bath maintained at 66°C (151°F) with an immersion or sous vide heater.

12. Quickly chill the mixture and refrigerate it at 4°C (39°F) or less.
    - Quick chilling, such as in an ice bath, is necessary to minimize the time the mixture remains in the danger zone for bacterial growth.
    - Typically you can chill 1 kilogram of base in the refrigerator because the mixture will cool quickly enough to not exceed the maximum time in the danger zone.
    - The danger zone is between 60°C and 4°C[12] (140°F and 39°F).

13. Mature the mixture for 24 hours at 4°C (39°F) or less.
    - You have some leeway here; the general range for maturation is 12 to 48 hours unless gelatin is being used, in which case 24 hours is needed.

14. When you are ready to freeze the gelato, weigh the base and add cold water to compensate for loss to evaporation during pasteurization.
    - This is where keeping the base in the pot and knowing the weight of the pot comes in handy.
    - Add any last-minute ingredients such as fruit juice, fruit puree, and so on, to the base.
        - Note that some ingredients, such as rice, should be added after blending, and others, such as liquor, should be added part-way through freezing.
    - Add together the weight of all ingredients in the base to this point.
    - Add the weight of the ingredients to the weight of the pot. Add cold water to bring the weight to the calculated batch weight.

15. Thoroughly blend the base with an immersion blender.

16. Taste and adjust salt.

17. Add any ingredients that cannot be blended, such as cooked rice that is intended to remain whole.

18. Freeze the gelato in a batch freezer.
    - Follow the manufacturer's instructions for the batch freezer.
    - If you are using a vertical batch freezer, remove the gelato when it is slightly firmer than soft-serve ice cream.
    - If you are using a horizontal batch freezer, the machine will signal when the gelato is ready to be extruded.
    - Be sure that the tub into which the gelato will be placed has been well-chilled in the freezer so that the gelato does not melt on contact.

---

[12] Food Safety and Inspection Service (2017).

- If the batch freezer extrudes the gelato through a chute in the bottom of the freezing cylinder, remove the gelato this way. Smooth the gelato as it is extruded into the tub.
- If the batch freezer doesn't have a chute, remove the gelato through the top of the batch freezer, smoothing it as it is added to the tub.

19. If you're adding ingredients (such as nuts, chocolate chips, or sauces), add them successively as you put the gelato into the tub. Gently mix and swirl the gelato with a silicone spatula.
20. Transfer the gelato to a blast freezer or a deep freezer to harden it.
    - It is best to let the gelato thoroughly harden before moving it to a display case or service freezer at serving temperature. This will typically take more than 2 hours in a blast freezer and more than 4 hours in a deep freezer.
    - If you need to serve the gelato quickly, in a pinch you can let it freeze enough in the freezer to get to serving consistency and serve it immediately.
        - In this case the gelato will be colder near the edges of the tub than on the inside, unlike holding it at serving temperature in a display case where the temperature will be uniform throughout.
        - You will need to mix the gelato as you serve it to get a consistent temperature and the right texture.

Adding Flavoring Ingredients

You add flavoring ingredients at different times during the process depending on the type of ingredient. Each gelato formula in this book has specific directions, but these are some general rules.

- Ingredients that will not be negatively affected by heat can be added with the milk and sucrose. Such ingredients include infusions like brewed coffee and canned coconut milk, as well as sweeteners used for their flavor such as maple syrup, honey, and dulce de leche.
- Cocoa can be cooked gently with water to fully hydrate before being mixed with the milk and sugar. This hydration process will decrease grittiness, though I find that with good quality cocoa, it is not always necessary.
- Solid chocolate is usually added before the skim milk powder and completely melted before adding other ingredients.
- Nut pastes are added after the mixture has been removed from the heat following pasteurization but while the base is still hot.
    - The residual heat of the just-pasteurized gelato base helps to soften the nut paste and makes it easier to incorporate.

- Because nut pastes are high in fat, cream is often not added. In this case, pasteurization will be completed in the same step as hydrating the stabilizers at 85°C (185°F).
- Fruit purees, fruit juices, and other ingredients that might be adversely affected by the heat of pasteurization are added after the mixture has been chilled and just before it is frozen.
  - Adding ingredients that might otherwise curdle the milk, like citrus and pomegranate juices, yogurt, and sour cream, is possible using this method.
- Ingredients that should not be subjected to immersion blending, such as cooked rice, are added to the base after blending and just before freezing.
- Alcoholic ingredients are usually added while the gelato is in the batch freezer and has partially frozen.

The Small-Scale Process for Egg-Based Gelato

The process differs somewhat for egg-based gelato. Follow these steps for creating egg-based gelato on a small scale:

1. If egg is in the gelato base, keep the maximum temperature below 72°C (162°F), and preferably not more than 69°C (157°F).
   - Temperatures above this risk cooking the egg (i.e., denaturing the egg proteins) and creating an unpleasant texture.
   - In addition, the "eggy" taste becomes more pronounced as eggs are heated above this temperature.

2. In general, when making egg-based gelato, beat the eggs or egg yolks with sugar until they are very pale. Thereafter add the milk and all ingredients that can be heated to 69°C (157°F). Pasteurize the base by gently heating it to 69°C (157°F) and holding it for 30 minutes,[13] making sure to keep it well below the maximum of 72°C (162°F).
   - This is best done by partially immersing the covered pot in a water bath heated with an immersion heater or sous vide heater, as this will produce more even, gentle heat than a stove top.
   - This step can also be completed using a stand mixer with induction heating, though this type of equipment is rare in a home or other small-scale environment.

3. Add the flavor ingredients that cannot be heated after maturation, as with non–egg-based gelato.

Notes on the Process of Small-Scale Production

Take note of these special considerations for the small-scale gelato process:

---

[13] Food and Drug Administration (2019), 91–92.

- Pasteurization is most important for dairy ingredients and eggs. Non-dairy, non-egg ingredients such as nut pastes and fruit can be added after pasteurization, but only if you verify that they are microbiologically safe.

- As milk and cream are heated, the proteins begin to denature. This process helps create a creamier gelato through emulsification. However, heating milk and cream to 90°C (194°F) or higher risks creating grittiness from excessively denatured proteins.

- Fermented or acidic dairy products, such as yogurt and sour cream, will likely curdle the gelato base unless they are added just before freezing the gelato.

- Locust bean gum hydrates at a range of different temperatures depending on where it is sourced and how it is manufactured. In practical terms, 85°C (185°F) is the temperature at which it is completely hydrated, regardless of these factors. Thus, if locust bean gum is in the base, the initial heating step is at 85°C (185°F).

- All ingredients added to the gelato after it has been chilled or while it is in the batch freezer should be as cold as possible.

- Though there are some exceptions, the best flavor is usually obtained from fruit, juices, and purees that have not been heated.
    - Heat treatment is necessary for some fruits due to chemical or enzymatic activity that adversely affects dairy ingredients. Pineapple is one such ingredient.
    - Some gelatieri feel that fruits, such as apples and pears, taste better when they are heat-treated.

Commercial-Scale Artisan Gelato Production

Commercial-scale production is not industrial production. It can include producing gelato for one or more gelato shops in the same area, for one or more restaurants, or for large-scale catering operations, in addition to other scenarios. In larger batches, pasteurization and the timing of ingredient additions are different from small-scale gelato production. One can easily make 12-kilogram batches of gelato using the process described for small-scale production, but as batch volume increases, the process can become unwieldy. Perhaps the biggest difference in commercial-scale gelato production is the use of a dedicated pasteurizer.

Commercial Production of Non–Egg-Based Gelato

The basic steps for making large-batch non-egg-based gelato are as follows:

1. Weigh out all ingredients.
    - Ingredients used in quantities greater than 100 grams can be weighed using a scale that measures in 1-gram increments.
    - Ingredients used in quantities less than 100 grams should be weighed using a scale that measures in 0.01-gram increments.

2. Place the dry ingredients in a large container, one by one, starting with the sugars.

- After adding the sucrose, dextrose, and fructose, add the stabilizers.
- Using a large wire balloon whisk, thoroughly distribute the stabilizers throughout the sugars.
- Add any remaining dry ingredients, such as nonfat milk powder.

3. Put the liquid ingredients in the pasteurizer and begin the heating cycle.
4. At approximately 35°C (95°F), gently sprinkle in the dry ingredients.
5. Allow the cycle to complete, which typically means it needs to reach 85°C (185°F).
6. If you are adding mascarpone or cream cheese, cool the mixture to 66°C (151°F) or less before adding them.
7. Once the cheese is added, heat the base to 66°C (151°F).
   - These cheeses can separate at temperatures above 66°C (151°F).
   - Pasteurize the mixture at 66°C (151°F) for 30 minutes.
8. Quickly chill the mixture to 4°C (39°F) or less.
   - If the pasteurizer does not have built-in refrigeration capabilities, remove the base and use a dedicated chiller or else chill it in an ice bath.
9. Mature the mixture for 24 hours at 4°C (39°F) or less.
   - If the pasteurizer has built-in refrigeration, maturation can be completed in the same equipment.
   - You have some leeway here; the general range for maturation is 12 to 48 hours unless gelatin is being used, in which case 24 hours is needed.
10. When you are ready to freeze the gelato, add any last-minute ingredients such as fruit juice, fruit puree, and so on, to the base.
    - If the base has been matured in the pasteurizer or in a dedicated chiller that continuously mixes the base, the additional ingredients can be added directly, as the pasteurizer will blend them into the base.
    - If the base has been matured in a refrigerator, it will need to be blended with a large immersion blender after these ingredients are added.
    - Note that some ingredients, such as rice, should be added after blending and others, such as liquor, should be added part-way through freezing.
11. Taste and adjust salt.
12. After removing the base from the pasteurizer, or after blending if the base was matured in a refrigerator, add any ingredients that cannot be blended, such as cooked rice that is intended to remain whole.
13. Freeze the gelato in a batch freezer.
    - Follow the manufacturer's instructions for the batch freezer.
    - If you are using a vertical batch freezer, remove the gelato from the batch freezer when it is slightly firmer than soft-serve ice cream.

- If you are using a horizontal batch freezer, the machine will signal when the gelato is ready to be extruded.
- Be sure that the tub into which the gelato will be placed has been well-chilled in the freezer so that the gelato does not melt on contact.
- If the batch freezer extrudes the gelato through a chute in the bottom of the freezing cylinder, remove the gelato this way. Smooth the gelato as it is extruded into the tub.
- If the batch freezer doesn't have a chute, remove the gelato through the top of the batch freezer, smoothing it as it is added to the tub.

14. If you're adding ingredients (such as nuts, chocolate chips, or sauces), add them successively as you place the gelato into the tub. Gently mix and swirl the gelato with a silicone spatula.
15. Transfer the gelato to a blast freezer to harden it.
    - It is best to let the gelato thoroughly harden before moving it to a display case or service freezer at serving temperature.

The Large-Scale Process for Egg-Based Gelato

The process differs somewhat for egg-based gelato. Follow these steps for creating egg-based gelato on a large scale:

1. If egg is included in the gelato base, the maximum temperature should be below 72°C (162°F) and preferably not more than 69°C (157°F).
   - Temperatures above this risk cooking the eggs (i.e., denaturing the egg proteins) and creating an unpleasant texture.
   - In addition, the "eggy" taste becomes more pronounced as eggs are heated above this temperature.
2. In general, when making egg-based gelato, beat the eggs or egg yolks with sugar until they are very pale.
3. In the pasteurizer, combine the milk and all ingredients that can be heated to 69°C (157°F).
4. Add the egg yolk–sugar mixture.
5. Pasteurize the base at 69°C (157°F) for 30 minutes,[14] making sure to keep it well below the maximum of 72°C (162°F).
6. Add the flavor ingredients that cannot be heated after maturation, as with non–egg-based gelato.

Once you have a basic understanding of the ingredients, equipment, and processes for making artisan gelato, you will be ready to move on to the truly creative and fulfilling activity of *making it* from the recipes that follow in the next part of the book!

---

[14] Food and Drug Administration (2019), 91–92.

PART TWO

Making Gelato: The Recipies

Gelato Formulas and Recipes for Component Ingredients

If you know how to make gelato and you want to jump right in, you'll love the formulas that follow. Each contains a list of ingredients and information on their percentages out of the total mixture, balance data, *potere anticongelante* (PAC) information (anti-freezing power in English), *potere dolcificante* (POD) information (sweetening power in English), and estimated serving temperature.

PAC is a method of determining the approximate serving temperature of gelato from the ingredients and their quantities. POD is a method for estimating the sweetness of gelato from the different sugars in the gelato. PAC and POD are covered in more detail in Chapter 7, "Freezing Point Depression," and Chapter 9, "Sweetening Power," respectively. You can make wonderful artisan Italian gelato without understanding these concepts, but the deeper you get into your gelato journey, especially if you want to develop your own flavors, the more useful they will become.

This chapter also includes brief directions aimed at home or small-scale gelato production. The process of making gelato varies somewhat if it is being made at large scale, such as enough to stock a gelateria. As mentioned in the Introduction, what does not change is the formula — the *proportions* of the ingredients in the total mixture.

Because the process of making gelato is standardized from flavor to flavor, with minor variations based on the inclusion of components such as eggs, sour cream, yogurt, mascarpone, cream cheese, fruit purees, and infusions, the directions presented for each flavor are brief and are focused on small-scale production. The processes for commercial production are described in Chapter 3, "The Process of Making Gelato." Once you have made gelato several times, the brief directions will be more than adequate. You can always refer to Chapter 3 for a refresher and detailed directions.

When I work with gelato masters in Italy, directions are rarely written out. They usually use just a list of ingredients and proportions that they convert to quantities based on the amount of gelato they want to make. Once you know the basic process, and the variations based on some of the ingredients, you really know how to make any gelato based on ingredient quantities alone.

All gelato formulas in this book are balanced. However, a few ingredients vary significantly from producer to producer. Mascarpone comes to mind, as its fat content can vary from about 35% to 50%. This is enough variation that it can affect the balance of the gelato. For ingredients that are likely to vary significantly from one producer to another, I provide information on composition or even specific brands.

In addition, the table in Appendix B, "Ingredient Composition," provides the component breakdown of every ingredient used in this book and many other common gelato ingredients. It is always a good idea to compare manufactured products you intend to use (such as chocolate and nut butters) with this table to confirm that there are no significant differences.

I try to achieve an estimated serving temperature of approximately −13.5°C (8°F) for all my gelato formulas. This is not possible for some gelato flavors, especially ones that contain alcohol, where the estimated serving temperature is lower. Some fruits contain so much fructose and/or dextrose that it is not possible to get a serving temperature of approximately −13.5°C (8°F) while including enough fruit to create good flavor.[15] In a gelateria, a separate display case set at a different temperature can be used for flavors that require a lower serving temperature.

Whenever I create a formula, I use a standardized batch size of 1000 grams. There are several advantages to this. Among them is the ability to enter my standard quantities for stabilizers that are used in minute quantities. Also, because I know the weight of all the ingredients will sum to 1000 grams, I have a reasonable starting point for deciding on the quantities of other ingredients.

Some ingredients, such as stabilizers, are included in amounts that might include fractions of a gram. That means that some other ingredients might end up requiring a fraction of a gram to reach a total of 1000 grams. I usually add the fractions of a gram to an ingredient present in large quantities, such as milk, cream, and sucrose, where a fraction of a gram in one direction or another will not be of any consequence. When weighing these ingredients, if your large digital scale (see Chapter 4, "Basic Equipment for Gelato Production," for recommendations) does not measure fractions of a gram, just round up.

> If you are not at ease with the metric system, weigh out each ingredient in metric then before removing it from the scale, switch the scale to pounds and ounces. This will quickly give you a sense of the relationship between the two systems. In no time, you'll be comfortable working with metric.

Occasionally, I list "off-balance ingredients" in the formulas that follow. These are ingredients that do not figure into the balance as they have no significant effect. Many of these are added in small quantities to the gelato just before you put it into the batch freezer. For small-scale production, I always recommend adding water to the base to compensate for evaporation during production — what I call "topping up" the gelato. Due to equipment differences, evaporation during large-scale production is less of a concern and I do not suggest topping up gelato made this way. If I am adding a flavoring, such as vanilla extract, I might list it as an off-balance ingredient and add it as part of the water that I use to top up the gelato. For large-scale production, I simply add the off-balance ingredient because there is no topping up.

Every batch freezer has an ideal batch size range. Initially, look at the range that is published in the instruction manual and aim to produce batches of gelato near the middle — not at the extremes — of the range. A little trial and error will guide you to the best batch size for

---

[15] The reasons for this are explained in Chapter 7, "Freezing Point Depression."

your machine. A batch size that is too large will increase freezing time, which can lead to the formation of large ice crystals,[16] an undesirable condition for any gelato.

If the ideal batch size for your batch freezer is not 1 kilogram, the standard size for all gelato formulas in this book, you will need to upsize (or possibly downsize) the ingredient quantities keeping the proportions constant.

What You'll Need to Make Gelato at a Small Scale

More information on the equipment needed for making gelato can be found in Chapter 3, "The Process of Making Gelato," but as a quick check before you begin, here's a brief list of what you will need for most recipes in this section:

- Digital scale capable of weighing up to 8 kilograms in increments of 1 gram
- Digital scale capable of weighing up to 200 grams in increments of 0.01 grams
- Lightweight containers for weighing ingredients
- Highest quality stainless-steel pot of 3- to 4-liter capacity
- Stainless-steel balloon whisk
- Silicone spatula
- Digital instant-read thermometer with increments of 0.1°C (0.2°F)
- Immersion blender
- Ice bath setup for quickly cooling the gelato base
- Refrigerator that will reliably hold a temperature of 4°C (39°F) or less
- Gelato batch freezer (a "gelato machine")
- Containers for the finished gelato
- Freezer to quickly chill and store gelato

---

[16] See Chapter 5, "Troubleshooting: What Happened to My Gelato?"

Gelato al Croccante di Mandorle

Almond Brittle Gelato

Ingredient	Quantity	Percent
Milk, 2%	550 g	55.00%
Heavy Cream (36% fat)	220 g	22.00%
Sucrose	162 g	16.20%
Powdered Skim Milk	40 g	4.00%
Guar Gum	1.25 g	0.125%
Locust Bean Gum	1.25 g	0.125%
Salt	0.5 g	0.05%
Dark Rum, 80 proof	25 g	2.50%
Batch Weight	1000 g	
Serving Temperature	−14.16°C	

Mix-In Ingredient	Quantity
Croccante, finely crushed	200 g

Component	Percent
Fats	9.02%
Sugars	16.20%
MSNF	10.15%
Other Solids	0.28%
Water	64.36%
Total Solids	35.64%
POD	17.05
PAC	28.32

Many years before I studied artisan Italian gelato in Italy, I was making this gelato at home. It called for gelatin, which is a stabilizer with a long history in the production of gelato, rather than guar and locust bean gums. If you are making this gelato in a gelato batch freezer from which you remove the gelato from the top of the machine, you can add the crushed croccante to the gelato just before removing it from the batch freezer, letting it mix through for several rotations of the dasher before removing the gelato. Otherwise, sprinkle the croccante into the gelato as it is being put into the pan.

1. In a small bowl, combine 30 grams of sucrose, guar gum, locust bean gum, and salt in a bowl. Mix well. Reserve.
2. Combine milk and remaining sucrose in a stainless-steel pot. Heat to 35°C (95°F), whisking occasionally.
3. Add skim milk powder and whisk to dissolve completely.
4. Continuing to heat the milk mixture, slowly sprinkle in the sucrose mixture, whisking constantly to avoid lumps and keeping the temperature below 45°C (113°F). After the sucrose mixture is incorporated, heat to 85°C (185°F), stirring constantly and scraping the bottom of the pot with a rubber spatula.
5. Add cream. Mix well. Heat to 75°C (167°F), stirring constantly, and hold for 15 seconds.
6. Chill quickly, preferably in an ice bath. Allow to mature overnight, covered and refrigerated at 4°C (39°F) or less.
7. Meanwhile, weigh out the rum, cover tightly, and refrigerate.
8. Just before freezing the gelato, add water to return the base to the calculated batch weight less the weight of the rum (975 grams for a single batch). Blend with an immersion blender. Taste and adjust salt, if necessary.
9. Freeze in a batch freezer. When the gelato is partially frozen and is mounding over the blades, add the cold rum and finish freezing.
10. Transfer the gelato from the batch freezer to a tub, stopping occasionally to sprinkle in some of the crushed croccante, swirling a bit with a silicone spatula.
11. Harden in a blast freezer or deep freezer.

Gelato alla Mandorla
Almond Gelato

In Italy, most nut gelati are made with nut pastes that are ground exceedingly finely. We have nothing approaching these pastes in the United States. Although the texture is slightly different, nut butters make very good nut gelati. The characteristic flavor of almonds comes from bitter almonds, which are essentially unavailable in the United States. A little pure almond extract compensates well. Be sure to use an almond butter that is pure almonds, preferably without salt. If you have access to Italian almond paste, you can use it to replace the almond butter.

1. In a small bowl, combine dextrose, guar gum, locust bean gum, and salt. Mix well. Reserve.
2. In a stainless-steel pot, combine milk and sucrose. Heat to 35°C (95°F), whisking occasionally.
3. Add skim milk powder and whisk to dissolve completely.
4. Continuing to heat the milk mixture, slowly sprinkle in the dextrose mixture, whisking constantly to avoid lumps and keeping the temperature below 45°C (113°F). After all the dextrose mixture is incorporated, heat to 85°C (185°F), stirring constantly and scraping the bottom of the pot with a rubber spatula.
5. Remove from heat. Stir in the almond butter then almond extract.
6. Chill quickly, preferably in an ice bath. Allow to mature overnight, covered and refrigerated at 4°C (39°F) or less.
7. Just before freezing the gelato, add water to return the base to the calculated batch weight. Blend with an immersion blender. Taste and adjust salt, if necessary.
8. Freeze in a batch freezer.
9. Transfer the gelato from the batch freezer to a tub
10. Harden in a blast freezer or deep freeze.

Ingredient	Quantity	Percent
Milk, 2%	647.4 g	64.74%
Almond Butter	130 g	13.00%
Sucrose	143 g	14.30%
Dextrose	36 g	3.60%
Powdered Skim Milk	39 g	3.90%
Guar Gum	1 g	0.10%
Locust Bean Gum	1 g	0.10%
Almond Extract	1.6 g	0.16%
Salt	1 g	0.10%
Batch Weight	1000 g	
Serving Temperature	-13.73°C	

Component	Percent
Fats	8.47%
Sugars	18.19%
MSNF	9.54%
Other Solids	5.49%
Water	58.30%
Total Solids	41.70%
POD	18.17
PAC	27.46

Gelato all'Amarena

Amarena Cherry Gelato

A gelato in which one ingredient is swiped in as the gelato is being extruded is known as a *gelato variegato*. The most famous variegato is probably Stracciatella (Fiordilatte with Dark Chocolate). If you look carefully at a gelato showcase in Italy, you will see that many flavors are Fiordilatte with different swipe-ins. This one is slightly different in that I add some of the syrup from the cherries to the gelato base. This recipe was standardized with Toschi Amarena cherries. Another brand might produce a different serving temperature.

Ingredient	Quantity	Percent
Milk, 2%	519 g	51.90%
Heavy Cream (36% fat)	248 g	24.80%
Sucrose	137.5 g	13.75%
Dextrose	5 g	0.50%
Syrup from Cherries	50 g	5.00%
Powdered Skim Milk	37 g	3.70%
Guar Gum	1.25 g	0.125%
Locust Bean Gum	1.25 g	0.125%
Salt	1 g	0.10%
Batch Weight	1000 g	
Serving Temperature	−13.97°C	

Mix-In Ingredient	Quantity
Amarena Cherries, chopped	100 g

Component	Percent
Fats	9.97%
Sugars	16.86%
MSNF	9.76%
Other Solids	0.33%
Water	63.09%
Total Solids	36.91%
POD	21.04
PAC	27.93

1. In a small bowl, combine dextrose, 30 grams of the sucrose, guar gum, locust bean gum, and salt. Mix well. Reserve.
2. Combine milk and sucrose in a stainless-steel pot. Heat to 35°C (95°F), whisking occasionally.
3. Add skim milk powder and whisk to dissolve completely.
4. Continuing to heat the milk mixture, slowly sprinkle in the dextrose mixture, whisking constantly to avoid lumps and keeping the temperature below 45°C (113°F). After the dextrose mixture is incorporated, heat to 85°C (185°F), stirring constantly and scraping the bottom of the pot with a rubber spatula.
5. Add cream. Mix well. Heat to 75°C (167°F), stirring constantly, and hold for 15 seconds.
6. Chill quickly, preferably in an ice bath. Allow to mature overnight, covered and refrigerated at 4°C (39°F) or less.
7. Meanwhile, drain the Amarena cherries and coarsely chop. Weigh out the required amount, cover tightly, and refrigerate.
8. Just before freezing the gelato, add water to return the base to the calculated batch weight. Blend with an immersion blender. Taste and adjust salt, if necessary.
9. Freeze in a batch freezer.
10. Transfer the gelato from the batch freezer to a tub, stopping periodically to sprinkle in some of the chopped cherries, swirling a bit with a silicone spatula.
11. Harden in a blast freezer or deep freezer.

Ingredient	Quantity	Percent
Milk, 2%	611.5 g	61.15%
Almond Butter	130 g	13.00%
Sucrose	150 g	15.00%
Powdered Skim Milk	45 g	4.50%
Guar Gum	1.25 g	0.125%
Locust Bean Gum	1.25 g	0.125%
Salt	1 g	0.10%
Amaretto Disaronno	60 g	6.00%
Batch Weight	1000 g	
Serving Temperature	−17.54°C	

Off-Balance Ingredient	Quantity
Almond Extract, if desired	1.75 g

Component	Percent
Fats	8.41%
Sugars	16.18%
MSNF	9.79%
Other Solids	5.53%
Water	60.08%
Total Solids	39.92%
POD	17.01
PAC	35.07

Gelato all'Amaretto

Amaretto Gelato

Different brands of amaretto contain varying amounts of alcohol. Most contain less than Amaretto Disaronno, so this formula should work with any brand of amaretto. My favorite brands are Disaronno and Lazzaroni, the company that makes the classic amaretti cookies. If you can find it, Italian almond paste will create a smoother gelato than American almond butter. Be sure the only ingredient in the almond butter or paste is almonds. If you want to increase the taste of almonds, you can add almond extract when tasting for salt before freezing. Note that the recommended serving temperature for this gelato is less than is customary due to the alcohol.

1. In a small bowl, combine 30 grams of the sucrose, guar gum, locust bean gum, and salt. Mix well. Reserve.
2. Combine milk and remaining sucrose in a stainless-steel pot. Heat to 35°C (95°F), whisking occasionally.
3. Add skim milk powder and whisk to dissolve completely.
4. Continuing to heat the milk mixture, slowly sprinkle in the sucrose mixture, whisking constantly to avoid lumps and keeping the temperature below 45°C (113°F). After the sucrose mixture is incorporated, heat to 85°C (185°F), stirring constantly and scraping the bottom of the pot with a rubber spatula.
5. Remove from heat. Stir in the almond butter.
6. Chill quickly, preferably in an ice bath. Allow to mature overnight, covered and refrigerated at 4°C (39°F) or less.
7. Meanwhile, weigh out the amaretto, cover tightly, and refrigerate.
8. Just before freezing the gelato, add almond extract to base, if desired.
9. Add water to return the base to the calculated batch weight less the weight of the amaretto (940 grams for a single batch). Blend with an immersion blender. Taste and adjust salt, if necessary.
10. Freeze in a batch freezer. When the gelato is partially frozen and is mounding over the blades, add the cold amaretto and finish freezing.
11. Transfer the gelato from the batch freezer to a tub.
12. Harden in a blast freezer or deep freezer.

Ingredient	Quantity	Percent
Milk, 2%	117 g	11.70%
Heavy Cream (36% fat)	230 g	23.0%
Sucrose	100 g	10.00%
Dextrose	15 g	1.50%
Powdered Skim Milk	70 g	7.00%
Guar Gum	1.25 g	0.125%
Locust Bean Gum	1.25 g	0.125%
Salt	1 g	0.10%
Apple Puree	464.5 g	46.45%
Batch Weight	1000 g	
Serving Temperature	−13.55°C	

Component	Percent
Fats	8.64%
Sugars	16.07%
MSNF	9.17%
Other Solids	1.76%
Water	64.37%
Total Solids	35.63%
POD	17.51
PAC	27.11

Gelato alla Mela e Cannella

Apple Cinnamon Gelato

I prefer using Saigon or Ceylon cinnamon in the apple puree for this gelato for their more delicate flavor. Though slightly different, they are both more floral and less pungent than cassia, which is what is typically labelled "cinnamon" in the United States. In the end, the choice of cinnamon and the quantity is up to your personal taste. Choose a very flavorful apple for this gelato. The directions for the apple puree are in the "Component Ingredients" section at the end of this chapter.

1. In a small bowl, combine dextrose, guar gum, locust bean gum, and salt. Mix well. Reserve.
2. Combine milk and sucrose in a stainless-steel pot. Heat to 35°C (95°F), whisking occasionally.
3. Add skim milk powder and whisk to dissolve completely.
4. Continuing to heat the milk mixture, slowly sprinkle in the dextrose mixture, whisking constantly to avoid lumps and keeping the temperature below 45°C (113°F). After the dextrose mixture is incorporated, heat to 85°C (185°F), stirring constantly and scraping the bottom of the pot with a rubber spatula.
5. Add cream. Mix well. Heat to 75°C (167°F), stirring constantly, and hold for 15 seconds.
6. Chill quickly, preferably in an ice bath. Allow to mature overnight, covered and refrigerated at 4°C (39°F) or less.
7. Just before freezing the gelato, add 929 grams of apple puree to the mature base.
8. Add water to return the base to the calculated batch weight. Blend with an immersion blender. Taste and adjust salt, if necessary.
9. Freeze in a batch freezer.
10. Transfer the gelato from the batch freezer to a tub.
11. Harden in a blast freezer or deep freezer.

Gelato all'Albicocca

Apricot Gelato

Made with ripe, in-season apricots, this gelato is a delight. Be sure to peel and thoroughly puree the apricots but do not strain them. A food processor, high-powered blender, or commercial immersion blender can be used to puree the apricots.

1. In a small bowl, combine dextrose, guar gum, locust bean gum, and salt. Mix well. Reserve.
2. Combine milk and sucrose in a stainless-steel pot. Heat to 35°C (95°F), whisking occasionally.
3. Add skim milk powder and whisk to dissolve completely.
4. Continuing to heat the milk mixture, slowly sprinkle in the dextrose mixture, whisking constantly to avoid lumps and keeping the mixture below 45°C (113°F). After the dextrose mixture is incorporated, heat to 85°C (185°F), stirring constantly and scraping the bottom of the pot with a rubber spatula.
5. Add cream. Mix well. Heat to 75°C (167°F), stirring constantly, and hold for 15 seconds.
6. Chill quickly, preferably in an ice bath. Allow to mature overnight, covered and refrigerated at 4°C (39°F) or less.
7. Meanwhile, put the apricots in the refrigerator.
8. Just before freezing the gelato, peel, pit, and puree the chilled apricots using a high-powered blender, food processor, or commercial immersion blender. Weigh out the correct amount and add it to the mature base.
9. Add water to return the base to the calculated batch weight. Blend with an immersion blender. Taste and adjust salt, if necessary.
10. Freeze in a batch freezer.
11. Transfer the gelato from the batch freezer to a tub.
12. Harden in a blast freezer or deep freezer.

Ingredient	Quantity	Percent
Milk, 2%	140 g	14.00%
Heavy Cream (36% fat)	236.5 g	23.65%
Sucrose	125 g	12.50%
Dextrose	20 g	2.00%
Powdered Skim Milk	75 g	7.50%
Guar Gum	1.25 g	0.125%
Locust Bean Gum	1.25 g	0.125%
Salt	1 g	0.10%
Fresh Apricot Puree	400 g	40.00%
Batch Weight	1000 g	
Serving Temperature	−13.59°C	

Component	Percent
Fats	9.01%
Sugars	18.04%
MSNF	9.90%
Other Solids	1.92%
Water	61.14%
Total Solids	38.86%
POD	18.33
PAC	27.18

Gelato alla Banana

Banana Gelato

Ingredient	Quantity	Percent
Milk, 2%	224.5 g	22.45%
Heavy Cream (36% fat)	232 g	23.20%
Sucrose	90 g	9.00%
Dextrose	9 g	0.90%
Powdered Skim Milk	49 g	4.90%
Guar Gum	1.25 g	0.125%
Locust Bean Gum	1.25 g	0.125%
Salt	1 g	0.10%
Fresh Banana Puree	392 g	39.20%
Batch Weight	1000 g	
Serving Temperature	−13.14°C	

Component	Percent
Fats	9.04%
Sugars	16.02%
MSNF	8.15%
Other Solids	3.67%
Water	63.11%
Total Solids	36.89%
POD	17.15
PAC	26.28

This gelato tastes just like fresh bananas. It is important to chill the bananas and to puree them at the last possible moment. Chilling the bananas will prevent the base from warming, which would extend freezing time. Pureeing at the last minute will minimize oxidation that will turn the bananas a gray color. If desired, you can add powdered citric acid equal to 0.2% of the weight of the bananas to the pureed bananas to slow oxidation.

1. In a small bowl, combine dextrose, 20 grams of sucrose, guar gum, locust bean gum, and salt. Mix well. Reserve.
2. Combine milk and sucrose in a stainless-steel pot. Heat to 35°C (95°F), whisking occasionally.
3. Add skim milk powder and whisk to dissolve completely.
4. Continuing to heat the milk mixture, slowly sprinkle in the dextrose mixture, whisking constantly to avoid lumps and keeping the mixture below 45°C (113°F). After the dextrose mixture is incorporated, heat to 85°C (185°F), stirring constantly and scraping the bottom of the pot with a rubber spatula.
5. Add cream. Mix well. Heat to 75°C (167°F), stirring constantly, and hold for 15 seconds.
6. Chill quickly, preferably in an ice bath. Allow to mature overnight, covered and refrigerated at 4°C (39°F) or less.
7. Meanwhile, refrigerate the whole, unpeeled bananas.
8. Just before freezing the gelato, puree the chilled bananas using a high-powered blender, food processor, or commercial immersion blender. Weigh out the correct amount and add it to the mature base.
9. Add water to return the base to the calculated batch weight. Blend with an immersion blender. Taste and adjust salt, if necessary.
10. Freeze in a batch freezer.
11. Transfer the gelato from the batch freezer to a tub.
12. Harden in a blast freezer or deep freezer.

Ingredient	Quantity	Percent
Milk, 2%	318.5 g	31.85%
Heavy Cream (36% fat)	200 g	20.00%
Sucrose	100 g	10.00%
Dextrose	6 g	0.60%
Powdered Skim Milk	47 g	4.70%
Brewed Vietnamese Coffee	50 g	5.00%
Dulce de Leche	125 g	12.50%
Banana Puree	150 g	15.00%
Guar Gum	1.25 g	0.125%
Locust Bean Gum	1.25 g	0.125%
Salt	1 g	0.10%
Batch Weight	1000 g	
Serving Temperature	−13.38°C	

Component	Percent
Fats	8.87%
Sugars	18.69%
MSNF	10.07%
Other Solids	2.42%
Water	59.95%
Total Solids	40.05%
POD	18.88
PAC	26.77

Gelato al Banoffi

Banoffi Gelato

This gelato was inspired by Ian Dowding's original recipe for Banoffi Pie. It was developed at the now-shuttered Hungry Monk Restaurant in the Jevington, East Sussex, United Kingdom, in 1971. The original recipe included cooking cans of condensed milk to make the toffee. For this recipe, I use canned dulce de leche, which has the same flavor profile. True to the original recipe, I like just a hint of coffee flavor. To achieve this, I use the instructions for making Vietnamese coffee in the "Component Ingredients" section later in this chapter, except that I use ground espresso rather than Vietnamese coffee. This recipe was balanced using La Lechera Dulce de Leche, but it should work with most brands due to the limited quantity involved.

1. In a small bowl, combine dextrose, 25 grams of sucrose, guar gum, locust bean gum, and salt. Mix well. Reserve.
2. Combine milk, dulce de leche, coffee, and remaining sucrose in a stainless-steel pot. Heat to 35°C (95°F), whisking occasionally.
3. Add skim milk powder and whisk to dissolve completely.
4. Continuing to heat the milk mixture, slowly sprinkle in the dextrose mixture, whisking constantly to avoid lumps and keeping the mixture below 45°C (113°F). After the dextrose mixture is incorporated, heat to 85°C (185°F), stirring constantly and scraping the bottom of the pot with a rubber spatula.
5. Add cream. Mix well. Heat to 75°C (167°F), stirring constantly, and hold for 15 seconds.
6. Chill quickly, preferably in an ice bath. Allow to mature overnight, covered and refrigerated at 4°C (39°F) or less.
7. Meanwhile, refrigerate the unpeeled bananas.
8. Just before freezing the gelato, peel and puree the chilled bananas using a high-powered blender, food processor, or commercial immersion blender. Weigh out the correct amount and add it to the mature base.
9. Add water to return the base to the calculated batch weight. Blend with an immersion blender. Taste and adjust salt, if necessary.
10. Freeze in a batch freezer.
11. Transfer the gelato from the batch freezer to a tub.
12. Harden in a blast freezer or deep freezer.

Gelato Formulas and Recipes for Component Ingredients

Ingredient	Quantity	Percent
Milk, 2%	258.5 g	25.85%
Heavy Cream (36% fat)	230 g	23.00%
Sucrose	152 g	15.20%
Dextrose	17 g	1.70%
Powdered Skim Milk	65 g	6.50%
Guar Gum	1.25 g	0.125%
Locust Bean Gum	1.25 g	0.125%
Salt	1 g	0.10%
Strained Pureed Blackberries	274 g	27.40%
Batch Weight	1000 g	
Serving Temperature	−13.52°C	

Component	Percent
Fats	8.98%
Sugars	18.10%
MSNF	9.97%
Other Solids	2.09%
Water	60.86%
Total Solids	39.14%
POD	18.69
PAC	27.03

Gelato alla Mora

Blackberry Gelato

Blackberries have a lot of seeds. I recommend pureeing them thoroughly and then passing the puree through a fine sieve to remove the seeds. You will need about 350 grams of blackberries to get enough puree for a single batch of this gelato.

1. In a small bowl, combine dextrose, guar gum, locust bean gum, and salt. Mix well. Reserve.
2. Combine milk and sucrose in a stainless-steel pot. Heat to 35°C (95°F), whisking occasionally.
3. Add skim milk powder and whisk to dissolve completely.
4. Continuing to heat the milk mixture, slowly sprinkle in the dextrose mixture, whisking constantly to avoid lumps and keeping the mixture below 45°C (113°F). After the dextrose mixture is incorporated, heat to 85°C (185°F), stirring constantly and scraping the bottom of the pot with a rubber spatula.
5. Add cream. Mix well. Heat to 75°C (167°F), stirring constantly, and hold for 15 seconds.
6. Chill quickly, preferably in an ice bath. Allow to mature overnight, covered and refrigerated at 4°C (39°F) or less.
7. Meanwhile, refrigerate the blackberries.
8. Just before freezing the gelato, puree the chilled blackberries using a high-powered blender, food processor, or commercial immersion blender and pass the puree through a sieve. Weigh out the correct amount and add it to the mature base.
9. Add water to return the base to the calculated batch weight. Blend with an immersion blender. Taste and adjust salt, if necessary.
10. Freeze in a batch freezer.
11. Transfer the gelato from the batch freezer to a tub.
12. Harden in a blast freezer or deep freezer.

Gelato al Mirtillo
Blueberry Gelato

The blueberry skin will leave little blue flecks in the gelato. For me, this is a reminder that the gelato was made with fresh fruit, not flavoring. If you do not like the blue flecks, you can strain the blueberry puree through a fine sieve before adding it to the base. It is important to chill the blueberries. This will prevent the base from warming, which can extend freezing time.

1. In a small bowl, combine dextrose, guar gum, locust bean gum, and salt. Mix well. Reserve.
2. Combine milk and sucrose in a stainless-steel pot. Heat to 35°C (95°F), whisking occasionally.
3. Add skim milk powder and whisk to dissolve completely.
4. Continuing to heat the milk mixture, slowly sprinkle in the dextrose mixture, whisking constantly to avoid lumps and keeping the mixture below 45°C (113°F). After the dextrose mixture is incorporated, heat to 85°C (185°F), stirring constantly and scraping the bottom of the pot with a rubber spatula.
5. Add cream and cinnamon. Mix well. Heat to 75°C (167°F), stirring constantly, and hold for 15 seconds.
6. Chill quickly, preferably in an ice bath. Allow to mature overnight, covered and refrigerated at 4°C (39°F) or less.
7. Meanwhile, refrigerate the blueberries.
8. Just before freezing the gelato, puree the chilled blueberries using a high-powered blender, food processor, or commercial immersion blender. Weigh out the required amount and add it to the mature base.
9. Add water to return the base to the calculated batch weight. Blend with an immersion blender. Taste and adjust salt, if necessary.
10. Freeze in a batch freezer.
11. Transfer the gelato from the batch freezer to a tub.
12. Harden in a blast freezer or deep freezer.

Ingredient	Quantity	Percent
Milk, 2%	334.4 g	33.44%
Heavy Cream (36% fat)	190 g	19.00%
Sucrose	120 g	12.00%
Dextrose	17 g	1.70%
Powdered Skim Milk	48 g	4.80%
Guar Gum	1.25 g	0.125%
Locust Bean Gum	1.25 g	0.125%
Salt	1 g	0.10%
Cinnamon, ground	0.1 g	0.01%
Fresh Blueberry Puree	287 g	28.70%
Batch Weight	1000 g	
Serving Temperature	−13.07°C	

Component	Percent
Fats	7.62%
Sugars	16.42%
MSNF	8.78%
Other Solids	1.92%
Water	65.25%
Total Solids	34.75%
POD	17.13
PAC	26.14

Gelato al Bourbon Old Fashioned

Bourbon Old Fashioned Gelato

The estimated serving temperature of this gelato is lower than the typical temperature of a gelato display case. This is due to the anti-freezing property of the alcohol, which limits the amount that can be added. Brown sugar helps to amplify the caramel flavor profile of the bourbon. Italian brown sugar comes in large free-flowing crystals called *zucchero di canna*. It is similar to turbinado sugar. See the instructions for making candied orange peel in the "Component Ingredients" section at the end of this chapter.

1. In a small bowl, combine 30 grams of the sucrose with guar gum, locust bean gum, and salt. Mix well. Reserve.
2. Combine milk, remaining sucrose, and turbinado sugar in a stainless-steel pot. Heat to 35°C (95°F), whisking occasionally.
3. Add skim milk powder and whisk to dissolve completely.
4. Continuing to heat the milk mixture, slowly sprinkle in the sucrose mixture, whisking constantly to avoid lumps and keeping the mixture below 45°C (113°F). After the dextrose mixture is incorporated, heat to 85°C (185°F), stirring constantly and scraping the bottom of the pot with a rubber spatula.
5. Add cream. Mix well. Heat to 75°C (167°F), stirring constantly, and hold for 15 seconds.
6. Chill quickly, preferably in an ice bath. Allow to mature overnight, covered and refrigerated at 4°C (39°F) or less.
7. Meanwhile, drain the cherries, cut in eighths, weigh out the required amount, and cover tightly. Finely dice the orange peel, weigh out the required amount, and cover tightly. Weigh out the required amount of bourbon and cover tightly. Refrigerate the cherries, candied orange peel, and bourbon.
8. Just before freezing the gelato, add water to return the base to the calculated batch weight less the weight of the bourbon (950 grams for a single batch). Blend with an immersion blender. Taste and adjust salt, if necessary.
9. Freeze in a batch freezer. When the gelato is partially frozen and is mounding over the blades, add the cold bourbon and finish freezing.
10. Transfer the gelato from the batch freezer to a tub, stopping periodically to sprinkle in some of the chopped Amarena cherries and candied orange peel, swirling a bit with a silicone spatula.
11. Harden in a blast freezer or deep freezer.

Ingredient	Quantity	Percent
Milk, 2%	515 g	51.50%
Heavy Cream (36% fat)	230 g	23.00%
Sucrose	85 g	8.50%
Turbinado Sugar	77 g	7.70%
Powdered Skim Milk	40 g	4.00%
Guar Gum	1.25 g	0.125%
Locust Bean Gum	1.25 g	0.125%
Salt	0.5 g	0.05%
Bourbon, 80 proof	50 g	5.00%
Batch Weight	1000 g	
Serving Temperature	−17.16°C	

Mix-In Ingredients	Quantity
Amarena Cherries, chopped	50 g
Candied Orange Peel, chopped	37.5 g

Component	Percent
Fats	9.31%
Sugars	16.14%
MSNF	9.89%
Other Solids	0.34%
Water	64.32%
Total Solids	35.79%
POD	16.97
PAC	34.32

56   *Make Your Own Artisan Italian Gelato*

Gelato al Burro Rosolato e Noci Pecan

Brown Butter Pecan Gelato

Ingredient	Quantity	Percent
Milk, 2%	630 g	63.00%
Heavy Cream (36% fat)	32 g	3.20%
Sucrose	158.5 g	15.85%
Dextrose	20 g	2.00%
Powdered Skim Milk	63 g	6.30%
Browned Butter	93 g	9.30%
Guar Gum	1.25 g	0.125%
Locust Bean Gum	1.25 g	0.125%
Salt	1 g	0.10%
Batch Weight	1000 g	
Serving Temperature	−13.42°C	

Mix-In Ingredient	Quantity
Chopped Toasted Pecans	60 g

Component	Percent
Fats	11.70%
Sugars	17.69%
MSNF	11.88%
Other Solids	0.33%
Water	58.41%
Total Solids	41.59%
POD	18.24
PAC	26.84

Browned butter keeps well in the refrigerator so do not be concerned about leftovers. If you do not use it for another batch of gelato, it is a great addition to steamed vegetables. See the instructions for making browned butter and toasting pecans in the "Component Ingredients" section at the end of this chapter.

1. In a small bowl, combine dextrose, guar gum, locust bean gum, and salt. Mix well. Reserve.
2. Combine milk and sucrose in a stainless-steel pot. Heat to 35°C (95°F), whisking occasionally.
3. Add skim milk powder and whisk to dissolve completely.
4. Continuing to heat the milk mixture, slowly sprinkle in the dextrose mixture, whisking constantly to avoid lumps and keeping the mixture below 45°C (113°F). After the dextrose mixture is incorporated, heat to 85°C (185°F), stirring constantly and scraping the bottom of the pot with a rubber spatula.
5. Add cream and browned butter. Mix well. Heat to 75°C (167°F), stirring constantly, and hold for 15 seconds.
6. Chill quickly, preferably in an ice bath. Allow to mature overnight, covered and refrigerated at 4°C (39°F) or less.
7. Just before freezing the gelato, add water to return the base to the calculated batch weight. Blend with an immersion blender. Taste and adjust salt, if necessary.
8. Freeze in a batch freezer.
9. Transfer the gelato from the batch freezer to a tub, stopping periodically to sprinkle in some of the toasted pecans, swirling a bit with a silicone spatula.
10. Harden in a blast freezer or deep freezer.

Ingredient	Quantity	Percent
Milk, 2%	200 g	20.00%
Heavy Cream (36% fat)	85 g	8.50%
Sucrose	155.5 g	15.55%
Dextrose	36 g	3.60%
Powdered Skim Milk	20 g	2.00%
Guar Gum	1.25 g	0.125%
Locust Bean Gum	1.25 g	0.125%
Salt	1 g	0.10%
Ricotta	500 g	50.00%
Batch Weight	1000 g	
Serving Temperature	−13.53°C	

Mix-In Ingredients	Quantity
Crushed Roasted Pistachios	30 g
Semi-sweet Chocolate Chips	15 g
Maraschino Cherries	50 g

Component	Percent
Fats	8.96%
Sugars	18.86%
MSNF	9.96%
Other Solids	0.33%
Water	61.88%
Total Solids	38.11%
POD	18.68
PAC	27.06

Gelato ai Cannoli

Cannoli Gelato

Ricotta is traditionally made from whey plus an acid, such as vinegar and salt. Milk and cream are sometimes added to increase the yield, as it takes a tremendous amount of whey to make a small amount of ricotta. Try to find ricotta that does not have any added stabilizers or thickeners. You can use Amarena cherries in place of maraschino cherries, but I prefer the flavor of the latter in this gelato.

1. In a small bowl, combine dextrose, guar gum, locust bean gum, and salt. Mix well. Reserve.
2. Combine milk, cream, and sucrose in a stainless-steel pot. Heat to 35°C (95°F), whisking occasionally.
3. Add skim milk powder and whisk to dissolve completely.
4. Continuing to heat the milk mixture, slowly sprinkle in the dextrose mixture, whisking constantly to avoid lumps and keeping the mixture below 45°C (113°F). After the dextrose mixture is incorporated, heat to 85°C (185°F), stirring constantly and scraping the bottom of the pot with a rubber spatula.
5. Chill quickly, preferably in an ice bath. Allow to mature overnight, covered and refrigerated at 4°C (39°F) or less.
6. Meanwhile, cut the cherries in half and gently squeeze to remove excess liquid. Cover tightly and refrigerate.
7. Just before freezing the gelato, add the ricotta.
8. Add water to return the base to the calculated batch weight. Blend with an immersion blender. Taste and adjust salt, if necessary.
9. Freeze in a batch freezer.
10. Transfer the gelato from the batch freezer to a tub, stopping periodically to sprinkle in some of the pistachios, chocolate chips, and cherries, swirling a bit with a silicone spatula.
11. Harden in a blast freezer or deep freezer.

Ingredient	Quantity	Percent
Milk, 2%	160 g	16.00%
Heavy Cream (36% fat)	237.5 g	23.75%
Sucrose	130 g	13.00%
Dextrose	20 g	2.00%
Powdered Skim Milk	75 g	7.50%
Guar Gum	1.25 g	0.125%
Locust Bean Gum	1.25 g	0.125%
Salt	1 g	0.10%
Fresh Cantaloupe Puree	374 g	37.40%
Batch Weight	1000 g	
Serving Temperature	−13.68°C	

Component	Percent
Fats	9.00%
Sugars	17.79%
MSNF	10.08%
Other Solids	0.98%
Water	62.15%
Total Solids	37.85%
POD	18.40
PAC	27.37

Gelato al Melone

Cantaloupe Gelato

Melone simply means melon in Italian, but Gelato al Melone is usually cantaloupe. If you make several types of melon gelato, you can refer to this one more specifically as Gelato al Cantalupo.

1. In a small bowl, combine dextrose, guar gum, locust bean gum, and salt. Mix well. Reserve.
2. Combine milk and sucrose in a stainless-steel pot. Heat to 35°C (95°F), whisking occasionally.
3. Add skim milk powder and whisk to dissolve completely.
4. Continuing to heat the milk mixture, slowly sprinkle in the dextrose mixture, whisking constantly to avoid lumps and keeping the mixture below 45°C (113°F). After the dextrose mixture is incorporated, heat to 85°C (185°F), stirring constantly and scraping the bottom of the pot with a rubber spatula.
5. Add cream. Mix well. Heat to 75°C (167°F), stirring constantly, and hold for 15 seconds.
6. Chill quickly, preferably in an ice bath. Allow to mature overnight, covered and refrigerated at 4°C (39°F) or less.
7. Meanwhile, peel and cube enough cantaloupe to yield 374 grams after pureeing. Refrigerate.
8. Just before freezing the gelato, puree the chilled cantaloupe using a high-powered blender, food processor, or commercial immersion blender. Weigh out the correct amount and add it to the mature base.
9. Add water to return the base to the calculated batch weight. Blend with an immersion blender. Taste and adjust salt, if necessary.
10. Freeze in a batch freezer.
11. Transfer the gelato from the batch freezer to a tub.
12. Harden in a blast freezer or deep freezer.

Gelato alla Torta di Carote

Carrot Cake Gelato

Ingredient	Quantity	Percent
Milk, 2%	350 g	35.00%
Water	85.5 g	8.55 g
Turbinado Sugar	155 g	15.50%
Carrots, chopped	100 g	10.00%
Dextrose	25 g	2.50%
Powdered Skim Milk	50 g	5.00%
Guar Gum	0.5 g	0.05%
Locust Bean Gum	0.125 g	0.0125%
Salt	1 g	0.10%
Cream Cheese, Philadelphia	232.88 g	23.29%
Batch Weight	1000 g	
Serving Temperature	-13.29°C	

Off-Balance Ingredients	Quantity
Cinnamon, ground	1.5 g
Allspice, ground	0.75 g
Cloves, ground	0.25 g
Nutmeg, ground	0.5 g

Mix In Ingredients	Quantity
Candied Carrots	30 g
Raisins in Syrup	45 g
Pecans, chopped and toasted	30 g

Component	Percent
Fats	9.04%
Sugars	18.15%
MSNF	10.22%
Other Solids	1.36%
Water	61.23%
Total Solids	38.77%
POD	18.40
PAC	26.58

Like pasta shapes, gelato flavors are constantly evolving in Italy. This is most definitely an American flavor profile, but the formula meets all the requirements of artisan Italian gelato. When I teach in Italy, each student is required to develop a gelato flavor to be produced by the end of the week. We get some unique flavors as students come from all around the world. Because cream cheese contains stabilizers, the amounts of guar gum and locust bean gum are less than usual. Directions to prepare candied carrots and raisins in syrup can be found in the "Component Ingredients" section at the end of this chapter.

1. In a small bowl, combine dextrose, guar gum, locust bean gum, and salt. Mix well. Reserve.
2. Puree the chopped carrots, water, and some of the milk using a high-powered blender, food processor, or commercial immersion blender. Use the remaining milk to rinse out the blender container.
3. Combine carrot puree, turbinado sugar, and spices in a stainless-steel pot. Heat mixture to 35°C (95°F), whisking occasionally.
4. Add skim milk powder and whisk to dissolve completely.
5. Continuing to heat the milk mixture, slowly sprinkle in the dextrose mixture, whisking constantly to avoid lumps and keeping the mixture below 45°C (113°F). After the dextrose mixture is incorporated, heat to 85°C (185°F), stirring constantly and scraping the bottom of the pot with a rubber spatula.
6. Add cream cheese. Mix well. Heat to 66°C (151°F), stirring constantly. Hold at 66°C (151°F) for 30 minutes, stirring if needed. (If the 30-minute hold is in a water bath or in a commercial pasteurizer, no stirring is needed. If the 30-minute hold is on the cooktop, occasional stirring will be needed to equalize the temperature.)
7. Chill quickly, preferably in an ice bath. Allow to mature overnight, covered and refrigerated at 4°C (39°F) or less.
8. Just before freezing the gelato, add water to return the base to the calculated batch weight plus the weight of the spices. Blend with an immersion blender. Taste and adjust salt, if necessary.
9. Freeze in a batch freezer.
10. Transfer the gelato from the batch freezer to a tub, stopping periodically to sprinkle in some of the candied carrots, raisins, and toasted pecans, swirling a bit with a silicone spatula.
11. Harden in a blast freezer or deep freezer.

Ingredient	Quantity	Percent
Milk, 2%	381.5 g	38.15%
Cream Cheese, Philadelphia	250 g	25.00%
Sucrose	160 g	16.00%
Dextrose	28 g	2.80%
Powdered Skim Milk	27.5 g	2.75%
Sour Cream	75 g	7.50%
Water	76 g	7.60%
Guar Gum	0.5 g	0.05%
Salt	1.5 g	0.15%
Batch Weight	1000 g	
Serving Temperature	−13.54°C	

Off-Balance Ingredient	Quantity
Vanilla Extract	5 g

Component	Percent
Fats	11.12%
Sugars	18.58%
MSNF	8.97%
Other Solids	0.76%
Water	60.57%
Total Solids	39.43%
POD	18.64
PAC	27.09

Gelato alla Cheesecake
Cheesecake Gelato

This gelato is based on the quintessentially simple (and my favorite) cheesecake recipe from the now-shuttered Three Sisters of Spain restaurant in Santa Fe, New Mexico. Cream cheese contains locust bean gum as well as other stabilizers. Because of this, locust bean gum has been removed from the formula and the amount of guar gum is less than usual. I like to top each serving with crushed whole wheat cinnamon spice cookies to create a flavor reminiscent of graham cracker crust.

1. In a small bowl, combine dextrose, guar gum, and salt. Mix well. Reserve.
2. Combine milk, sucrose, and water in a stainless-steel pot. Heat to 35°C (95°F), whisking occasionally.
3. Add skim milk powder and whisk to dissolve completely.
4. Continuing to heat the milk mixture, slowly sprinkle in the dextrose mixture, whisking constantly to avoid lumps and keeping the mixture below 45°C (113°F). After the dextrose mixture is incorporated, heat to 85°C (185°F), stirring constantly and scraping the bottom of the pot with a rubber spatula.
5. Add cream cheese and whisk to incorporate while continuing to heat to 66°C (151°F). Hold at 66°C (151°F) for 30 minutes, stirring if needed. (If the 30-minute hold is in a water bath or in a commercial pasteurizer, no stirring is needed. If the 30-minute hold is on the cooktop, occasional stirring will be needed to equalize the temperature.)
6. Chill quickly, preferably in an ice bath. Allow to mature overnight, covered and refrigerated at 4°C (39°F) or less.
7. Just before freezing the gelato, add sour cream and vanilla extract.
8. Add water to return the base to the calculated batch weight. Blend with an immersion blender. Taste and adjust salt, if necessary.
9. Freeze in a batch freezer.
10. Transfer the gelato from the batch freezer to a tub.
11. Harden in a blast freezer or deep freezer.
12. When serving, sprinkle with crushed whole wheat spice cookies, if desired.

Ingredient	Quantity	Percent
Milk, 2%	192.75 g	19.28%
Heavy Cream (36% fat)	230 g	23.00%
Sucrose	112.5 g	11.25%
Powdered Skim Milk	60 g	6.00%
Guar Gum	1.25 g	0.125%
Locust Bean Gum	1.25 g	0.125%
Salt	1 g	0.10%
Pure Almond Extract	1.25 g	0.125%
Pureed Sweet Cherries	400 g	40.00%
Batch Weight	1000 g	
Serving Temperature	−13.57°C	

Mix-In Ingredient	Quantity
Chopped Sweet Cherries	100 g

Component	Percent
Fats	8.90%
Sugars	16.38%
MSNF	8.90%
Other Solids	2.24%
Water	63.68%
Total Solids	36.32%
POD	17.41
PAC	27.14

Gelato alla Ciliegia

Cherry Gelato

I started developing my formula for cherry gelato using cherries from the tree of close friends. It was always a challenge to get enough ripe cherries before the birds had their fill. I like the addition of pure almond extract to boost the cherry flavor. If you wish, you can omit it and make up the difference with 2% milk.

1. In a small bowl, combine 30 grams of the sucrose, guar gum, locust bean gum, and salt. Mix well. Reserve.
2. Combine milk and remaining sucrose in a stainless-steel pot. Heat to 35°C (95°F), whisking occasionally.
3. Add skim milk powder and whisk to dissolve completely.
4. Continuing to heat the milk mixture, slowly sprinkle in the sucrose mixture, whisking constantly to avoid lumps and keeping the mixture below 45°C (113°F). After the sucrose mixture is incorporated, heat to 85°C (185°F), stirring constantly and scraping the bottom of the pot with a rubber spatula.
5. Add cream and almond extract. Mix well. Heat to 75°C (167°F), stirring constantly, and hold for 15 seconds.
6. Chill quickly, preferably in an ice bath. Allow to mature overnight, covered and refrigerated at 4°C (39°F) or less.
7. Meanwhile, pit enough cherries to make the required amount of puree. Cover and refrigerate.
8. Just before freezing the gelato, puree the chilled cherries using a high-powered blender, food processor, or commercial immersion blender. Weigh out the correct amount and add it to the mature base.
9. Add water to return the base to the calculated batch weight. Blend with an immersion blender. Taste and adjust salt, if necessary.
10. Freeze in a batch freezer.
11. Transfer the gelato from the batch freezer to a tub, stopping periodically to sprinkle in some of the chopped cherries, swirling a bit with a silicone spatula.
12. Harden in a blast freezer or deep freezer.

Gelato al Cioccolato
Chocolate Gelato #1

This gelato gets its chocolate flavor from cocoa. Cocoa is what is left when most of the cocoa butter is pressed out of roasted, ground cacao nibs also known as cacao mass. Cocoa, as opposed to cocoa butter, contains most of the chocolate flavor so this is a very chocolatey gelato. Cocoa can add a slight grittiness to gelato. The low temperature pasteurization at 66°C for 30 minutes helps to fully hydrate the cocoa, minimizing grittiness. Most cocoa comes in one of two ranges for fat content: 22% to 24% or 10% to 12%. This formula is balanced for cocoa with 22% to 24% fat. Mascarpone varies in fat content from approximately 36% to 50%. This formula will remain balanced for any mascarpone within this range.

Ingredient	Quantity	Percent
Milk, 2%	553 g	55.30%
Mascarpone, 42% fat	150 g	15.00%
Sucrose	132 g	13.20%
Dextrose	41 g	4.10%
Powdered Skim Milk	47 g	4.70%
Water	41 g	4.10%
Cocoa Powder, 22–24% fat	32 g	3.20%
Guar Gum	1.25 g	0.125%
Locust Bean Gum	1.25 g	0.125%
Salt	1.5 g	0.15%
Batch Weight	1000 g	
Serving Temperature	−13.94°C	

Component	Percent
Fats	8.25%
Sugars	17.02%
MSNF	10.69%
Other Solids	3.29%
Water	60.76%
Total Solids	39.24%
POD	16.98
PAC	27.87

1. In a small bowl, combine dextrose, guar gum, locust bean gum, and salt. Mix well. Reserve.
2. In a stainless-steel pot, whisk together the cocoa and water until smooth.
3. Slowly whisk in milk until the cocoa is fully dispersed and no lumps remain.
4. Add sucrose. Heat to 35°C (95°F), whisking occasionally.
5. Add skim milk powder and whisk to dissolve completely.
6. Continuing to heat the milk mixture, slowly sprinkle in the dextrose mixture, whisking constantly to avoid lumps and keeping the mixture below 45°C (113°F). After the dextrose mixture is incorporated, heat to 85°C (185°F), stirring constantly and scraping the bottom of the pot with a rubber spatula.
7. Off the heat, add mascarpone. Use a whisk to fully incorporate the mascarpone.
8. Heat to 66°C (151°F), stirring constantly. Hold at 66°C (151°F) for 30 minutes, stirring if needed. (If the 30-minute hold is in a water bath or in a commercial pasteurizer, no stirring is needed. If the 30-minute hold is on the cooktop, occasional stirring will be needed to equalize the temperature.)
9. Chill quickly, preferably in an ice bath. Allow to mature overnight, covered and refrigerated at 4°C (39°F) or less.
10. Just before freezing the gelato, add water to return the base to the calculated batch weight. Blend with an immersion blender. Taste and adjust salt, if necessary.
11. Freeze in a batch freezer.
12. Transfer the gelato from the batch freezer to a tub.
13. Harden in a blast freezer or deep freezer.

Ingredient	Quantity	Percent
Milk, 2%	500 g	50.00%
Mascarpone, 42% fat	100 g	10.00%
Sucrose	116 g	11.60%
Dextrose	25 g	2.50%
Powdered Skim Milk	50 g	5.00%
Chocolate, 72% Cocoa Solids	105 g	10.50%
Water	100 g	10.00%
Guar Gum	1.25 g	0.125%
Locust Bean Gum	1.25 g	0.125%
Salt	1.5 g	0.15%
Batch Weight	1000 g	
Serving Temperature	−13.60°C	

Component	Percent
Fats	9.34%
Sugars	16.61%
MSNF	10.09%
Other Solids	4.47%
Water	59.50%
Total Solids	40.50%
POD	18.25
PAC	27.20

Gelato al Fondente

Chocolate Gelato #2

This gelato is flavored with solid chocolate, which is called *fondente* in Italian. Use very high-quality chocolate in bar, tablet, or lozenge form. Do not use chocolate chips as they frequently do not melt well. I think that chocolate with 72% cocoa solids strikes a good balance of chocolate flavor and intensity, though you can use chocolate with slightly more or less cocoa solids and still have a balanced formula. This formula uses mascarpone in place of cream, as does the recipe for Chocolate Gelato #1.

1. In a small bowl, combine dextrose, guar gum, locust bean gum, and salt. Mix well. Reserve.
2. Combine milk and sucrose in a stainless-steel pot. Heat to 35°C (95°F), whisking occasionally.
3. Add the chocolate, broken into pieces, and stir until melted, keeping the temperature below 45°C (113°F).
4. Add skim milk powder and whisk to dissolve completely.
5. Continuing to heat the milk mixture, slowly sprinkle in the dextrose mixture, whisking constantly to avoid lumps and keeping the mixture below 45°C (113°F). After the dextrose mixture is incorporated, heat to 85°C (185°F), stirring constantly and scraping the bottom of the pot with a rubber spatula.
6. Off the heat, add mascarpone. Use a whisk to fully incorporate the mascarpone.
7. Heat to 66°C (151°F), stirring constantly. Hold at 66°C (151°F) for 30 minutes, stirring if needed. (If the 30-minute hold is in a water bath or in a commercial pasteurizer, no stirring is needed. If the 30-minute hold is on the cooktop, occasional stirring will be needed to equalize the temperature.)
8. Chill quickly, preferably in an ice bath. Allow to mature overnight, covered and refrigerated at 4°C (39°F) or less.
9. Just before freezing the gelato, add water to return the base to the calculated batch weight. Blend with an immersion blender. Taste and adjust salt, if necessary.
10. Freeze in a batch freezer.
11. Transfer the gelato from the batch freezer to a tub.
12. Harden in a blast freezer or deep freezer.

Make Your Own Artisan Italian Gelato

Gelato al Cioccolato e Burro di Arachidi

Chocolate Peanut Butter Gelato

Ingredient	Quantity	Percent
Milk, 2%	510 g	51.00%
Heavy Cream (36% fat)	75 g	7.50%
Sucrose	150 g	15.00%
Dextrose	10 g	1.00%
Fructose	10 g	1.00%
Cocoa Powder (22–24% fat)	20 g	2.00%
Water	81.5 g	8.15%
Natural Peanut Butter, Smooth	90 g	9.00%
Powdered Skim Milk	50 g	5.00%
Guar Gum	1 g	0.10%
Locust Bean Gum	1 g	0.10%
Salt	1.5 g	0.15%
Batch Weight	1000 g	
Serving Temperature	−13.10°C	

Mix-In Ingredient	Quantity
Roasted Unsalted Peanuts	30 g

Component	Percent
Fats	8.67%
Sugars	17.48%
MSNF	9.83%
Other Solids	5.77%
Water	58.25%
Total Solids	41.75%
POD	18.59
PAC	26.19

This gelato was developed to be reminiscent of milk chocolate peanut butter cups. Use a smooth, not chunky, natural peanut butter that contains only peanuts. A trace of added salt is okay, too. Do not use peanut butter that has added vegetable fats of any sort as these fats will negatively affect the mouthfeel of the gelato. I typically use Laura Scudder's Natural Peanut Butter. Try topping each serving with miniature chocolate peanut butter cups or chopped-up larger ones.

1. In a small bowl, combine dextrose, fructose, guar gum, locust bean gum, and salt. Mix well. Reserve.
2. In a stainless-steel pot, whisk together the cocoa and water until smooth.
3. Slowly whisk in milk until the cocoa is fully dispersed and no lumps remain.
4. Add sucrose. Heat to 35°C (95°F), whisking occasionally.
5. Add skim milk powder and whisk to dissolve completely.
6. Continuing to heat the milk mixture, slowly sprinkle in the dextrose mixture, whisking constantly to avoid lumps and keeping the mixture below 45°C (113°F). After the dextrose mixture is incorporated, heat to 85°C (185°F), stirring constantly and scraping the bottom of the pot with a rubber spatula.
7. Add cream. Mix well. Hold at 75°C (167°F) or above for 15 seconds.
8. Remove from heat. Whisk in the peanut butter until thoroughly combined.
9. Chill quickly, preferably in an ice bath. Allow to mature overnight, covered and refrigerated at 4°C (39°F) or less.
10. Just before freezing the gelato, add water to return the base to the calculated batch weight. Blend with an immersion blender. Taste and adjust salt, if necessary.
11. Freeze in a batch freezer.
12. Transfer the gelato from the batch freezer to a tub, stopping periodically to sprinkle in the roasted peanuts, swirling a bit with a spatula.
13. Harden in a blast freezer or deep freezer.

Ingredient	Quantity	Percent
Milk, 2%	336.5 g	33.65%
Aroy-D Coconut Cream, 70%	400 g	40.00%
Sucrose	180 g	18.00%
Dextrose	10 g	1.00%
Powdered Skim Milk	70 g	7.00%
Guar Gum	1.25 g	0.125%
Locust Bean Gum	1.25 g	0.125%
Salt	1 g	0.10%
Batch Weight	1000 g	
Serving Temperature	−13.03°C	

Component	Percent
Fats	9.18%
Sugars	18.92%
MSNF	9.69%
Other Solids	0.33%
Water	61.88%
Total Solids	38.12%
POD	19.51
PAC	26.07

Gelato al Cocco

Coconut Gelato

Many years ago at university, I had a group of friends from all around the world. Many of them liked to cook. I got quite an education in the cuisines of the world and, because of longstanding friendships, did a deep dive into Sri Lankan and Caribbean cooking. By the age of 19, I became proficient at making coconut milk by hand. In the days before food processors, this involved a hand-crank coconut grater and a sieve. I did not think I would get many takers if I based my coconut gelato on freshly made coconut milk, so I opted to devise a formula using a high-quality canned product. I balanced this recipe using Aroy-D canned coconut cream, which contains 70% coconut extractives. The only other ingredient in the coconut cream is water. If you use a different brand or strength you may need to rebalance the formula. Try to avoid any coconut milk that contains thickeners or any ingredients other than coconut and water.

1. In a small bowl, combine dextrose, 20 grams of sucrose, guar gum, locust bean gum, and salt. Mix well. Reserve.
2. Combine milk and remaining sucrose in a stainless-steel pot. Heat to 35°C (95°F), whisking occasionally. Add skim milk powder and whisk to dissolve completely.
3. Continuing to heat the milk mixture, slowly sprinkle in the dextrose mixture, whisking constantly to avoid lumps and keeping the mixture below 45°C (113°F). After the dextrose mixture is incorporated, heat to 85°C (185°F), stirring constantly and scraping the bottom of the pot with a rubber spatula.
4. Remove from heat. Add coconut cream. Mix well.
5. Chill quickly, preferably in an ice bath. Allow to mature overnight, covered and refrigerated at 4°C (39°F) or less.
6. Just before freezing the gelato, add water to return the base to the calculated batch weight. Blend with an immersion blender. Taste and adjust salt, if necessary.
7. Freeze in a batch freezer.
8. Transfer the gelato from the batch freezer to a tub.
9. Harden in a blast freezer or deep freezer.

Ingredient	Quantity	Percent
Milk, 2%	203 g	20.30%
Heavy Cream (36% fat)	235 g	23.50%
Sucrose	170 g	17.00%
Dextrose	25 g	2.50%
Powdered Skim Milk	63.5 g	6.35%
Brewed Espresso Coffee	300 g	30.00%
Guar Gum	1.25 g	0.125%
Locust Bean Gum	1.25 g	0.125%
Salt	1 g	0.10%
Batch Weight	1000 g	
Serving Temperature	−13.70°C	

Mix-In Ingredient	Quantity
Espresso Beans, freshly ground	3 g

Component	Percent
Fats	8.97%
Sugars	19.30%
MSNF	9.36%
Other Solids	0.94%
Water	61.44%
Total Solids	38.56%
POD	19.50
PAC	27.40

Gelato al Caffè
Coffee Gelato

When I learned to make coffee gelato in Italy, the coffee flavor came from hand-pulled espresso shots. It takes a lot of espresso shots to get the amount required for this gelato. In the United States, I don't have a kitchen assistant to pull espresso so I devised a method that is much easier while still delivering the same depth of flavor. If you are up for it, though, by all means hand-pull your own espresso. Just make it strong! Otherwise, see the process for making steeped espresso in the "Component Ingredients" section at the end of this chapter.

1. In a small bowl, combine dextrose, guar gum, locust bean gum, and salt. Mix well. Reserve.
2. Combine milk, brewed espresso, and sucrose in a stainless-steel pot. Heat to 35°C (95°F), whisking occasionally.
3. Add skim milk powder and whisk to dissolve completely.
4. Continuing to heat the milk mixture, slowly sprinkle in the dextrose mixture, whisking constantly to avoid lumps and keeping the mixture below 45°C (113°F). After the dextrose mixture is incorporated, heat to 85°C (185°F), stirring constantly and scraping the bottom of the pot with a rubber spatula.
5. Add cream. Mix well. Heat to 75°C (167°F), stirring constantly, and hold for 15 seconds.
6. Chill quickly, preferably in an ice bath. Allow to mature overnight, covered and refrigerated at 4°C (39°F) or less.
7. Just before freezing the gelato, add water to return the base to the calculated batch weight.
8. Add ground espresso. Blend with an immersion blender. Taste and adjust salt, if necessary.
9. Freeze in a batch freezer.
10. Transfer the gelato from the batch freezer to a tub.
11. Harden in a blast freezer or deep freezer.

Ingredient	Quantity	Percent
Milk, 2%	440 g	44.00%
Heavy Cream (36% fat)	45 g	4.50%
Sucrose	139 g	13.90%
Fructose	20 g	2.00%
Dextrose	10 g	1.00%
Cocoa Mass	120 g	12.00%
Powdered Skim Milk	60 g	6.00%
Water	162 g	16.20%
Guar Gum	1.25 g	0.125%
Locust Bean Gum	1.25 g	0.125%
Salt	1.5 g	0.15%
Base Weight	1000 g	
Serving Temperature	−13.24°C	

Mix-In Ingredient	Quantity
Candied Orange Peel, chopped	50 g

Component	Percent
Fats	8.90%
Sugars	16.82%
MSNF	9.96%
Other Solids	5.98%
Water	58.33%
Total Solids	41.67%
POD	18.44
PAC	26.49

Gelato al Cioccolato Extra-Fondente e Scorze d'Arancia Candite

Dark Chocolate & Candied Orange Peel Gelato

Cocoa mass is pure cocoa beans that have been roasted and ground. It is the beginning point for producing solid chocolate, such as bars and lozenges. The difference is that cocoa mass does not have added sugar or other ingredients. It is the darkest and purest form of chocolate available. The recipe for candied orange peel can be found in the "Component Ingredients" section at the end of this chapter.

1. In a small bowl, combine fructose, dextrose, guar gum, locust bean gum, and salt. Mix well. Reserve.
2. Combine milk, water, and sucrose in a stainless-steel pot. Heat to 35°C, whisking occasionally.
3. Add cocoa mass, broken into pieces if not in lozenge or chip form, and stir until melted, keeping the temperature below 45°C (113°F).
4. Add skim milk powder and whisk to dissolve completely.
5. Continuing to heat the milk mixture, slowly sprinkle in the fructose mixture, whisking constantly to avoid lumps and keeping the mixture below 45°C (113°F). After the fructose mixture is incorporated, heat to 85°C (185°F), stirring constantly and scraping the bottom of the pot with a rubber spatula.
6. Add cream. Mix well. If the mixture is not at or above 75°C (167°F), heat to that temperature, stirring constantly, and hold for 15 seconds.
7. Chill quickly, preferably in an ice bath. Allow to mature overnight, covered and refrigerated at 4°C (39°F) or less.
8. Just before freezing the gelato, add water to return the base to the calculated batch weight. Blend with an immersion blender. Taste and adjust salt, if necessary.
9. Freeze in a batch freezer.
10. Transfer the gelato from the batch freezer to a tub, stopping periodically to sprinkle in some of the candied orange peel, swirling a bit with a spatula.
11. Harden in a blast freezer or deep freezer.

Ingredient	Quantity	Percent
Milk, 2%	491.5 g	49.15%
Heavy Cream (36% fat)	220 g	22.00%
Sucrose	40 g	4.00%
Deglet Noor Dates, pitted	200 g	20.00%
Powdered Skim Milk	45 g	4.50%
Guar Gum	1.25 g	0.125%
Locust Bean Gum	1.25 g	0.125%
Salt	1 g	0.10%
Batch Weight	1000 g	
Serving Temperature	−15.13°C	

Component	Percent
Fats	8.99%
Sugars	16.68%
MSNF	10.10%
Other Solids	3.47%
Water	60.77%
Total Solids	39.23%
POD	18.48
PAC	30.26

Gelato al Dattero di Deglet Noor

Deglet Noor Date Gelato

Deglet Noor dates and Medjool dates are two of the most commonly available date varieties in the United States. They have different sugar contents and, thus, different gelato formulas. Although this gelato formula is balanced, with sugar on the low side, the amount of glucose and fructose in dates means that the serving temperature is lower than the norm.

1. In a small bowl, combine 30 grams of the sucrose, guar gum, locust bean gum, and salt. Mix well. Reserve.
2. Coarsely chop the dates.
1. Puree the dates as thoroughly as possible with half of the milk using a high-powered blender, food processor, or commercial immersion blender. Pour the puree into a stainless-steel pot.
3. Use the remaining milk to rinse out the blender jar or food processor container and add to the puree.
4. Add remaining sucrose to the date puree. Heat to 35°C (95°F), whisking occasionally.
5. Add skim milk powder and whisk to dissolve completely.
6. Continuing to heat the milk mixture, slowly sprinkle in the sucrose mixture, whisking constantly to avoid lumps and keeping the mixture below 45°C (113°F). After the sucrose mixture is incorporated, heat to 85°C (185°F), stirring constantly and scraping the bottom of the pot with a rubber spatula.
7. Add cream. Mix well. Heat to 75°C (167°F), stirring constantly, and hold for 15 seconds.
8. Chill quickly, preferably in an ice bath. Allow to mature overnight, covered and refrigerated at 4°C (39°F) or less.
9. Just before freezing the gelato, add water to return the base to the calculated batch weight. Blend with an immersion blender. Taste and adjust salt, if necessary.
10. Freeze in a batch freezer.
11. Transfer the gelato from the batch freezer to a tub.
12. Harden in a blast freezer or deep freezer.

Gelato Formulas and Recipes for Component Ingredients

Gelato al Dulce de Leche

Dulce de Leche Gelato

Ingredient	Quantity	Percent
Milk, 2%	457 g	45.70%
Heavy Cream (36% fat)	138 g	13.80%
Sucrose	25 g	2.50%
Dextrose	6 g	0.60%
Powdered Skim Milk	23 g	2.30%
Dulce de Leche, La Lachera	347.5 g	34.75%
Guar Gum	1.25 g	0.125%
Locust Bean Gum	1.25 g	0.125%
Salt	1 g	0.10%
Batch Weight	1000 g	
Serving Temperature	−12.75°C	

Component	Percent
Fats	8.54%
Sugars	19.09%
MSNF	11.26%
Other Solids	2.31%
Water	58.80%
Total Solids	41.20%
POD	17.78
PAC	25.50

Although dulce de leche is from Latin America, it is a popular gelato flavor in Italy. La Lechera is a commonly available brand of dulce de leche in the United States. If using another brand, the formula may need to be rebalanced.

1. In a small bowl, combine dextrose, 20 grams of sucrose, guar gum, locust bean gum, and salt. Mix well. Reserve.
2. Combine milk, remaining sucrose, and dulce de leche in a stainless-steel pot. Heat to 35°C (95°F), whisking occasionally.
3. Add skim milk powder and whisk to dissolve completely.
4. Continuing to heat the milk mixture, slowly sprinkle in the dextrose mixture, whisking constantly to avoid lumps and keeping the mixture below 45°C (113°F). After the dextrose mixture is incorporated, heat to 85°C (185°F), stirring constantly and scraping the bottom of the pot with a rubber spatula.
5. Add cream. Mix well. Heat to 75°C (167°F), stirring constantly, and hold for 15 seconds.
6. Chill quickly, preferably in an ice bath. Allow to mature overnight, covered and refrigerated at 4°C (39°F) or less.
7. Just before freezing the gelato, add water to return the base to the calculated batch weight. Blend with an immersion blender. Taste and adjust salt, if necessary.
8. Freeze in a batch freezer.
9. Transfer the gelato from the batch freezer to a tub.
10. Harden in a blast freezer or deep freezer.

Gelato alla Crema Pasticcera
Egg Cream Gelato

Crema is a flavor but also a style of gelato popular in northern Italy. It contains egg yolks, which are rare in gelato made in southern Italy. Egg yolk functions as a stabilizer, so no added stabilizers are needed. With a high-powered blender, the whole vanilla bean can be used, not just the seeds. This will provide more flecks of vanilla in the gelato that look and taste just like vanilla seeds. Instead of a vanilla bean, you can add vanilla extract or vanilla bean paste to the mature base just before freezing.

1. Puree the chopped vanilla bean with some of the milk in a high-powered blender. Pour the puree into a stainless-steel pot.
2. Use the remaining milk to rinse out the blender jar and add to the puree.
3. Beat the eggs and sucrose until very pale, almost white.
4. Combine beaten egg yolk–sugar mixture and all other ingredients in the pot with the milk.
5. Heat the mixture to 69°C (157°F), stirring constantly. Hold at 69°C (157°F) for 30 minutes, stirring if needed. (If the 30-minute hold is in a water bath or in a commercial pasteurizer, no stirring is needed. If the 30-minute hold is on the cooktop, occasional stirring will be needed to equalize the temperature.)
6. Chill quickly, preferably in an ice bath. Allow to mature overnight, covered and refrigerated at 4°C (39°F) or less.
7. Just before freezing the gelato, add water to return the base to the calculated batch weight. Blend with an immersion blender. Taste and adjust salt, if necessary.
8. Freeze in a batch freezer.
9. Transfer the gelato from the batch freezer to a tub.
10. Harden in a blast freezer or deep freezer.

Ingredient	Quantity	Percent
Milk, 2%	537 g	53.70%
Heavy Cream (36% fat)	160 g	16.00%
Sucrose	155 g	15.50%
Dextrose	25 g	2.50%
Powdered Skim Milk	30 g	3.00%
Egg Yolk	92 g	9.20%
Salt	1 g	0.10%
Batch Weight	1000 g	
Serving Temperature	−12.86°C	

Off-Balance Ingredient	Quantity
Vanilla Bean, chopped	½ bean

Component	Percent
Fats	9.26%
Sugars	17.85%
MSNF	8.70%
Other Solids	2.00%
Water	62.20%
Total Solids	37.80%
POD	18.00
PAC	25.71

Ingredient	Quantity	Percent
Milk, 2%	460 g	46.00%
Heavy Cream (36% fat)	220 g	22.00%
Sucrose	125 g	12.50%
Powdered Skim Milk	47 g	4.70%
Water	47 g	4.70%
Dried Figs, stems removed	100 g	10.00%
Salt	1 g	0.10%
Batch Weight	1000 g	
Serving Temperature	−14.00°C	

Component	Percent
Fats	8.94%
Sugars	17.29%
MSNF	10.00%
Other Solids	2.22%
Water	61.55%
Total Solids	38.45%
POD	18.65
PAC	28.01

Gelato ai Fichi Secchi

Fig Gelato

I have made this gelato with both California mission figs and Turkish Smyrna figs. Both make excellent gelato. The mission figs make the gelato a little darker and with a slightly more pronounced taste. The usual stabilizers are absent from this formula because the solids in the figs stabilize the mixture. In fact, they do this so well that the gelato retains its texture at the usual serving temperature of −13°C (9°F) even though the calculated serving temperature, based on PAC, is −14°C (7°F). My goal in creating this gelato was to be reminiscent of the classic American fig-filled cookies.

1. Coarsely chop the figs.
2. Puree the figs as thoroughly as possible with half of the milk using a high-powered blender, food processor, or commercial immersion blender. Pour the puree into a stainless-steel pot.
3. Use the remaining milk and the water to rinse out the blender jar or food processor container and add to the puree.
4. Add the sucrose and salt. Heat to 35°C (95°F), whisking occasionally.
5. Add skim milk powder and whisk to dissolve completely.
6. Add cream. Mix well. Heat to 75°C (167°F), stirring constantly, and hold for 15 seconds.
7. Chill quickly, preferably in an ice bath. Allow to mature overnight, covered and refrigerated at 4°C (39°F) or less.
8. Just before freezing the gelato, add water to return the base to the calculated batch weight. Blend with an immersion blender. Taste and adjust salt, if necessary.
9. Freeze in a batch freezer.
10. Transfer the gelato from the batch freezer to a tub.
11. Harden in a blast freezer or deep freezer.

Gelato al Fiordilatte
Fiordilatte Gelato

Fiordilatte gelato is the most straightforward gelato to make. It is pure dairy. It does not even contain any vanilla. Although ingredient quality is always important for gelato, it is of consummate importance for fiordilatte, as it does not contain any flavors other than lightly sweetened dairy. As fiordilatte gelato is the foundation of many other flavors of gelato, I suggest making it before embarking on making any of the other flavors.

1. In a small bowl, combine dextrose, guar gum, locust bean gum, and salt. Mix well. Reserve.
2. Combine milk, sucrose, and fructose in a stainless-steel pot. Heat to 35°C (95°F), whisking occasionally.
3. Add skim milk powder and whisk to dissolve completely.
4. Continuing to heat the milk mixture, slowly sprinkle in the dextrose mixture, whisking constantly to avoid lumps and keeping the mixture below 45°C (113°F). After the dextrose mixture is incorporated, heat to 85°C (185°F), stirring constantly and scraping the bottom of the pot with a rubber spatula.
5. Add cream. Mix well. Heat to 75°C (167°F), stirring constantly, and hold for 15 seconds.
6. Chill quickly, preferably in an ice bath. Allow to mature overnight, covered and refrigerated at 4°C (39°F) or less.
7. Just before freezing the gelato, add water to return the base to the calculated batch weight. Blend with an immersion blender. Taste and adjust salt, if necessary.
8. Freeze in a batch freezer.
9. Transfer the gelato from the batch freezer to a tub.
10. Harden in a blast freezer or deep freezer.

Ingredient	Quantity	Percent
Milk, 2%	525 g	52.50%
Heavy Cream (36% fat)	263 g	26.30%
Sucrose	135 g	13.50%
Dextrose	20 g	2.00%
Fructose	20 g	2.00%
Powdered Skim Milk	34 g	3.40%
Guar Gum	1.25 g	0.125%
Locust Bean Gum	1.25 g	0.125%
Salt	0.50 g	0.05%
Batch Weight	1000 g	
Serving Temperature	−13.21°C	

Component	Percent
Fats	10.52%
Sugars	17.34%
MSNF	9.62%
Other Solids	0.28%
Water	62.24%
Total Solids	37.76%
POD	18.69
PAC	26.42

Ingredient	Quantity	Percent
Milk, 2%	250.5 g	25.05%
Heavy Cream (36% fat)	231 g	23.10%
Sucrose	100 g	10.00%
Powdered Skim Milk	65 g	6.50%
Guar Gum	1.25 g	0.125%
Locust Bean Gum	1.25 g	0.125%
Salt	1 g	0.10%
Pureed Red Seedless Grapes	350 g	35.00%
Batch Weight	1000 g	
Serving Temperature	−13.93°C	

Component	Percent
Fats	8.86%
Sugars	16.07%
MSNF	9.90%
Other Solids	1.89%
Water	63.28%
Total Solids	36.72%
POD	17.78
PAC	27.85

Gelato all'Uva

Grape Gelato

Grapes contain lots of dextrose and fructose, two simple sugars that significantly lower the freezing point of the gelato base. Because of this, no dextrose is added to this mixture and the maximum quantity of grapes that can be added is limited by their anti-freezing power. If you live in an area where you can get concord grapes, by all means use them in this gelato in place of red grapes.

1. In a small bowl, combine 30 grams of sucrose, guar gum, locust bean gum, and salt. Mix well. Reserve.
2. Combine milk and remaining sucrose in a stainless-steel pot. Heat to 35°C (95°F), whisking occasionally.
3. Add skim milk powder and whisk to dissolve completely.
4. Continuing to heat the milk mixture, slowly sprinkle in the sucrose mixture, whisking constantly to avoid lumps and keeping the mixture below 45°C (113°F). After the sucrose mixture is incorporated, heat to 85°C (185°F), stirring constantly and scraping the bottom of the pot with a rubber spatula.
5. Add cream. Mix well. Heat to 75°C, stirring constantly, and hold for 15 seconds.
6. Chill quickly, preferably in an ice bath. Allow to mature overnight, covered and refrigerated at 4°C (39°F) or less.
7. Meanwhile, quarter the grapes and remove any seeds. There will be some seeds even in seedless grapes. Refrigerate the grapes.
8. Just before freezing the gelato, puree the chilled grapes using a high-powered blender, food processor, or commercial immersion blender. Weigh out the correct amount and add it to the mature base.
9. Add water to return the base to the calculated batch weight. Blend with an immersion blender. Taste and adjust salt, if necessary.
10. Freeze in a batch freezer.
11. Transfer the gelato from the batch freezer to a tub.
12. Harden in a blast freezer or deep freezer.

Make Your Own Artisan Italian Gelato

Ingredient	Quantity	Percent
Milk, 2%	186 g	18.60%
Heavy Cream (36% fat)	215 g	21.50%
Sucrose	110 g	11.00%
Fructose	20 g	2.00%
Powdered Skim Milk	64 g	6.40%
Guar Gum	1.25 g	0.125%
Locust Bean Gum	1.25 g	0.125%
Salt	1 g	0.10%
Guava Puree	400 g	40.00%
Amoretti Guava Extract	1.5 g	0.15%
Batch Weight	1000 g	
Serving Temperature	−13.33°C	

Component	Percent
Fats	8.66%
Sugars	16.70%
MSNF	9.12%
Other Solids	4.02%
Water	61.50%
Total Solids	38.50%
POD	18.58
PAC	26.65

Gelato alla Guava

Guava Gelato

If you do not live somewhere where guavas grow, try buying frozen guava puree. It is often available in stores that sell Latin and Caribbean food products. Be sure to buy *pure* guava puree, with no ingredients other than guava, and not a guava concentrate. If you want to amplify the guava flavor, use the Amoretti guava extract, which also is pure. I cannot recommend any other brands. If you do not use the guava extract, just add more milk to compensate.

1. In a small bowl, combine fructose, guar gum, locust bean gum, and salt. Mix well. Reserve.
2. Combine milk and sucrose in a stainless-steel pot. Heat to 35°C (95°F), whisking occasionally.
3. Add skim milk powder and whisk to dissolve completely.
4. Continuing to heat the milk mixture, slowly sprinkle in the fructose mixture, whisking constantly to avoid lumps and keeping the mixture below 45°C (113°F). After the fructose mixture is incorporated, heat to 85°C (185°F), stirring constantly and scraping the bottom of the pot with a rubber spatula.
5. Add cream. Mix well. Heat to 75°C (167°F), stirring constantly, and hold for 15 seconds.
6. Chill quickly, preferably in an ice bath. Allow to mature overnight, covered and refrigerated at 4°C (39°F) or less.
7. Meanwhile, prepare guava puree or allow frozen puree to melt in the refrigerator.
8. Just before freezing the gelato, add guava puree and guava extract, if using.
9. Add water to return the base to the calculated batch weight. Blend with an immersion blender. Taste and adjust salt, if necessary.
10. Freeze in a batch freezer.
11. Transfer the gelato from the batch freezer to a tub.
12. Harden in a blast freezer or deep freezer.

Ingredient	Quantity	Percent
Milk, 2%	651.5 g	65.15%
Sucrose	125 g	12.50%
Dextrose	25 g	2.50%
Powdered Skim Milk	40 g	4.00%
Guar Gum	1 g	0.10%
Locust Bean Gum	1 g	0.10%
Salt	1.5 g	0.15%
Chocolate, 72% Cacao	70 g	7.00%
Hazelnut Paste	85 g	8.50%
Batch Weight	1000 g	
Serving Temperature	−13.61°C	

Component	Percent
Fats	9.50%
Sugars	17.13%
MSNF	9.68%
Other Solids	4.85%
Water	58.85%
Total Solids	41.15%
POD	18.23
PAC	27.22

Gelato al Gianduia

Hazelnut Chocolate Gelato

Hazelnuts from Italy's Piedmont region are prized throughout the country. Consequently, hazelnut paste from Piedmont is typically more expensive that that from other regions. Italian nut pastes, including hazelnut paste, are smoother and silkier than American nut butters. If possible, use pure hazelnut paste from Italy for this classic gelato.

1. In a small bowl, combine dextrose, guar gum, locust bean gum, and salt. Mix well. Reserve.
2. Combine milk and sucrose in a stainless-steel pot. Heat to 35°C (95°F), whisking occasionally.
3. Add the chocolate, broken into pieces, and stir until melted, keeping the temperature below 45°C (113°F).
4. Add skim milk powder and whisk to dissolve completely.
5. Continuing to heat the milk mixture, slowly sprinkle in the dextrose mixture, whisking constantly to avoid lumps and keeping the mixture below 45°C (113°F). After the dextrose mixture is incorporated, heat to 85°C (185°F), stirring constantly and scraping the bottom of the pot with a rubber spatula.
6. Remove from heat. Whisk in hazelnut paste until thoroughly blended.
7. Chill quickly, preferably in an ice bath. Allow to mature overnight, covered and refrigerated at 4°C (39°F) or less.
8. Just before freezing the gelato, add water to return the base to the calculated batch weight. Blend with an immersion blender. Taste and adjust salt, if necessary.
9. Freeze in a batch freezer.
10. Transfer the gelato from the batch freezer to a tub.
11. Harden in a blast freezer or deep freezer.

Ingredient	Quantity	Percent
Milk, 2%	649 g	64.90%
Hazelnut Paste	130 g	13.00%
Sucrose	144 g	14.40%
Dextrose	30 g	3.00%
Powdered Skim Milk	44 g	4.40%
Guar Gum	1 g	0.10%
Locust Bean Gum	1 g	0.10%
Salt	1 g	0.10%
Batch Weight	1000 g	
Serving Temperature	−13.63°C	

Component	Percent
Fats	9.72%
Sugars	17.96%
MSNF	10.03%
Other Solids	3.39%
Water	58.91%
Total Solids	41.09%
POD	18.05
PAC	27.26

Gelato alla Nocciola

Hazelnut Gelato

Hazelnut gelato is one of the handful of absolutely classic gelato flavors in Italy. It is a perennial favorite. In general, nut-based gelati are expensive to make due to the cost of the nut pastes. Italian nut pastes are ground so finely that they do not impart any grittiness to the gelato. Be sure that any hazelnut paste you use contains only one ingredient: hazelnuts. Hazelnuts from Piedmont are the most prized in Italy.

1. In a small bowl, combine dextrose, guar gum, locust bean gum, and salt. Mix well. Reserve.
2. Combine milk and sucrose in a stainless-steel pot. Heat to 35°C (95°F), whisking occasionally.
3. Add skim milk powder and whisk to dissolve completely.
4. Continuing to heat the milk mixture, slowly sprinkle in the dextrose mixture, whisking constantly to avoid lumps and keeping the mixture below 45°C (113°F). After the dextrose mixture is incorporated, heat to 85°C (185°F), stirring constantly and scraping the bottom of the pot with a rubber spatula.
5. Remove from heat. Stir in the hazelnut paste.
6. Chill quickly, preferably in an ice bath. Allow to mature overnight, covered and refrigerated at 4°C (39°F) or less.
7. Just before freezing the gelato, add water to return the base to the calculated batch weight. Blend with an immersion blender. Taste and adjust salt, if necessary.
8. Freeze in a batch freezer.
9. Transfer the gelato from the batch freezer to a tub.
10. Harden in a blast freezer or deep freezer.

Gelato all'Ibisco

Hibiscus Gelato

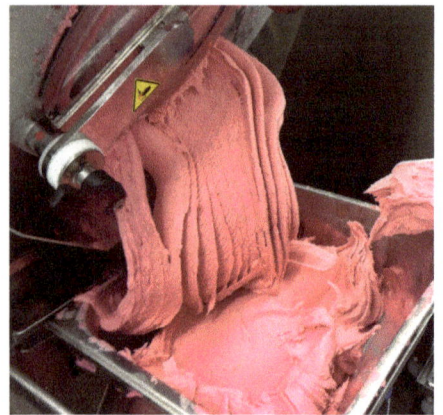

Dried hibiscus flowers are used to make a bright red drink throughout the Caribbean and Central America. The flowers can be purchased in markets catering to customers from those areas. In Spanish, the flowers are referred to as *Flor de Jamaica*. In the English-speaking West Indies, the flowers and the drink are referred to as *sorrel*. Cloves and cinnamon are commonly included in the drink. I prefer to use Ceylon or Saigon cinnamon sticks for their more floral flavor. The hibiscus infusion is made by steeping dried hibiscus flowers and spices in water. The directions can be found in the "Component Ingredients" section at the end of this chapter. The flowers and spices do not add an appreciable amount of solids to the gelato so the infusion is treated as if it were water.

Ingredient	Quantity	Percent
Milk, 2%	199.5 g	19.95%
Heavy Cream (36% fat)	236 g	23.60%
Sucrose	166 g	16.60%
Fructose	20 g	2.00%
Powdered Skim Milk	75 g	7.50%
Guar Gum	1.25 g	0.125%
Locust Bean Gum	1.25 g	0.125%
Salt	1 g	0.10%
Hibiscus Infusion, chilled	300 g	30.00%
Batch Weight	1000 g	
Serving Temperature	−13.49°C	

Component	Percent
Fats	8.95%
Sugars	18.60%
MSNF	10.43%
Other Solids	0.33%
Water	61.69%
Total Solids	38.31%
POD	20.47
PAC	26.99

1. In a small bowl, combine fructose, guar gum, locust bean gum, salt. Mix well. Reserve.
2. Combine milk and sucrose in a stainless-steel pot. Heat to 35°C (95°F), whisking occasionally.
3. Add skim milk powder and whisk to dissolve completely.
4. Continuing to heat the milk mixture, slowly sprinkle in the fructose mixture, whisking constantly to avoid lumps and keeping the mixture below 45°C (113°F). After the fructose mixture is incorporated, heat to 85°C (185°F), stirring constantly and scraping the bottom of the pot with a rubber spatula.
5. Add cream. Mix well. Heat to 75°C (167°F), stirring constantly, and hold for 15 seconds.
6. Chill quickly, preferably in an ice bath. Allow to mature overnight, covered and refrigerated at 4°C (39°F) or less.
7. Just before freezing the gelato, add the cold hibiscus infusion to the mature gelato base.
8. Add water to return the base to the calculated batch weight. Blend with an immersion blender. Taste and adjust salt, if necessary.
9. Freeze in a batch freezer.
10. Transfer the gelato from the batch freezer to a tub.
11. Harden in a blast freezer or deep freezer.

Ingredient	Quantity	Percent
Milk, 2%	572.5 g	57.25%
Heavy Cream (36% fat)	215 g	21.50%
Honey	80 g	8.00%
Sucrose	95 g	9.50%
Powdered Skim Milk	34 g	3.40%
Guar Gum	1.25 g	0.125%
Locust Bean Gum	1.25 g	0.125%
Salt	1 g	0.10%
Batch Weight	1000 g	
Serving Temperature	−14.06°C	

Component	Percent
Fats	8.87%
Sugars	16.07%
MSNF	9.75%
Other Solids	0.39%
Water	64.92%
Total Solids	35.08%
POD	17.64
PAC	28.11

Gelato al Miele

Honey Gelato

The sugars in honey are almost exclusively fructose and dextrose. These lower the freezing point of the gelato much more than sucrose, limiting the amount of honey that can be incorporated into the gelato. It is best to use a very flavorful honey if you want the honey flavor to shine. Even a mild honey, though, will produce a wonderful gelato.

1. In a small bowl, combine 30 grams of the sucrose, guar gum, locust bean gum, and salt. Mix well. Reserve.
2. Combine milk, honey, and remaining sucrose in a stainless-steel pot. Heat to 35°C (95°F), whisking occasionally.
3. Add skim milk powder and whisk to dissolve completely.
4. Continuing to heat the milk mixture, slowly sprinkle in the sucrose mixture, whisking constantly to avoid lumps and keeping the mixture below 45°C (113°F). After the sucrose mixture is incorporated, heat to 85°C (185°F), stirring constantly and scraping the bottom of the pot with a rubber spatula.
5. Add cream. Mix well. Heat to 75°C (167°F), stirring constantly, and hold for 15 seconds.
6. Chill quickly, preferably in an ice bath. Allow to mature overnight, covered and refrigerated at 4°C (39°F) or less.
7. Just before freezing the gelato, add water to return the base to the calculated batch weight. Blend with an immersion blender. Taste and adjust salt, if necessary.
8. Freeze in a batch freezer.
9. Transfer the gelato from the batch freezer to a tub.
10. Harden in a blast freezer or deep freezer.

Gelato al Caffè Irlandese
Irish Coffee Gelato

Ingredient	Quantity	Percent
Milk, 2%	294.5 g	29.45%
Heavy Cream (36% fat)	230 g	23.00%
Sucrose	85 g	8.50%
Turbinado Sugar	77 g	7.70%
Powdered Skim Milk	60 g	6.00%
Brewed Espresso Coffee	200 g	20.00%
Guar Gum	1.25 g	0.125%
Locust Bean Gum	1.25 g	0.125%
Salt	1 g	0.10%
Irish Whisky, 80 proof	50 g	5.00%
Batch Weight	1000 g	
Serving Temperature	−17.41°C	

Component	Percent
Fats	8.94%
Sugars	16.14%
MSNF	9.82%
Other Solids	0.79%
Water	64.31%
Total Solids	35.69%
POD	16.96
PAC	34.83

The ideal serving temperature of this gelato is lower than the typical temperature of a gelato display case. This is due to the anti-freezing property of the alcohol, which limits the amount that can be added. Italian brown sugar comes in large free-flowing crystals called *zucchero di canna*. It is similar to turbinado sugar. You can pull your own espresso shots or you can use the technique for steeped espresso in the "Component Ingredients" section at the end of this chapter to get a similar flavor with much less work.

1. In a small bowl, combine 30 grams of sucrose, guar gum, locust bean gum, and salt. Mix well. Reserve.
2. Combine milk, coffee, remaining sucrose, and turbinado sugar in a stainless-steel pot. Heat to 35°C (95°F), whisking occasionally.
3. Add skim milk powder and whisk to dissolve completely.
4. Continuing to heat the milk mixture, slowly sprinkle in the sucrose mixture, whisking constantly to avoid lumps and keeping the mixture below 45°C (113°F). After the sucrose mixture is incorporated, heat to 85°C (185°F), stirring constantly and scraping the bottom of the pot with a rubber spatula.
5. Add cream. Mix well. Heat to 75°C (167°F), stirring constantly, and hold for 15 seconds.
6. Chill quickly, preferably in an ice bath. Allow to mature overnight, covered and refrigerated at 4°C (39°F) or less.
7. Meanwhile, weigh out the Irish whisky, cover tightly, and refrigerate.
8. Just before freezing the gelato, add water to return the base to the calculated batch weight less the weight of the whisky (950 grams for a single batch). Blend with an immersion blender. Taste and adjust salt, if necessary.
9. Freeze in a batch freezer. When the gelato is partially frozen and is mounding over the blades, add the cold whisky and finish freezing.
10. Transfer the gelato from the batch freezer to a tub.
11. Harden in a blast freezer or deep freezer.

Ingredient	Quantity	Percent
Milk, 2%	524.5 g	52.45%
Heavy Cream (36% fat)	263 g	26.30%
Sucrose	135 g	13.50%
Dextrose	20 g	2.00%
Fructose	20 g	2.00%
Powdered Skim Milk	34 g	3.40%
Guar Gum	1.25 g	0.125%
Locust Bean Gum	1.25 g	0.125%
Salt	1 g	0.10%
Batch Weight	1000 g	
Serving Temperature	−13.50°C	

Off-Balance Ingredient	Quantity
Dried Lavender Flowers	4.5 g

Component	Percent
Fats	10.52%
Sugars	17.34%
MSNF	9.62%
Other Solids	0.33%
Water	62.20%
Total Solids	37.80%
POD	18.69
PAC	27.00

Gelato alla Lavanda

Lavender Gelato

The culinary use of lavender extends back many centuries. English lavender is the most common variety used for cooking. You may not be able to be determine what variety you are buying, but be certain you buy a food-grade lavender. Too much lavender can cause a soapy and/or bitter taste. Feel free to adjust the amount of lavender to your taste and to the strength of the particular lavender flowers you are using. During the infusion process, water will evaporate from the milk. This water is replaced with more water.

1. Combine milk and lavender in a stainless-steel pot. Note the total weight of the pot and contents.
2. Heat the milk and lavender mixture to 85°C (185°F). Cover and infuse for 1 hour off the heat.
3. Meanwhile, combine dextrose, guar gum, locust bean gum, and salt. Mix well. Reserve.
4. After the milk and lavender have infused for 1 hour, add enough water to return the pot with its contents to the weight noted in step 1.
5. Strain the milk, pressing lightly on the lavender flowers. Add enough additional milk to the lavender-infused milk to equal the required quantity (524.5 grams for a single batch).
6. Combine infused milk, sucrose, and fructose in a stainless-steel pot. If the mixture is below 35°C, heat it to that temperature, whisking occasionally. If it is at 35°C (95°F) or above, proceed with the next step.
7. Add skim milk powder and whisk to dissolve completely.
8. Continuing to heat the milk mixture, if needed, slowly sprinkle in the dextrose mixture, whisking constantly to avoid lumps and keeping the mixture below 45°C (113°F). After the dextrose mixture is incorporated, heat to 85°C (185°F), stirring constantly and scraping the bottom of the pot with a rubber spatula.
9. Add cream. Mix well. Heat to 75°C (167°F), stirring constantly, and hold for 15 seconds.
10. Chill quickly, preferably in an ice bath. Allow to mature overnight, covered and refrigerated at 4°C (39°F) or less.
11. Just before freezing the gelato, add water to return the base to the calculated batch weight. Blend with an immersion blender. Taste and adjust salt, if necessary.
12. Freeze in a batch freezer.
13. Transfer the gelato from the batch freezer to a tub.
14. Harden in a blast freezer or deep freezer.

Gelato Formulas and Recipes for Component Ingredients

Ingredient	Quantity	Percent
Milk, 2%	225 g	22.50%
Heavy Cream (36% fat)	226.5 g	22.65%
Sucrose	150 g	15.00%
Dextrose	20 g	2.00%
Powdered Skim Milk	75 g	7.50%
Guar Gum	1.25 g	0.125%
Locust Bean Gum	1.25 g	0.125%
Salt	1 g	0.10%
Lemon Juice, freshly squeezed	300 g	30.00%
Batch Weight	1000 g	
Serving Temperature	−13.25°C	

Off-Balance Ingredient	Quantity
Zest of 3 Lemons, in strips	

Mix-In Ingredient	Quantity
Zest of 1 Lemon, grated	

Component	Percent
Fats	8.73%
Sugars	17.60%
MSNF	10.60%
Other Solids	1.81%
Water	61.26%
Total Solids	38.74%
POD	18.11
PAC	26.50

Gelato al Limone
Lemon Gelato

Lemon is more commonly found as a flavor in sorbetto and granita–frozen treats with no dairy. However, lemon makes luscious gelato. This formula makes a tart gelato. You can make it less tart by swapping out some of the lemon juice for water. The formula will remain balanced even if you replace half the lemon juice with water. During the infusion process, water will evaporate from the milk. This water is replaced with more water. Once the lemon zest is removed, add a bit more milk to compensate for what is lost. Lemon zest provides more lemon flavor than could be obtained by juice alone. Pare it carefully to avoid any bitter white pith.

1. Combine the milk and strips of lemon zest in a stainless-steel pot. Note the total weight of the pot and contents.
2. Heat the milk and lemon zest to 85°C (185°F). Cover and allow to infuse for 1 hour off heat.
3. Meanwhile, combine dextrose, guar gum, locust bean gum, and salt. Mix well. Reserve.
4. After the milk and lemon zest have infused for 1 hour, add enough water to return the pot with its contents to the weight noted in step 1.
5. Strain the milk. Add enough additional milk to the lemon-infused milk to equal the required quantity (525 grams for a single batch).
6. Combine the infused milk and sucrose in a stainless-steel pot. If the mixture is below 35°C (95°F), heat it to that temperature, whisking occasionally. If it is at 35°C (95°F) or above, proceed with the next step.
7. Add skim milk powder and whisk to dissolve completely.
8. Continuing to heat the milk mixture, if needed, slowly sprinkle in the dextrose mixture, whisking constantly to avoid lumps and keeping the mixture below 45°C (113°F). After the dextrose mixture is incorporated, heat to 85°C (185°F), stirring constantly and scraping the bottom of the pot with a rubber spatula.
9. Add cream. Mix well. Heat to 75°C (167°F), stirring constantly, and hold for 15 seconds.
10. Chill quickly, preferably in an ice bath. Allow to mature overnight, covered and refrigerated at 4°C (39°F) or less.

(Continued)

11. Meanwhile, refrigerate the lemons. About an hour before freezing the gelato, squeeze the lemons. Strain the juice, weigh out the required amount, and refrigerate.
12. Just before freezing the gelato, add the cold lemon juice to the mature base.
13. Add water to return the base to the calculated batch weight. Add the grated lemon zest. Blend with an immersion blender. Taste and adjust salt, if necessary.
14. Freeze in a batch freezer.
15. Transfer the gelato from the batch freezer to a tub.
16. Harden in a blast freezer or deep freezer.

Gelato alla Liquirizia

Licorice Gelato

Ingredient	Quantity	Percent
Milk, 2%	492.5 g	49.25%
Heavy Cream (36% fat)	250 g	25.00%
Sucrose	135 g	13.50%
Dextrose	20 g	2.00%
Fructose	20 g	2.00%
Powdered Skim Milk	34 g	3.40%
Ground Licorice Root	45 g	4.50%
Guar Gum	1.25 g	0.125%
Locust Bean Gum	1.25 g	0.125%
Salt	1 g	0.10%
Base Weight	1000 g	
Serving Temperature	−13.40°C	

Off-Balance Ingredient	Quantity
Anise Oil	2.5 g

Component	Percent
Fats	9.99%
Sugars	17.34%
MSNF	9.25%
Other Solids	4.83%
Water	58.60%
Total Solids	41.40%
POD	18.65
PAC	26.81

Licorice is a popular flavor for gelato in Italy, especially in Calabria. There is actually very little licorice in most licorice candy sold around the world, though the amount varies by region. This gelato is made with pure, ground licorice root. Anise oil enhances the flavor of licorice. Do not use anise extract as it is not potent enough. The anise oil adds an inconsequential amount of fat and carbohydrate to the gelato base, so I do not include it in the balance calculations. I add it in place of a bit of water when I am topping up the base just before freezing.

1. In a small bowl, combine dextrose, guar gum, locust bean gum, and salt. Mix well. Reserve.
2. Combine milk, sucrose, and fructose in a stainless-steel pot. Add ground licorice root and whisk until fully moistened and combined. Heat to 35°C (95°F), whisking occasionally.
3. Add skim milk powder and whisk to dissolve completely.
4. Continuing to heat the milk mixture, slowly sprinkle in the dextrose mixture, whisking constantly to avoid lumps and keeping the mixture below 45°C (113°F). After the dextrose mixture is incorporated, heat to 85°C (185°F), stirring constantly and scraping the bottom of the pot with a rubber spatula.
5. Add cream. Mix well. Heat to 75°C (167°F), stirring constantly, and hold for 15 seconds.
6. Chill quickly, preferably in an ice bath. Allow to mature overnight, covered and refrigerated at 4°C (39°F) or less.
7. Just before freezing the gelato, add anise oil.
8. Add water to return the base to the calculated batch weight. Blend with an immersion blender. Taste and adjust salt, if necessary.
9. Freeze in a batch freezer.
10. Transfer the gelato from the batch freezer to a tub.
11. Harden in a blast freezer or deep freezer.

Ingredient	Quantity	Percent
Milk, 2%	385 g	38.50%
Heavy Cream (36% fat)	226.5 g	22.65%
Sucrose	145 g	14.50%
Dextrose	20 g	2.00%
Fructose	10 g	1.00%
Powdered Skim Milk	60 g	6.00%
Guar Gum	1.25 g	0.125%
Locust Bean Gum	1.25 g	0.125%
Salt	1 g	0.10%
Lime Juice, freshly squeezed	150 g	15.00%
Batch Weight	1000 g	
Serving Temperature	−13.51°C	

Off-Balance Ingredient	Quantity
Zest of 3 Limes, in strips	

Mix-In Ingredient	Quantity
Zest of 1 Lime, grated	

Component	Percent
Fats	8.96%
Sugars	17.59%
MSNF	10.61%
Other Solids	1.45%
Water	61.39%
Total Solids	38.61%
POD	18.54
PAC	27.03

Gelato al Lime

Lime Gelato

This lime gelato is refreshing but not too tart. Mexican or Key limes are more tart than ordinary limes (often called Persian limes). This recipe has been standardized using Persian limes. Squeeze the lime juice just before using it and strain it to remove any pulp. Lime zest provides more lime flavor than could be obtained by juice alone. Pare it carefully to avoid any bitter white pith.

1. Combine the milk and strips of lime zest in a stainless-steel pot. Note the total weight of the pot and contents.
2. Heat the milk and lime zest to 85°C (185°F). Cover and allow to infuse for 1 hour off heat.
3. Meanwhile, combine dextrose, guar gum, locust bean gum, and salt. Mix well. Reserve.
4. After the milk and lime zest have infused for 1 hour, add enough water to return the pot with its contents to the weight noted in step 1.
5. Strain the milk. Add enough additional milk to the lime-infused milk to equal the required quantity (385 grams for a single batch).
6. Combine the infused milk, sucrose, and fructose in a stainless-steel pot. If the mixture is below 35°C (95°F), heat it to that temperature, whisking occasionally. If it is at 35°C (95°F) or above, proceed with the next step.
7. Add skim milk powder and whisk to dissolve completely.
8. Continuing to heat the milk mixture, if needed, slowly sprinkle in the dextrose mixture, whisking constantly to avoid lumps and keeping the mixture below 45°C (113°F). After the dextrose mixture is incorporated, heat to 85°C (185°F), stirring constantly and scraping the bottom of the pot with a rubber spatula.
9. Add cream. Mix well. Heat to 75°C (167°F), stirring constantly, and hold for 15 seconds.
10. Chill quickly, preferably in an ice bath. Allow to mature overnight, covered and refrigerated at 4°C (39°F) or less.
11. Meanwhile, refrigerate the limes. About an hour before freezing the gelato, squeeze the limes. Strain the juice, weigh out the required amount, and refrigerate.
12. Just before freezing the gelato, add the cold lime juice to the mature base.
13. Add water to return the base to the calculated batch weight. Add the grated lime zest. Blend with an immersion blender. Taste and adjust salt, if necessary.
14. Freeze in a batch freezer.
15. Transfer the gelato from the batch freezer to a tub.
16. Harden in a blast freezer or deep freezer.

Gelato al Mango

Mango Gelato

It is important to use ripe, flavorful mangos for this gelato. Put the mangoes in the refrigerator at least several hours before pureeing them so that they are as cold as possible. A warm gelato base takes longer to freeze in the batch freezer.

1. In a small bowl, combine dextrose, 20 grams of sucrose, guar gum, locust bean gum, and salt. Mix well. Reserve.
2. Combine milk and remaining sucrose in a stainless-steel pot. Heat to 35°C (95°F), whisking occasionally.
3. Add skim milk powder and whisk to dissolve completely.
4. Continuing to heat the milk mixture, slowly sprinkle in the dextrose mixture, whisking constantly to avoid lumps and keeping the mixture below 45°C (113°F). After the dextrose mixture is incorporated, heat to 85°C (185°F), stirring constantly and scraping the bottom of the pot with a rubber spatula.
5. Add cream. Mix well. Heat to 75°C (167°F), stirring constantly, and hold for 15 seconds.
6. Chill quickly, preferably in an ice bath. Allow to mature overnight, covered and refrigerated at 4°C (39°F) or less.
7. Meanwhile, refrigerate the mangoes.
8. Just before freezing the gelato, peel, coarsely chop, and puree the mangoes using a high-powered blender, food processor, or commercial immersion blender. Weigh out the correct amount and add it to the mature base.
9. Just before freezing the gelato, add water to return the base to the calculated batch weight. Blend with an immersion blender. Taste and adjust salt, if necessary.
10. Freeze in a batch freezer.
11. Transfer the gelato from the batch freezer to a tub.
12. Harden in a blast freezer or deep freezer.

Ingredient	Quantity	Percent
Milk, 2%	215 g	21.50%
Heavy Cream (36% fat)	215 g	21.50%
Sucrose	118 g	11.80%
Dextrose	12 g	1.20%
Powdered Skim Milk	55 g	5.50%
Guar Gum	1.25 g	0.125%
Locust Bean Gum	1.25 g	0.125%
Salt	0.5 g	0.05%
Fresh Mango Puree	382 g	38.20%
Base Weight	1000 g	
Serving Temperature	−13.22°C	

Component	Percent
Fats	8.36%
Sugars	18.14%
MSNF	8.53%
Other Solids	1.20%
Water	63.77%
Total Solids	36.23%
POD	19.26
PAC	26.43

Ingredient	Quantity	Percent
Milk, 2%	455 g	45.50%
Heavy Cream (36% fat)	225 g	22.50%
Maple Syrup	250 g	25.00%
Fructose	20 g	2.00%
Powdered Skim Milk	46 g	4.60%
Guar Gum	1.25 g	0.125%
Locust Bean Gum	1.25 g	0.125%
Salt	1.5 g	0.15%
Batch Weight	1000 g	
Serving Temperature	−13.16°C	

Mix-In Ingredient	Quantity
Chopped Toasted Pecans	30 g

Component	Percent
Fats	9.04%
Sugars	17.13%
MSNF	9.89%
Other Solids	2.14%
Water	61.81%
Total Solids	38.19%
POD	18.90
PAC	26.32

Gelato all'Acero e Noci Pecan

Maple Pecan Gelato

The sugar in maple syrup is almost all sucrose, hence there is no added sucrose in this gelato. Try to find an especially flavorful maple syrup. If you can find Grade B, or equivalent, it should have more flavor than the Grade A that is typically available at most retailers.

1. In a small bowl, combine fructose, guar gum, locust bean gum, and salt. Mix well. Reserve.
2. Combine milk and maple syrup in a stainless-steel pot. Heat to 35°C (95°F), whisking occasionally.
3. Add skim milk powder and whisk to dissolve completely.
4. Continuing to heat the milk mixture, slowly sprinkle in the fructose mixture, whisking constantly to avoid lumps and keeping the mixture below 45°C (113°F). After the fructose mixture is incorporated, heat to 85°C (185°F), stirring constantly and scraping the bottom of the pot with a rubber spatula.
5. Add cream. Mix well. Heat to 75°C (167°F), stirring constantly, and hold for 15 seconds.
6. Chill quickly, preferably in an ice bath. Allow to mature overnight, covered and refrigerated at 4°C (39°F) or less.
7. Just before freezing the gelato, add water to return the base to the calculated batch weight. Blend with an immersion blender. Taste and adjust salt, if necessary.
8. Freeze in a batch freezer.
9. Transfer the gelato from the batch freezer to a tub, stopping periodically to sprinkle in some of the toasted pecans, swirling a bit with a silicone spatula.
10. Harden in a blast freezer or deep freezer.

Gelato Formulas and Recipes for Component Ingredients

Gelato all'Acero, Rum e Uvetta
Maple Rum Raisin Gelato

Try to find an especially flavorful maple syrup. If you can find Grade B, or equivalent, it should have more flavor than the Grade A that is typically available at most retailers. The day before freezing the gelato, generously cover the raisins with rum and allow them to soak up the rum and soften at room temperature. The rum will keep the raisins from becoming too hard in the freezer.

1. Cover the raisins with a generous amount of rum and allow to soften, covered, at room temperature for 24 hours.
2. In a small bowl, combine fructose, guar gum, locust bean gum, and salt. Mix well. Reserve.
3. Combine milk and maple syrup in a stainless-steel pot. Heat to 35°C (95°F), whisking occasionally.
4. Add skim milk powder and whisk to dissolve completely.
5. Continuing to heat the milk mixture, slowly sprinkle in the fructose mixture, whisking constantly to avoid lumps and keeping the mixture below 45°C (113°F). After the fructose mixture is incorporated, heat to 85°C (185°F), stirring constantly and scraping the bottom of the pot with a rubber spatula.
6. Add cream. Mix well. Heat to 75°C (167°F), stirring constantly, and hold for 15 seconds.
7. Chill quickly, preferably in an ice bath. Allow to mature overnight, covered and refrigerated at 4°C (39°F) or less.
8. Just before freezing the gelato, add water to return the base to the calculated batch weight. Blend with an immersion blender. Taste and adjust salt, if necessary.
9. Freeze in a batch freezer.
10. Meanwhile, drain the raisins.
11. Transfer the gelato from the batch freezer to a tub, stopping periodically to sprinkle in some of the rum-soaked, drained raisins, swirling a bit with a spatula.
12. Harden in a blast freezer or deep freezer.

Ingredient	Quantity	Percent
Milk, 2%	455 g	45.50%
Heavy Cream (36% fat)	225 g	22.50%
Maple Syrup	250 g	25.00%
Fructose	20 g	2.00%
Powdered Skim Milk	46 g	4.60%
Guar Gum	1.25 g	0.125%
Locust Bean Gum	1.25 g	0.125%
Salt	1.5 g	0.15%
Batch Weight	1000 g	
Serving Temperature	−13.16°C	

Mix-In Ingredient	Quantity
Raisins	70 g
Rum to cover raisins	

Component	Percent
Fats	9.04%
Sugars	17.13%
MSNF	9.89%
Other Solids	2.14%
Water	61.81%
Total Solids	38.19%
POD	18.90
PAC	26.32

Ingredient	Quantity	Percent
Milk, 2%	511 g	51.10%
Mascarpone, 36% fat	250 g	25.00%
Sucrose	170 g	17.00%
Dextrose	16 g	1.60%
Powdered Skim Milk	50 g	5.00%
Guar Gum	1.25 g	0.125%
Locust Bean Gum	1.25 g	0.125%
Salt	0.5	0.05%
Batch Weight	1000 g	
Serving Temperature	−13.07°C	

Component	Percent
Fats	10.01%
Sugars	18.47%
MSNF	11.56%
Other Solids	0.28%
Water	59.68%
Total Solids	40.32%
POD	19.02
PAC	26.13

Gelato al Mascarpone

Mascarpone Gelato

Mascarpone, a soft, fresh cheese, makes this gelato a little more tangy than fiordilatte gelato. This particular formula is balanced for mascarpone consisting of 36% fat. If using mascarpone with 42% to 43% fat, decrease the mascarpone to 210 grams and increase the 2% milk to 551 grams.

1. In a small bowl, combine dextrose, guar gum, locust bean gum, and salt. Mix well. Reserve.
2. Combine milk and sucrose in a stainless-steel pot. Heat to 35°C (95°F), whisking occasionally.
3. Add skim milk powder and whisk to dissolve completely.
4. Continuing to heat the milk mixture, slowly sprinkle in the dextrose mixture, whisking constantly to avoid lumps and keeping the mixture below 45°C (113°F). After the dextrose mixture is incorporated, heat to 85°C (185°F), stirring constantly and scraping the bottom of the pot with a rubber spatula.
5. Add mascarpone. Use a whisk to completely incorporate the mascarpone.
6. Heat to 66°C (151°F), stirring constantly. Hold at 66°C (151°F) for 30 minutes, stirring if needed. (If the 30-minute hold is in a water bath or in a commercial pasteurizer, no stirring is needed. If the 30-minute hold is on the cooktop, occasional stirring will be needed to equalize the temperature.)
7. Chill quickly, preferably in an ice bath. Allow to mature overnight, covered and refrigerated at 4°C (39°F) or less.
8. Just before freezing the gelato, add water to return the base to the calculated batch weight. Blend with an immersion blender. Taste and adjust salt, if necessary.
9. Freeze in a batch freezer.
10. Transfer the gelato from the batch freezer to a tub.
11. Harden in a blast freezer or deep freezer.

Ingredient	Quantity	Percent
Milk, 2%	516.5 g	51.65%
Heavy Cream (36% fat)	220 g	22.00%
Sucrose	65 g	6.50%
Medjool Dates, pitted	150 g	15.00%
Powdered Skim Milk	45 g	4.50%
Guar Gum	1.25 g	0.125%
Locust Bean Gum	1.25 g	0.125%
Salt	1 g	0.10%
Batch Weight	1000 g	
Serving Temperature	−15.97°C	

Component	Percent
Fats	8.98%
Sugars	16.48%
MSNF	10.32%
Other Solids	2.14%
Water	62.09%
Total Solids	37.91%
POD	18.45
PAC	31.93

Gelato al Dattero di Medjool

Medjool Date Gelato

Medjool dates and Deglet Noor dates are two of the most commonly available date varieties in the United States. They have different sugar contents and, thus, different gelato formulas. Although this gelato formula is balanced, with sugar on the low side, the amount of glucose and fructose in dates means that the serving temperature is lower than the norm.

1. In a small bowl, combine 30 grams of the sucrose, guar gum, locust bean gum, and salt. Mix well. Reserve.
2. Coarsely chop the dates.
3. Puree the dates as thoroughly as possible with half of the milk using a high-powered blender, food processor, or commercial immersion blender. Pour the puree into a stainless-steel pot.
4. Use the remaining milk to rinse out the blender jar or food processor container and add to the puree.
5. Add remaining sucrose to the date puree. Heat to 35°C (95°F), whisking occasionally.
6. Add skim milk powder and whisk to dissolve completely.
7. Continuing to heat the milk mixture, slowly sprinkle in the sucrose mixture, whisking constantly to avoid lumps and keeping the mixture below 45°C (113°F). After the sucrose mixture is incorporated, heat to 85°C (185°F), stirring constantly and scraping the bottom of the pot with a rubber spatula.
8. Add cream. Mix well. Heat to 75°C (167°F), stirring constantly, and hold for 15 seconds.
9. Chill quickly, preferably in an ice bath. Allow to mature overnight, covered and refrigerated at 4°C (39°F) or less.
10. Just before freezing the gelato, add water to return the base to the calculated batch weight. Blend with an immersion blender. Taste and adjust salt, if necessary.
11. Freeze in a batch freezer.
12. Transfer the gelato from the batch freezer to a tub.
13. Harden in a blast freezer or deep freezer.

Gelato al Cioccolato al Latte

Milk Chocolate Gelato

Dark chocolate can seem serious. Milk chocolate is quite the opposite. This gelato starts with dark chocolate but the proportion is less than is used in dark chocolate gelato. The lower percentage of chocolate and the higher percentage of dairy turn it into milk chocolate.

1. In a small bowl, combine dextrose, guar gum, locust bean gum, and salt. Mix well. Reserve.
2. Combine milk and sucrose in a stainless-steel pot. Heat to 35°C (95°F), whisking occasionally.
3. Add the chocolate and stir until melted, keeping the temperature below 45°C (113°F).
4. Add skim milk powder and whisk to dissolve completely.
5. Continuing to heat the milk mixture, slowly sprinkle in the dextrose mixture, whisking constantly to avoid lumps and keeping the mixture below 45°C (113°F). After the dextrose mixture is incorporated, heat to 85°C (185°F), stirring constantly and scraping the bottom of the pot with a rubber spatula.
6. Add cream. Mix well. Heat to 75°C (167°F), stirring constantly, and hold for 15 seconds.
7. Chill quickly, preferably in an ice bath. Allow to mature overnight, covered and refrigerated at 4°C (39°F) or less.
8. Just before freezing the gelato, add water to return the base to the calculated batch weight. Blend with an immersion blender. Taste and adjust salt, if necessary.
9. Freeze in a batch freezer.
10. Transfer the gelato from the batch freezer to a tub.
11. Harden in a blast freezer or deep freezer.

Ingredient	Quantity	Percent
Milk, 2%	600 g	60.00%
Heavy Cream (36% fat)	131 g	13.10%
Sucrose	125 g	12.50%
Dextrose	25 g	2.50%
Powdered Skim Milk	40 g	4.00%
Chocolate, 72% Cocoa Solids	75 g	7.50%
Guar Gum	1.25 g	0.125%
Locust Bean Gum	1.25 g	0.125%
Salt	1.5 g	0.15%
Batch Weight	1000 g	
Serving Temperature	−13.42°C	

Component	Percent
Fats	8.80%
Sugars	16.74%
MSNF	10.04%
Other Solids	3.04%
Water	61.39%
Total Solids	38.61%
POD	17.98
PAC	26.85

Gelato Formulas and Recipes for Component Ingredients

Gelato al Cioccolato al Latte Variegato al Burro di Arachidi

Milk Chocolate Peanut Butter Ripple Gelato

Ingredient	Quantity	Percent
Milk, 2%	600 g	60.00%
Heavy Cream (36% fat)	131.5 g	13.15%
Sucrose	125 g	12.50%
Dextrose	25 g	2.50%
Powdered Skim Milk	40 g	4.00%
Chocolate, 72% Cocoa Solids	75 g	7.50%
Guar Gum	1.25 g	0.125%
Locust Bean Gum	1.25 g	0.125%
Salt	1 g	0.10%
Base Weight	1000 g	
Serving Temperature	−13.13°C	

Mix-In Ingredient	Quantity
Peanut Butter Sauce	150 g

Component	Percent
Fats	8.82%
Sugars	16.74%
MSNF	10.04%
Other Solids	3.00%
Water	61.41%
Total Solids	38.59%
POD	17.98
PAC	26.26

Unless I am making a super-dark chocolate gelato, I use chocolate with 72% cocoa solids for all my chocolate gelati. I find that 72% chocolate makes a dark chocolate that is balanced and not too bitter. Using a smaller quantity of chocolate and more milk and/or cream produces a milk chocolate gelato. Using a single type of chocolate simplifies the process of keeping key ingredients in stock and minimizes errors from using the wrong ingredient. The recipe for peanut butter sauce is in the "Component Ingredients" section at the end of this chapter.

1. In a small bowl, combine dextrose, guar gum, locust bean gum, and salt. Mix well. Reserve.
2. Combine milk and sucrose in a stainless-steel pot. Heat to 35°C (95°F), whisking occasionally.
3. Add the chocolate, broken into pieces, and stir until melted, keeping the temperature below 45°C (113°F).
4. Add skim milk powder and whisk to dissolve completely.
5. Continuing to heat the milk mixture, slowly sprinkle in the dextrose mixture, whisking constantly to avoid lumps and keeping the mixture below 45°C (113°F). After the dextrose mixture is incorporated, heat to 85°C (185°F), stirring constantly and scraping the bottom of the pot with a rubber spatula.
6. Add cream. Mix well. If the temperature is not at or above 75°C (167°F), heat to 75°C (167°F), stirring constantly, and hold for 15 seconds.
7. Chill quickly, preferably in an ice bath. Allow to mature overnight, covered and refrigerated at 4°C (39°F) or less.
8. Meanwhile, make the peanut butter sauce. When the sauce is cold, load it into a disposable pastry bag and refrigerate.
9. Just before freezing the gelato, add water to return the base to the calculated batch weight. Blend with an immersion blender. Taste and adjust salt, if necessary.
10. Freeze in a batch freezer.
11. Transfer the gelato from the batch freezer to a tub, stopping periodically to pipe in stripes of the peanut butter sauce, swirling a bit with a spatula.
12. Harden in a blast freezer or deep freezer.

Make Your Own Artisan Italian Gelato

Gelato alla Menta
Mint Gelato

Ingredient	Quantity	Percent
Milk, 2%	526 g	52.60%
Heavy Cream (36% fat)	261.5 g	26.15%
Sucrose	135 g	13.50%
Dextrose	20 g	2.00%
Fructose	20 g	2.00%
Powdered Skim Milk	34 g	3.40%
Guar Gum	1.25 g	0.125%
Locust Bean Gum	1.25 g	0.125%
Salt	1 g	0.10%
Batch Weight	1000 g	
Serving Temperature	−13.50°C	

Off-Balance Ingredient	Quantity
Fresh Mint Leaves and Stems	100 g

Component	Percent
Fats	10.47%
Sugars	17.34%
MSNF	9.62%
Other Solids	0.33%
Water	62.25%
Total Solids	37.75%
POD	18.69
PAC	27.00

If you like fresh mint, this gelato is for you. It is delightfully refreshing. If you are a gardener, you know that mint can overtake your garden. This is a great way to use it. If you like mint *and* chocolate, follow the process for stracciatella and drizzle chocolate into the mint gelato. Spearmint is my mint of choice, but feel free to try other types that strike your fancy.

1. Wash, dry, and coarsely chop mint leaves and stems.
2. Combine milk and mint in a stainless-steel pot. Note the weight of the pot and contents.
3. Heat the milk and mint to 85°C (185°F). Cover and allow to infuse for 30 minutes off heat.
4. Meanwhile, combine dextrose, guar gum, locust bean gum, and salt. Mix well. Reserve.
5. After the milk and mint have infused for 30 minutes, add enough water to return the pot with its contents to the weight noted in step 2.
6. Strain the milk, pressing on the mint to extract as much liquid as possible. Add additional milk, if needed, to the mint-infused milk to equal the required quantity (526 grams for a single batch).
7. Combine infused milk, sucrose, and fructose in a stainless-steel pot. If the mixture is below 35°C (95°F), heat it to that temperature, whisking occasionally. If it is at 35°C (95°F) or above, proceed with the next step.
8. Add skim milk powder and whisk to dissolve completely.
9. Continuing to heat the milk mixture, if needed, slowly sprinkle in the dextrose mixture, whisking constantly to avoid lumps and keeping the mixture below 45°C (113°F). After the dextrose mixture is incorporated, heat to 85°C (185°F), stirring constantly and scraping the bottom of the pot with a rubber spatula.
10. Add cream. Mix well. Heat to 75°C (167°F), stirring constantly, and hold for 15 seconds.
11. Chill quickly, preferably in an ice bath. Allow to mature overnight, covered and refrigerated at 4°C (39°F) or less.
12. Just before freezing the gelato, add water to return the base to the calculated batch weight. Blend with an immersion blender. Taste and adjust salt, if necessary.
13. Freeze in a batch freezer.
14. Transfer the gelato from the batch freezer to a tub.
15. Harden in a blast freezer or deep freezer.

Gelato ai Frutti di Bosco

Mixed Berry Gelato

Frutti di bosco is a perennial favorite gelato flavor in Italy. This formula uses blueberries, raspberries, and strawberries, but any combination of berries can be used. Other options include blackberries and red currants. If other berries are used, however, you will need to rebalance the formula to account for their varying compositions. I find raspberry seeds to be unpleasant in gelato, so I strain the raspberry puree before adding it to the base. I do not feel this way about strawberry seeds, so I do not strain the strawberry puree.

Ingredient	Quantity	Percent
Milk, 2%	150.5 g	15.05%
Heavy Cream (36% fat)	221 g	22.10%
Sucrose	130 g	13.00%
Dextrose	20 g	2.00%
Powdered Skim Milk	75 g	7.50%
Guar Gum	1.25 g	0.125%
Locust Bean Gum	1.25 g	0.125%
Salt	1 g	0.10%
Pureed Blueberries	125 g	12.50%
Pureed Raspberries	125 g	12.50%
Pureed Strawberries	150 g	15.00%
Batch Weight	1000 g	
Serving Temperature	−13.65°C	

Component	Percent
Fats	8.42%
Sugars	17.22%
MSNF	9.89%
Other Solids	2.96%
Water	61.51%
Total Solids	38.49%
POD	17.94
PAC	27.29

1. In a small bowl, combine dextrose, guar gum, locust bean gum, and salt. Mix well. Reserve.
2. Combine milk, cream, and sucrose in a stainless-steel pot. Heat milk mixture to 35°C (95°F).
3. Add skim milk powder and whisk to dissolve completely.
4. Continuing to heat the milk mixture, slowly sprinkle in the dextrose mixture, whisking constantly to avoid lumps and keeping the mixture below 45°C (113°F). After the dextrose mixture is incorporated, heat to 85°C (185°F), stirring constantly and scraping the bottom of the pot with a rubber spatula.
5. Add cream. Mix well. Heat to 75° (167°F) C, stirring constantly, and hold for 15 seconds.
6. Chill quickly, preferably in an ice bath. Allow to mature overnight, covered and refrigerated at 4˚C (39°F) or less.
7. Meanwhile, wash the berries and keep them refrigerated.
8. About an hour before freezing the gelato, hull the strawberries.
9. Puree each of the berries and weigh out the correct amount and refrigerate. Strain the raspberries before weighing if desired.
10. Just before freezing the gelato, add the pureed berries to the mature base.
11. Add water to return the base to the calculated batch weight. Blend with an immersion blender. Taste and adjust salt, if necessary.
12. Freeze in a batch freezer.
13. Transfer the gelato from the batch freezer to a tub.
14. Harden in a blast freezer or deep freezer.

Ingredient	Quantity	Percent
Milk, 2%	425 g	42.50%
Heavy Cream (36% fat)	140 g	14.00%
Sucrose	125 g	12.50%
Dextrose	25 g	2.50%
Powdered Skim Milk	56 g	5.60%
Brewed Espresso Coffee	150 g	15.00%
Chocolate, 72% Cocoa Solids	75 g	7.50%
Guar Gum	1.25 g	0.125%
Locust Bean Gum	1.25 g	0.125%
Salt	1.5 g	0.15%
Batch Weight	1000 g	
Serving Temperature	−13.41°C	

Component	Percent
Fats	8.83%
Sugars	16.74%
MSNF	10.04%
Other Solids	3.35%
Water	61.05%
Total Solids	38.95%
POD	17.97
PAC	26.82

Gelato al Moccacino

Mocha Gelato

The classic combination of chocolate and coffee is a real treat. You can pull espresso shots to make this gelato or you can follow my process for steeped espresso described in the "Component Ingredients" section at the end of this chapter.

1. In a small bowl, combine dextrose, guar gum, locust bean gum, and salt. Mix well. Reserve.
2. Combine milk, espresso, and sucrose in a stainless-steel pot. Heat to 35°C (95°F), whisking occasionally.
3. Add the chocolate, broken into pieces, and stir until melted, keeping the temperature below 45°C (113°F).
4. Add skim milk powder and whisk to dissolve completely.
5. Continuing to heat the milk mixture, slowly sprinkle in the dextrose mixture, whisking constantly to avoid lumps and keeping the mixture below 45°C (113°F). After the dextrose mixture is incorporated, heat to 85°C (185°F), stirring constantly and scraping the bottom of the pot with a rubber spatula.
6. Add cream. Mix well. Heat to 75°C (167°F), stirring constantly, and hold for 15 seconds.
7. Chill quickly, preferably in an ice bath. Allow to mature overnight, covered and refrigerated at 4°C (39°F) or less.
8. Just before freezing the gelato, add water to return the base to the calculated batch weight. Blend with an immersion blender. Taste and adjust salt, if necessary.
9. Freeze in a batch freezer.
10. Transfer the gelato from the batch freezer to a tub.
11. Harden in a blast freezer or deep freezer.

Gelato alla Crema di Arancia
Orange Cream Gelato

Ingredient	Quantity	Percent
Milk, 2%	70 g	7.00%
Heavy Cream (36% fat)	230 g	23.00%
Sucrose	127 g	12.70%
Dextrose	20 g	2.00%
Powdered Skim Milk	75 g	7.50%
Guar Gum	1.25 g	0.125%
Locust Bean Gum	1.25 g	0.125%
Salt	0.5 g	0.05%
Orange Juice, Fresh Squeezed	475 g	47.50%
Batch Weight	1000 g	
Serving Temperature	−13.55°C	

Off-Balance Ingredient	Quantity
Zest of 3 Oranges, in strips	

Component	Percent
Fats	8.55%
Sugars	18.51%
MSNF	9.22%
Other Solids	1.90%
Water	61.83%
Total Solids	38.17%
POD	19.07
PAC	27.11

This gelato is based on one made by Chef John Nocita of the Italian Culinary Institute in Staletti, Calabria. It is reminiscent of American dreamsicles and creamsicles, which are versions of an orange sherbet exterior covering a frozen dairy interior. The flavor, however, given the freshness of the ingredients and the serving temperature and consistency of gelato, is nothing that could ever be achieved by a dreamsicle or creamsicle! Orange zest provides more orange flavor than could be obtained by juice alone. Pare it carefully to avoid any bitter white pith.

1. Combine the milk and strips of orange zest in a stainless-steel pot. Note the total weight of the pot and contents.
2. Heat the milk and orange zest to 85°C (185°F). Cover the pot and allow to infuse for 1 hour off heat.
3. Meanwhile, combine dextrose, guar gum, locust bean gum, and salt. Mix well. Reserve.
4. After the milk and orange zest have infused for 1 hour, add enough water to return the pot with its contents to the weight noted in step 1.
5. Strain the milk. Add enough additional milk to the orange-infused milk to equal the required quantity (70 grams for a single batch).
6. Combine the infused milk, cream, and sucrose in a stainless-steel pot. Heat to 35°C (95°F), whisking occasionally.
7. Add skim milk powder and whisk to dissolve completely.
8. Continuing to heat the milk mixture, slowly sprinkle in the dextrose mixture, whisking constantly to avoid lumps and keeping the mixture below 45°C (113°F). After the dextrose mixture is incorporated, heat to 85°C (185°F), stirring constantly and scraping the bottom of the pot with a rubber spatula.
9. Chill quickly, preferably in an ice bath. Allow to mature overnight, covered and refrigerated at 4°C (39°F) or less.
10. Meanwhile, refrigerate the oranges. About an hour before freezing the gelato, squeeze the oranges. Strain the juice, weigh out the required amount, and refrigerate.
11. Just before freezing the gelato, add the cold orange juice to the mature base.
12. Add water to return the base to the calculated batch weight. Blend with an immersion blender. Taste and adjust salt, if necessary.
13. Freeze in a batch freezer.
14. Transfer the gelato from the batch freezer to a tub.
15. Harden in a blast freezer or deep freezer.

Make Your Own Artisan Italian Gelato

Ingredient	Quantity	Percent
Milk, 2%	140 g	14.00%
Heavy Cream (36% fat)	236.5 g	23.65%
Sucrose	125 g	12.50%
Dextrose	20 g	2.00%
Powdered Skim Milk	75 g	7.50%
Guar Gum	1.25 g	0.125%
Locust Bean Gum	1.25 g	0.125%
Salt	1 g	0.10%
Fresh Peach Puree	400 g	40.00%
Batch Weight	1000 g	
Serving Temperature	−13.46°C	

Component	Percent
Fats	8.97%
Sugars	17.70%
MSNF	9.90%
Other Solids	1.55%
Water	61.90%
Total Solids	38.10%
POD	18.13
PAC	26.92

Gelato alla Pesca

Peach Gelato

As with most fruit-based gelato flavors, ripe aromatic peaches are essential to producing a full-flavored gelato. Be sure to thoroughly puree the peaches but do not strain them. A food processor, high-powered blender, or commercial immersion blender can be used to puree the peaches.

1. In a small bowl, combine dextrose, guar gum, locust bean gum, and salt. Mix well. Reserve.
2. Combine milk and sucrose in a stainless-steel pot. Heat to 35°C (95°F), whisking occasionally.
3. Add skim milk powder and whisk to dissolve completely.
4. Continuing to heat the milk mixture, slowly sprinkle in the dextrose mixture, whisking constantly to avoid lumps and keeping the mixture below 45°C (113°F). After the dextrose mixture is incorporated, heat to 85°C (185°F), stirring constantly and scraping the bottom of the pot with a rubber spatula.
5. Add cream. Mix well. Heat to 75°C (167°F), stirring constantly, and hold for 15 seconds.
6. Chill quickly, preferably in an ice bath. Allow to mature overnight, covered and refrigerated at 4°C (39°F) or less.
7. Meanwhile, put the peaches in the refrigerator.
8. Just before freezing the gelato, peel, chop, and puree the peaches using a high-powered blender, food processor, or commercial immersion blender. Weigh out the correct amount and add it to the mature base.
9. Add water to return the base to the calculated batch weight. Blend with an immersion blender. Taste and adjust salt, if necessary.
10. Freeze in a batch freezer.
11. Transfer the gelato from the batch freezer to a tub.
12. Harden in a blast freezer or deep freezer.

Gelato al Burro di Arachidi e Marmellata

Peanut Butter and Jelly Gelato

Ingredient	Quantity	Percent
Milk, 2%	650 g	65.00%
Natural Peanut Butter	130 g	13.00%
Sucrose	143 g	14.30%
Dextrose	35 g	3.50%
Powdered Skim Milk	39 g	3.90%
Guar Gum	1 g	0.10%
Locust Bean Gum	1 g	0.10%
Salt	1 g	0.10%
Batch Weight	1000 g	
Serving Temperature	−13.77°C	

Mix-In Ingredient	Quantity
Strawberry Sauce	150 g

Component	Percent
Fats	7.86%
Sugars	18.33%
MSNF	9.56%
Other Solids	5.99%
Water	58.26%
Total Solids	41.74%
POD	18.35
PAC	27.55

This is a particularly American flavor combination but the parameters of the formula are strictly Italian. Because I do not live in an area where concord grapes grow, I make a strawberry sauce to play the part of the "jelly." A disposable pastry bag works well to pipe in the strawberry sauce but it can be drizzled in using a spoon. The directions for the strawberry sauce are in the "Component Ingredients" section at the end of this chapter.

1. In a small bowl, combine dextrose, guar gum, locust bean gum, and salt. Mix well. Reserve.
2. Combine milk and sucrose in a stainless-steel pot. Heat to 35°C (95°F), whisking occasionally.
3. Add skim milk powder and whisk to dissolve completely.
4. Continuing to heat the milk mixture, slowly sprinkle in the dextrose mixture, whisking constantly to avoid lumps and keeping the mixture below 45°C (113°F). After the dextrose mixture is incorporated, heat to 85°C (185°F), stirring constantly and scraping the bottom of the pot with a rubber spatula.
5. Remove from heat. Add peanut butter and whisk until thoroughly combined.
6. Chill quickly, preferably in an ice bath. Allow to mature overnight, covered and refrigerated at 4°C (39°F) or less.
7. Meanwhile, prepare the strawberry sauce. When the sauce is cold, load it into a disposable pastry bag and refrigerate.
8. Just before freezing the gelato, add water to return the base to the calculated batch weight. Blend with an immersion blender. Taste and adjust salt, if necessary.
9. Freeze in a batch freezer.
10. Transfer the gelato from the batch freezer to a tub.
11. As the gelato is being put into the tub, stop periodically and pipe in some of the strawberry sauce, swirling a bit with a silicone spatula.
12. Harden in a blast freezer or deep freezer.

Make Your Own Artisan Italian Gelato

Ingredient	Quantity	Percent
Milk, 2%	650 g	65.00%
Natural Peanut Butter	130 g	13.00%
Sucrose	143 g	14.30%
Dextrose	35 g	3.50%
Powdered Skim Milk	39 g	3.90%
Guar Gum	1 g	0.10%
Locust Bean Gum	1 g	0.10%
Salt	1 g	0.10%
Batch Weight	1000 g	
Serving Temperature	−13.77°C	

Component	Percent
Fats	7.86%
Sugars	18.33%
MSNF	9.56%
Other Solids	5.99%
Water	58.26%
Total Solids	41.74%
POD	18.35
PAC	27.55

Gelato al Burro di Arachidi

Peanut Butter Gelato

Use natural peanut butter for this gelato. That is, one that only contains peanuts or peanuts and salt. Do not use peanut butter with added fats, stabilizers, and/or emulsifiers of any kind, as the texture, once frozen, can be unpredictable. Nut-based gelato tends to require more salt than fruit gelato, so do not hesitate to salt the base to taste just before freezing it.

1. In a small bowl, combine dextrose, guar gum, locust bean gum, and salt. Mix well. Reserve.
2. Combine milk and sucrose in a stainless-steel pot. Heat to 35°C (95°F), whisking occasionally.
3. Add skim milk powder and whisk to dissolve completely.
4. Continuing to heat the milk mixture, slowly sprinkle in the dextrose mixture, whisking constantly to avoid lumps and keeping the mixture below 45°C (113°F). After the dextrose mixture is incorporated, heat to 85°C (185°F), stirring constantly and scraping the bottom of the pot with a rubber spatula.
5. Remove from heat. Add peanut butter and whisk until thoroughly combined.
6. Chill quickly, preferably in an ice bath. Allow to mature overnight, covered and refrigerated at 4°C (39°F) or less.
7. Just before freezing the gelato, add water to return the base to the calculated batch weight. Blend with an immersion blender. Taste and adjust salt, if necessary.
8. Freeze in a batch freezer.
9. Transfer the gelato from the batch freezer to a tub.
10. Harden in a blast freezer or deep freezer.

Gelato Formulas and Recipes for Component Ingredients

Ingredient	Quantity	Percent
Milk, 2%	162 g	16.20%
Heavy Cream (36% fat)	235 g	23.50%
Sucrose	125 g	12.50%
Powdered Skim Milk	75 g	7.50%
Guar Gum	1.25 g	0.125%
Locust Bean Gum	1.25 g	0.125%
Salt	0.5 g	0.05%
Fresh Persimmon Puree	400 g	40.00%
Base Weight	1000 g	
Serving Temperature	−13.65°C	

Component	Percent
Fats	8.92%
Sugars	17.52%
MSNF	10.08%
Other Solids	3.07%
Water	60.41%
Total Solids	39.59%
POD	18.92
PAC	27.29

Gelato ai Cachi

Persimmon Gelato

For this gelato, use Asian persimmons, also called astringent, Japanese, or Chinese persimmons. These are the persimmons that must be very soft in order to be edible. Non-astringent persimmons, such as Fuyu, have a texture closer to apples and have a slightly different composition.

1. In a small bowl, combine 30 grams of the sucrose, guar gum, locust bean gum, and salt. Mix well. Reserve.
2. Combine milk and remaining sucrose in a stainless-steel pot. Heat to 35°C (95°F), whisking occasionally.
3. Add skim milk powder and whisk to dissolve completely.
4. Continuing to heat the milk mixture, slowly sprinkle in the sucrose mixture, whisking constantly to avoid lumps and keeping the mixture below 45°C (113°F). After the sucrose mixture is incorporated, heat to 85°C (185°F), stirring constantly and scraping the bottom of the pot with a rubber spatula.
5. Add cream. Mix well. Heat to 75°C (167°F), stirring constantly, and hold for 15 seconds.
6. Chill quickly, preferably in an ice bath. Allow to mature overnight, covered and refrigerated at 4°C (39°F) or less.
7. Meanwhile, refrigerate the persimmons.
8. About an hour before freezing the gelato, peel the persimmons, remove the seeds, and puree the persimmons using a high-powered blender, food processor, or commercial immersion blender. Weigh out the required amount and return to the refrigerator.
9. Just before freezing the gelato, add the persimmon puree to the mature base.
10. Add water to return the base to the calculated batch weight. Blend with an immersion blender. Taste and adjust salt, if necessary.
11. Freeze in a batch freezer.
12. Transfer the gelato from the batch freezer to a tub.
13. Harden in a blast freezer or deep freezer.

Ingredient	Quantity	Percent
Milk, 2%	179.5 g	17.95%
Heavy Cream (36% fat)	60 g	6.00%
Sucrose	120 g	12.00%
Fructose	12 g	1.20%
Powdered Skim Milk	75 g	7.50%
Guar Gum	1.25 g	0.125%
Locust Bean Gum	1.25 g	0.125%
Salt	1 g	0.10%
Coconut Cream	250 g	25.00%
Pineapple, Canned in Juice	250 g	25.00%
Dark Rum, 80 proof	50 g	5.00%
Batch Weight	1000 g	
Serving Temperature	−18.75°C	

Component	Percent
Fats	8.41%
Sugars	16.88%
MSNF	9.14%
Other Solids	0.86%
Water	64.72%
Total Solids	35.28%
POD	18.49
PAC	37.51

Gelato alla Piña Colada

Piña Colada Gelato

The serving temperature of this "adult" gelato is lower than usual due to the inclusion of rum. I have never found the taste of gelato made with rum flavoring to be acceptable, though if you cannot use rum, the flavoring is an option. I balanced this using Kara Coconut Cream, which contains 23.3% fat. Another option is Aroy-D Coconut Cream, which contains 21% fat. Using canned pineapple ensures that the enzymes that break down casein in milk are deactivated. It also provides a ready source of great-tasting pineapple year-round.

1. In a small bowl, combine fructose, 20 grams of sucrose, guar gum, locust bean gum, and salt. Mix well. Reserve.
2. Combine milk, cream, and remaining sucrose in a stainless-steel pot. Heat to 35°C (95°F), whisking occasionally.
3. Add skim milk powder and whisk to dissolve completely.
4. Continuing to heat the milk mixture, slowly sprinkle in the fructose mixture, whisking constantly to avoid lumps and keeping the mixture below 45°C (113°F). After the fructose mixture is incorporated, heat to 85°C (185°F), stirring constantly and scraping the bottom of the pot with a rubber spatula.
5. Remove from heat. Stir in the coconut cream.
6. Chill quickly, preferably in an ice bath. Allow to mature overnight, covered and refrigerated at 4°C (39°F) or less.
7. Meanwhile, refrigerate the canned pineapple as well as the correct amount of rum.
8. Just before freezing the gelato, thoroughly drain the pineapple and puree the pineapple pulp using a high-powered blender, food processor, or commercial immersion blender. Weigh out the correct amount and add it to the mature base.
9. Add water to return the base to the calculated batch weight less the weight of the rum (950 grams for a single batch). Blend with an immersion blender. Taste and adjust salt, if necessary.
10. Freeze in a batch freezer. When the gelato is partially frozen and is mounding over the blades, add the cold rum and finish freezing.
11. Transfer the gelato from the batch freezer to a tub.
12. Harden in a blast freezer or deep freezer.

Gelato Formulas and Recipes for Component Ingredients

Ingredient	Quantity	Percent
Milk, 2%	213 g	21.30%
Heavy Cream (36% fat)	214 g	21.40%
Sucrose	130 g	13.00%
Dextrose	12 g	1.20%
Powdered Skim Milk	52 g	5.20%
Guar Gum	1.25 g	0.125%
Locust Bean Gum	1.25 g	0.125%
Salt	0.5 g	0.05%
Pineapple, Canned in Juice	376 g	37.60%
Batch Weight	1000 g	
Serving Temperature	−13.61°C	

Component	Percent
Fats	8.21%
Sugars	19.48%
MSNF	8.22%
Other Solids	1.07%
Water	63.03%
Total Solids	36.97%
POD	20.23
PAC	27.21

Gelato all'Ananas

Pineapple Gelato

Pineapple contains enzymes, most prominently bromelain, that break down casein, a major protein in milk. This can create an off taste and cause the milk to curdle. Heat-treating the pineapple deactivates the enzyme. Flavorful fresh pineapple can be difficult to find, but good quality pineapple canned in juice is always available and it is already heat-treated so it will not react with the milk.

1. In a small bowl, combine dextrose, 15 grams of sucrose, guar gum, locust bean gum, and salt. Mix well. Reserve.
2. Combine milk and remaining sucrose in a stainless-steel pot. Heat to 35°C (95°F), whisking occasionally.
3. Add skim milk powder and whisk to dissolve completely.
4. Continuing to heat the milk mixture, slowly sprinkle in the dextrose mixture, whisking constantly to avoid lumps and keeping the mixture below 45°C (113°F). After the dextrose mixture is incorporated, heat to 85°C (185°F), stirring constantly and scraping the bottom of the pot with a rubber spatula.
5. Add cream. Mix well. Heat to 75°C (167°F), stirring constantly, and hold for 15 seconds.
6. Chill quickly, preferably in an ice bath. Allow to mature overnight, covered and refrigerated at 4°C (39°F) or less.
7. Meanwhile, refrigerate the canned pineapple.
8. Just before freezing the gelato, thoroughly drain the pineapple and puree the pineapple pulp using a high-powered blender, food processor, or commercial immersion blender. Weigh out the correct amount and add it to the mature base.
9. Add water to return the base to the calculated batch weight. Blend with an immersion blender. Taste and adjust salt, if necessary.
10. Freeze in a batch freezer.
11. Transfer the gelato from the batch freezer to a tub.
12. Harden in a blast freezer or deep freezer.

Gelato al Pistacchio

Pistachio Gelato

Along with hazelnut, pistachio is one of the most popular nut gelati in Italy. The best pistachios come from Bronte in Sicily. Be sure that the pistachio paste you use does not have any ingredients other than pistachios.

1. In a small bowl, combine dextrose, guar gum, locust bean gum, and salt. Mix well. Reserve.
2. Combine milk and sucrose in a stainless-steel pot. Heat to 35°C (95°F), whisking occasionally.
3. Add skim milk powder and whisk to dissolve completely.
4. Continuing to heat the milk mixture, slowly sprinkle in the dextrose mixture, whisking constantly to avoid lumps and keeping the mixture below 45°C (113°F). After the dextrose mixture is incorporated, heat to 85°C (185°F), stirring constantly and scraping the bottom of the pot with a rubber spatula.
5. Remove from heat. Stir in the pistachio paste.
6. Chill quickly, preferably in an ice bath. Allow to mature overnight, covered and refrigerated at 4°C (39°F) or less.
7. Just before freezing the gelato, add water to return the base to the calculated batch weight. Blend with an immersion blender. Taste and adjust salt, if necessary.
8. Freeze in a batch freezer.
9. Transfer the gelato from the batch freezer to a tub.
10. Harden in a blast freezer or deep freezer.

Ingredient	Quantity	Percent
Milk, 2%	666.5 g	66.65%
Pistachio Paste	130 g	13.00%
Sucrose	140 g	14.00%
Dextrose	20 g	2.00%
Powdered Skim Milk	40 g	4.00%
Guar Gum	1 g	0.10%
Locust Bean Gum	1 g	0.10%
Salt	1.5 g	0.15%
Batch Weight	1000 g	
Serving Temperature	−13.22°C	

Component	Percent
Fats	8.46%
Sugars	17.10%
MSNF	9.81%
Other Solids	4.92%
Water	59.72%
Total Solids	40.28%
POD	17.50
PAC	26.43

Gelato Formulas and Recipes for Component Ingredients

Ingredient	Quantity	Percent
Milk, 2%	221.5 g	22.15%
Heavy Cream (36% fat)	235 g	23.50%
Sucrose	120 g	12.00%
Powdered Skim Milk	70 g	7.00%
Guar Gum	1.25 g	0.125%
Locust Bean Gum	1.25 g	0.125%
Salt	1 g	0.10%
Pomegranate Juice	350 g	35.00%
Batch Weight	1000 g	
Serving Temperature	−13.43°C	

Component	Percent
Fats	9.06%
Sugars	16.41%
MSNF	10.14%
Other Solids	0.72%
Water	63.67%
Total Solids	36.33%
POD	17.84
PAC	26.85

Gelato al Melograno

Pomegranate Gelato

If fresh pomegranate juice is not available, or you are not up to juicing your own pomegranates, you can use bottled pomegranate juice. The composition of a juice blend will be different and the gelato is likely to be unbalanced if you use something other than pure pomegranate juice. Most of the sugar in pomegranate juice is dextrose and fructose, so neither of these sugars is added to this gelato.

1. In a small bowl, combine 30 grams of sucrose, guar gum, locust bean gum, and salt. Mix well. Reserve.
2. Combine milk and remaining sucrose in a stainless-steel pot. Heat to 35°C (95°F), whisking occasionally.
3. Add skim milk powder and whisk to dissolve completely.
4. Continuing to heat the milk mixture, slowly sprinkle in the sucrose mixture, whisking constantly to avoid lumps and keeping the mixture below 45°C (113°F). After the sucrose mixture is incorporated, heat to 85°C (185°F), stirring constantly and scraping the bottom of the pot with a rubber spatula.
5. Add cream. Mix well. Heat to 75°C (167°F), stirring constantly, and hold for 15 seconds.
6. Chill quickly, preferably in an ice bath. Allow to mature overnight, covered and refrigerated at 4°C (39°F) or less.
7. Meanwhile, refrigerate the pomegranate juice.
8. Just before freezing the gelato, weigh out the correct amount of cold pomegranate juice and add it to the mature base.
9. Add water to return the base to the calculated batch weight. Blend with an immersion blender. Taste and adjust salt, if necessary.
10. Freeze in a batch freezer.
11. Transfer the gelato from the batch freezer to a tub.
12. Harden in a blast freezer or deep freezer.

Gelato alla Torta di Zucca

Pumpkin Pie Gelato

Proportions of guar gum and locust bean gum are reduced from my usual amounts as the pumpkin puree thickens the gelato base even though the total amount of solids is within range for a balanced gelato. I recommend using Saigon or Ceylon cinnamon rather than the more commonly available cassia cinnamon for a more delicate flavor. Pie pumpkins can be difficult to source. Using canned pumpkin puree ensures consistency from batch to batch. I balanced this formula using Libby's canned pumpkin, which is 100% pumpkin with no other ingredients. Sprinkle candied orange peel on top for a particularly Italian touch or, for something more American, use crushed spice cookies, such as Biscoff, to resemble pie crust.

Ingredient	Quantity	Percent
Milk, 2%	224.5 g	22.45%
Heavy Cream (36% fat)	230 g	23.00%
Sucrose	150 g	15.00%
Dextrose	18 g	1.80%
Powdered Skim Milk	69 g	6.90%
Canned Pumpkin Puree	305 g	30.50%
Ground Cinnamon	1 g	0.10%
Freshly Grated Nutmeg	0.25 g	0.025%
Guar Gum	0.5 g	0.05%
Locust Bean Gum	0.5 g	0.05%
Salt	1.25 g	0.125%
Batch Weight	1000 g	
Serving Temperature	−13.60°C	

Off-Balance Ingredient	Quantity
Vanilla Extract	5 g

Component	Percent
Fats	8.90%
Sugars	17.91%
MSNF	10.04%
Other Solids	2.02%
Water	61.13%
Total Solids	38.87%
POD	18.48
PAC	27.21

1. In a small bowl, combine dextrose, 10 grams of sucrose, guar gum, locust bean gum, and salt. Mix well. Reserve.
2. Combine milk and remaining sucrose in a stainless-steel pot. Heat to 35°C (95°F), whisking occasionally.
3. Add skim milk powder and whisk to dissolve completely.
4. Continuing to heat the milk mixture, slowly sprinkle in the dextrose mixture, whisking constantly to avoid lumps and keeping the mixture below 45°C (113°F).
5. After the dextrose mixture is incorporated, add the pumpkin puree and whisk to incorporate. Heat to 85°C (185°F), stirring constantly and scraping the bottom of the pot with a rubber spatula.
6. Add cream, cinnamon, and nutmeg. Mix well. Heat to 75°C (167°F), stirring constantly, and hold for 15 seconds.
7. Chill quickly, preferably in an ice bath. Allow to mature overnight, covered and refrigerated at 4°C (39°F) or less.
8. Just before freezing the gelato, add vanilla extract.
9. Add water to return the base to the calculated batch weight. Blend with an immersion blender. Taste and adjust salt, if necessary.
10. Freeze in a batch freezer.
11. Transfer the gelato from the batch freezer to a tub.
12. Harden in a blast freezer or deep freezer.

Gelato Formulas and Recipes for Component Ingredients

Gelato al Lampone
Raspberry Gelato

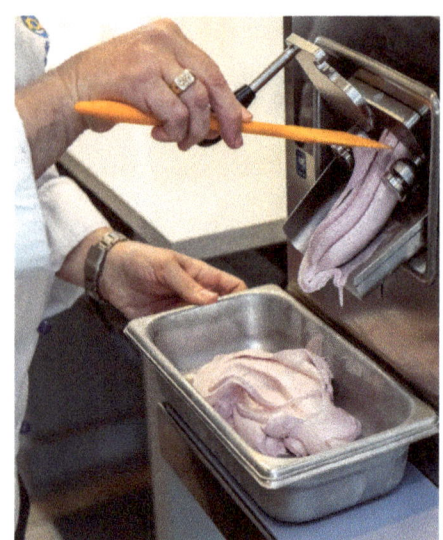

Raspberries make an especially flavorful gelato. To maximize flavor, the quantity of raspberry puree is at the practical upper limit. Because the formula contains just a small amount of liquid milk, you will need to add the cream at the beginning rather than after the stabilizers have been fully hydrated. After pureeing the raspberries, pass them through a fine sieve to remove the seeds. You will need 500 to 520 grams of raspberries to make 400 grams of puree after sieving.

1. In a small bowl, combine fructose, guar gum, locust bean gum, and salt. Mix well. Reserve.
2. Combine milk, cream, and sucrose in a stainless-steel pot. Heat to 35°C (95°F), whisking occasionally.
3. Add skim milk powder and whisk to dissolve completely.
4. Continuing to heat the milk mixture, slowly sprinkle in the fructose mixture, whisking constantly to avoid lumps and keeping the mixture below 45°C (113°F). After the fructose mixture is incorporated, heat to 85°C (185°F), stirring constantly and scraping the bottom of the pot with a rubber spatula.
5. Chill quickly, preferably in an ice bath. Allow to mature overnight, covered and refrigerated at 4°C (39°F) or less.
6. Meanwhile, refrigerate the raspberries.
7. Just before freezing the gelato, puree the chilled raspberries using a high-powered blender, food processor, or commercial immersion blender and pass through a fine sieve to remove the seeds.
8. Weigh out the correct amount of raspberry puree and add it to the mature base.
9. Add water to return the base to the calculated batch weight. Blend with an immersion blender. Taste and adjust salt, if necessary.
10. Freeze in a batch freezer.
11. Transfer the gelato from the batch freezer to a tub.
12. Harden in a blast freezer or deep freezer.

Ingredient	Quantity	Percent
Milk, 2%	120 g	12.00%
Heavy Cream (36% fat)	231.5 g	23.15%
Sucrose	150 g	15.00%
Fructose	20 g	2.00%
Powdered Skim Milk	75 g	7.50%
Guar Gum	1.25 g	0.125%
Locust Bean Gum	1.25 g	0.125%
Salt	1 g	0.10%
Fresh Raspberry Puree	400 g	40.00%
Batch Weight	1000 g	
Serving Temperature	−13.51°C	

Component	Percent
Fats	8.72%
Sugars	18.07%
MSNF	9.68%
Other Solids	4.94%
Water	58.59%
Total Solids	41.41%
POD	20.11
PAC	27.02

106   *Make Your Own Artisan Italian Gelato*

Ingredient	Quantity	Percent
Milk, 2%	350 g	35.00%
Heavy Cream (36% fat)	230 g	23.00%
Sucrose, divided	141 g	14.10%
Dextrose, divided	30 g	3.00%
Powdered Skim Milk	60 g	6.00%
Guar Gum	1 g	0.10%
Locust Bean Gum	1 g	0.10%
Salt, divided	2 g	0.20%
Water	154 g	15.40%
Arborio Rice, uncooked	31 g	3.10%
Batch Weight	1000 g	
Serving Temperature	−13.54°C	

Off-Balance Ingredients	Quantity
Vanilla Bean, chopped	½ bean
Zest of 1½ Lemons, in strips	

Component	Percent
Fats	9.02%
Sugars	16.86%
MSNF	10.31%
Other Solids	3.12%
Water	60.69%
Total Solids	39.31%
POD	17.03
PAC	27.07

Gelato al Riso e Vaniglia

Rice Pudding Gelato

This gelato might sound a bit unusual, but it is common in gelato display cases throughout Italy. It is like a gelato version of rice pudding. I like it with a pronounced vanilla flavor, but you could flavor it with cinnamon instead. The rice will exude starch, which is a stabilizer, so the quantities of guar gum and locust bean gum are less than usual. After cooking the rice, it is important to add water, as noted in the formula, so the mixture remains a pourable slurry when cold. I like flecks of vanilla in this gelato, so I prefer to use a whole vanilla bean. As an alternative you could use vanilla paste or even extract. If so, add the paste or extract just before freezing the gelato as you are blending the base with an immersion blender.

1. In a small bowl, combine 15 grams of the dextrose, guar gum, locust bean gum, and 1 gram of salt. Mix well. Reserve.
2. Puree the chopped vanilla bean with some of the milk in a high-powered blender. Use the remaining milk to rinse out the blender jar.
3. Combine the vanilla-infused milk and 115 grams of the sucrose in a stainless-steel pot. Heat to 35°C (95°F), whisking occasionally.
4. Add skim milk powder and whisk to dissolve completely.
5. Continuing to heat the milk mixture, slowly sprinkle in the dextrose mixture, whisking constantly to avoid lumps and keeping the mixture below 45°C (113°F). After the dextrose mixture is incorporated, heat to 85°C (185°F), stirring constantly and scraping the bottom of the pot with a rubber spatula.
6. Add cream. Mix well. Heat to 75°C (167°F), stirring constantly, and hold for 15 seconds.
7. Chill quickly, preferably in an ice bath. Allow to mature overnight, covered and refrigerated at 4°C (39°F) or less.
8. Meanwhile, weigh a small pot and record the weight.
9. Combine water, rice, the remaining 26 grams of sucrose, the remaining 15 grams of dextrose, the remaining 1 gram of salt, and lemon zest in the pot.
10. Cover and simmer till rice is tender but still whole and most of the liquid is absorbed, approximately 30 minutes.

(continued next page)

Gelato Formulas and Recipes for Component Ingredients

11. Cool slightly. Remove the lemon zest.
12. Add water to return the mixture to its pre-cooked weight: 227 grams[17] for a single batch (plus the weight of the pot).
13. Cover and refrigerate overnight at 4°C (39°F) or less.
14. Just before freezing the gelato, add water to return the base to the calculated batch weight less the weight of the rice (773 grams for a single batch). Blend with an immersion blender. Taste and adjust salt, if necessary.
15. Stir in the cold cooked rice mixture.
16. Freeze in a batch freezer.
17. Transfer the gelato from the batch freezer to a tub.
18. Harden in a blast freezer or deep freezer.

---

[17] 154 grams water + 31 grams rice + 26 grams sucrose + 15 grams dextrose + 1 gram salt = 227 grams.

Ingredient	Quantity	Percent
Milk, 2%	524.5 g	52.45%
Heavy Cream (36% fat)	263 g	26.30%
Sucrose	135 g	13.50%
Dextrose	20 g	2.00%
Fructose	20 g	2.00%
Powdered Skim Milk	34 g	3.40%
Guar Gum	1.25 g	0.125%
Locust Bean Gum	1.25 g	0.125%
Salt	1 g	0.10%
Batch Weight	1000 g	
Serving Temperature	−13.50°C	

Off-Balance Ingredients	Quantity
Vanilla Bean, chopped	½ bean
Malaga or Sweet Sherry	as needed

Mix-In Ingredients	Quantity
Raisins	70 g
Rum to cover raisins	

Component	Percent
Fats	10.52%
Sugars	17.34%
MSNF	9.62%
Other Solids	0.33%
Water	62.20%
Total Solids	37.80%
POD	18.69
PAC	27.00

Gelato al Malaga
Rum Raisin Gelato

In Italy, rum raisin gelato is referred to as *malaga*. Malaga happens to be the name of a fortified wine from Spain. It resembles sweet sherry. Some versions of Gelato al Malaga contain Malaga wine instead of rum. I like to use both: Malaga (or sweet sherry) in the gelato and rum in the raisins.

1. Cover the raisins with a generous amount of rum and allow to soften, covered, at room temperature for 24 hours.
2. In a small bowl, combine fructose, guar gum, locust bean gum, and salt. Mix well. Reserve.
3. Puree the chopped vanilla bean with some of the milk in a high-powered blender. Use the remaining milk to rinse out the blender jar.
4. Combine vanilla-infused milk, sucrose, and dextrose in a stainless-steel pot. Heat to 35°C (95°F), whisking occasionally.
5. Add skim milk powder and whisk to dissolve completely.
6. Continuing to heat the milk mixture, slowly sprinkle in the fructose mixture, whisking constantly to avoid lumps and keeping the mixture below 45°C (113°F). After the fructose mixture is incorporated, heat to 85°C (185°F), stirring constantly and scraping the bottom of the pot with a rubber spatula.
7. Add cream. Mix well. Heat to 75°C (167°F), stirring constantly, and hold for 15 seconds.
8. Chill quickly, preferably in an ice bath. Allow to mature overnight, covered and refrigerated at 4°C (39°F) or less.
9. Just before freezing the gelato, add Malaga or sweet sherry to return the base to the calculated batch weight.[18] Do not use more than 20 grams per kilogram of base. If more liquid is needed, use water. Blend with an immersion blender. Taste and adjust salt, if necessary.
10. Freeze in a batch freezer.
11. Meanwhile, drain the raisins.
12. Transfer the gelato from the batch freezer to a tub, stopping periodically to sprinkle in some of the rum-soaked, drained raisins, swirling a bit with a spatula.
13. Harden in a blast freezer or deep freezer.

---

[18] If making at a commercial scale using a pasteurizer and chiller, add 20 grams of Malaga or sweet sherry per kilogram of base.

Ingredient	Quantity	Percent
Milk, 2%	520 g	52.00%
Heavy Cream (36% fat)	223.38 g	22.34%
Sucrose	150 g	15.00%
Dextrose	30 g	3.00%
Powdered Skim Milk	43 g	4.30%
Guar Gum	1.25 g	0.125%
Locust Bean Gum	1.25 g	0.125%
Salt	1 g	0.10%
Powdered Saffron	0.12 g	0.012%
Rosewater	30 g	3.00%
Batch Weight	1000 g	
Serving Temperature	−13.38°C	

Mix-In Ingredients	Quantity
Chopped Roasted Pistachios	10 g

Component	Percent
Fats	9.08%
Sugars	17.76%
MSNF	10.18%
Other Solids	0.34%
Water	62.63%
Total Solids	37.37%
POD	17.93
PAC	26.76

Gelato allo Zafferano e Acqua di Rose

Saffron and Rosewater Gelato

In Italy, saffron is available finely pulverized in small, single-use packets of 0.1 to 0.12 grams. This makes it easy to incorporate the saffron into liquid. If using saffron threads, finely pulverize them with a mortar and pestle. Rosewater from the Middle East is needed for this gelato. Other more powerful rose extracts would overpower the flavor if used in the quantity noted. The flavor is subtle, but you can increase the rosewater and saffron if desired.

1. In a small bowl, combine dextrose, guar gum, locust bean gum, and salt. Mix well. Reserve.
2. Combine milk and sucrose in a stainless-steel pot. Heat to 35°C (95°F), whisking occasionally.
3. Add skim milk powder and whisk to dissolve completely.
4. Continuing to heat the milk mixture, slowly sprinkle in the dextrose mixture, whisking constantly to avoid lumps and keeping the mixture below 45°C (113°F). After the dextrose mixture is incorporated, heat to 85°C (185°F), stirring constantly and scraping the bottom of the pot with a rubber spatula.
5. Add saffron and cream. Whisk to fully disperse the saffron. Heat to 75°C (167°F), stirring constantly, and hold for 15 seconds.
6. Chill quickly, preferably in an ice bath. Allow to mature overnight, covered and refrigerated at 4°C (39°F) or less.
7. Just before freezing the gelato, add rosewater.
8. Add water to return the base to the calculated batch weight. Blend with an immersion blender. Taste and adjust salt, if necessary.
9. Freeze in a batch freezer.
10. Transfer the gelato from the batch freezer to a tub. Top with chopped pistachios, if desired.
11. Harden in a blast freezer or deep freezer.

Ingredient	Quantity	Percent
Milk, 2%	616 g	61.60%
Peanuts, Oil Roasted Salted	120 g	12.00%
Heavy Cream (36% fat)	50 g	5.00%
Sucrose	143 g	14.30%
Dextrose	25 g	2.50%
Powdered Skim Milk	44 g	4.40%
Guar Gum	1 g	0.10%
Locust Bean Gum	1 g	0.10%
Batch Weight	1000 g	
Serving Temperature	−12.27°C	

Component	Percent
Fats	9.31%
Sugars	17.10%
MSNF	10.05%
Other Solids	5.21%
Water	58.33%
Total Solids	41.67%
POD	17.39
PAC	24.55

Gelato alle Arachidi Salate

Salted Peanut Gelato

This gelato is a riff on classic Italian nut gelati but made with an iconic American ingredient: peanuts. Although the calculated serving temperature of this gelato is −12.27°C (9.9°F), in reality it is lower. The salt on the peanuts has not been factored into the calculation of PAC, as the amount of salt in any given batch of peanuts is unknown. Be certain not to include any loose salt from the bottom of the package. If you find that this gelato is too soft at serving temperature, you could rinse the salt off a portion of the peanuts for subsequent batches. Alternatively, you could serve the gelato from a service freezer that is set to a lower temperature to accommodate gelati that contain liquor.

1. In a small bowl, combine dextrose, guar gum, and locust bean gum. Mix well. Reserve.
2. Puree the peanuts with some of the milk in a high-powered blender. Use the remaining milk to rinse out the blender jar.
3. Combine milk-peanut mixture and sucrose in a stainless-steel pot. Heat to 35°C (95°F), whisking occasionally.
4. Add skim milk powder and whisk to dissolve completely.
5. Continuing to heat the milk mixture, slowly sprinkle in the dextrose mixture, whisking constantly to avoid lumps and keeping the mixture below 45°C (113°F). After the dextrose mixture is incorporated, heat to 85°C (185°F), stirring constantly and scraping the bottom of the pot with a rubber spatula.
6. Add cream. Mix well. The temperature will be above 75°C (167°F) after the cream is added due to the small amount of cream relative to the large amount of hot base.
7. Chill quickly, preferably in an ice bath. Allow to mature overnight, covered and refrigerated at 4°C (39°F) or less.
8. Just before freezing the gelato, add water to return the base to the calculated batch weight. Blend with an immersion blender. Taste and adjust salt, if necessary.
9. Freeze in a batch freezer.
10. Transfer the gelato from the batch freezer to a tub.
11. Harden in a blast freezer or deep freezer.

Gelato Formulas and Recipes for Component Ingredients

Gelato alla Stracciatella
Stracciatella Gelato

Stracciatella is fiordilatte gelato with melted chocolate mixed in. There are two ways to mix in the melted chocolate. One is to put the melted and cooled, but still liquid, chocolate directly into the gelato batch freezer for a few seconds just before removing the frozen gelato. The chocolate will harden and mix through the gelato in small pieces. The second method is to drizzle the chocolate into the gelato as the gelato is being put in the tub and then mixing with a spatula to break up the chocolate, which will harden almost immediately. You can use chocolate with more or less cocoa solids to suit your taste. You can also use a different quantity of chocolate, if desired.

Ingredient	Quantity	Percent
Milk, 2%	525 g	52.50%
Heavy Cream (36% fat)	263 g	26.30%
Sucrose	135 g	13.50%
Dextrose	20 g	2.00%
Fructose	20 g	2.00%
Powdered Skim Milk	34 g	3.40%
Guar Gum	1.25 g	0.125%
Locust Bean Gum	1.25 g	0.125%
Salt	0.50 g	0.05%
Batch Weight	1000 g	
Serving Temperature	−13.21°C	

Mix-In Ingredients	Quantity
Chocolate, 72% Cocoa Solids	90 g

Component	Percent
Fats	10.52%
Sugars	17.34%
MSNF	9.62%
Other Solids	0.28%
Water	62.24%
Total Solids	37.76%
POD	18.69
PAC	26.42

1. In a small bowl, combine dextrose, guar gum, locust bean gum, and salt. Mix well. Reserve.
2. Combine milk, sucrose, and fructose in a stainless-steel pot. Heat milk mixture to 35°C (95°F), whisking occasionally.
3. Add skim milk powder and whisk to dissolve completely.
4. Continuing to heat the milk mixture, slowly sprinkle in the dextrose mixture, whisking constantly to avoid lumps and keeping the mixture below 45°C (113°F). After the dextrose mixture is incorporated, heat to 85°C (185°F), stirring constantly and scraping the bottom of the pot with a rubber spatula.
5. Add cream. Mix well. Heat to 75°C (167°F), stirring constantly, and hold for 15 seconds.
6. Chill quickly, preferably in an ice bath. Allow to mature overnight, covered and refrigerated at 4°C (39°F) or less.
7. Just before freezing the gelato, add water to return the base to the calculated batch weight. Blend with an immersion blender. Taste and adjust salt, if necessary.
8. Freeze in a batch freezer.
9. As the gelato is freezing, melt the chocolate in a double boiler over boiling water or use a microwave on low power and stirring often so as to not scorch the chocolate. Allow the chocolate to cool, but not harden, as the gelato freezes.
10. Add the melted chocolate to the gelato using one of the two methods described above.
11. Transfer the gelato from the batch freezer to a tub.
12. Harden in a blast freezer or deep freezer.

Ingredient	Quantity	Percent
Milk, 2%	170 g	17.00%
Heavy Cream (36% fat)	215 g	21.50%
Sucrose	128 g	12.80%
Fructose	24 g	2.40%
Powdered Skim Milk	59.5 g	5.95%
Guar Gum	1.25 g	0.125%
Locust Bean Gum	1.25 g	0.125%
Salt	1 g	0.10%
Fresh Strawberry Puree	400 g	40.00%
Base Weight	1000 g	
Serving Temperature	−13.49°C	

Component	Percent
Fats	8.22%
Sugars	17.34%
MSNF	8.55%
Other Solids	1.67%
Water	64.23%
Total Solids	35.77%
POD	19.57
PAC	26.98

Gelato alla Fragola

Strawberry Gelato

This gelato is the essence of summer and one of the most traditional fruit-flavored gelati in Italy. If you can get fresh, local strawberries, by all means use them for this gelato. If you use commercially available ones, look for smaller, fully ripe berries. Unlike raspberries, I prefer to not strain the seeds out of the strawberry puree. Strawberries don't contain quite as many seeds, and they are smaller. Their presence is a reminder that this gelato is made with fresh fruit.

1. In a small bowl, combine fructose, guar gum, locust bean gum, and salt. Mix well. Reserve.
2. Combine milk and sucrose in a stainless-steel pot. Heat to 35°C (95°F), whisking occasionally.
3. Add skim milk powder and whisk to dissolve completely.
4. Continuing to heat the milk mixture, slowly sprinkle in the fructose mixture, whisking constantly to avoid lumps and keeping the mixture below 45°C (113°F). After the fructose mixture is incorporated, heat to 85°C (185°F), stirring constantly and scraping the bottom of the pot with a rubber spatula.
5. Add cream. Mix well. Heat to 75°C (167°F), stirring constantly, and hold for 15 seconds.
6. Chill quickly, preferably in an ice bath. Allow to mature overnight, covered and refrigerated at 4°C (39°F) or less.
7. Meanwhile, wash the strawberries and keep them refrigerated.
8. About an hour before freezing the gelato, hull the strawberries and puree using a high-powered blender, food processor, or commercial immersion blender. Weigh out the correct amount and return to the refrigerator.
9. Just before freezing the gelato, add the pureed strawberries to the mature base.
10. Add water to return the base to the calculated batch weight. Blend with an immersion blender. Taste and adjust salt, if necessary.
11. Freeze in a batch freezer.
12. Transfer the gelato from the batch freezer to a tub.
13. Harden in a blast freezer or deep freezer.

Ingredient	Quantity	Percent
Milk, 2%	41.5 g	4.15%
Heavy Cream (36% fat)	245 g	24.50%
Sucrose	125 g	12.50%
Powdered Skim Milk	85 g	8.50%
Guar Gum	1.25 g	0.125%
Locust Bean Gum	1.25 g	0.125%
Salt	1 g	0.10%
Tamarind Puree (22% Pulp)	500 g	50.00%
Batch Weight	1000 g	
Serving Temperature	−13.37°C	

Component	Percent
Fats	9.05%
Sugars	16.77%
MSNF	10.02%
Other Solids	3.54%
Water	60.63%
Total Solids	39.37%
POD	17.99
PAC	26.75

Gelato al Tamarindo

Tamarind Gelato

I pondered the process for making this gelato for quite a while. I ruled out using blocks of dried tamarind pulp. These always contain seeds and fiber making it difficult to portion reliably. I knew I would not use any tamarind concentrates, as they did not have the flavor I was looking for. I was going to use fresh tamarind, which can be found in some specialty markets. After cracking open the crunchy pod, it is relatively easy to separate the moist flesh from the seeds and fiber, making portioning easier. While shopping for tamarind pods, I noticed frozen tamarind puree that had no ingredients other than tamarind pulp and water. I instantly decided to use this product. The product I found contains 22% tamarind pulp, so if you want to use fresh tamarind instead of the prepared puree, use 22% of the amount listed below, making up the difference with water.

1. In a small bowl, combine 30 grams of the sucrose, guar gum, locust bean gum, and salt. Mix well. Reserve.
2. Combine milk, cream, and remaining sucrose in a stainless-steel pot. Heat to 35°C (95°F), whisking occasionally.
3. Add skim milk powder and whisk to dissolve completely.
4. Continuing to heat the milk mixture, slowly sprinkle in the sucrose mixture, whisking constantly to avoid lumps and keeping the mixture below 45°C (113°F). After the sucrose mixture is incorporated, heat to 85°C (185°F), stirring constantly and scraping the bottom of the pot with a rubber spatula.
5. Chill quickly, preferably in an ice bath. Allow to mature overnight, covered and refrigerated at 4°C (39°F) or less.
6. Meanwhile, put the tamarind puree in the refrigerator to thaw, if frozen. Alternatively, make the puree using 110 grams fresh tamarind pulp, seeds and hard bits removed, and 390 grams water and refrigerate.
7. Just before freezing the gelato, add the tamarind puree.
8. Add water to return the base to the calculated batch weight. Blend with an immersion blender. Taste and adjust salt, if necessary.
9. Freeze in a batch freezer.
10. Transfer the gelato from the batch freezer to a tub.
11. Harden in a blast freezer or deep freezer.

Ingredient	Quantity	Percent
Milk, 2%	511 g	51.10%
Mascarpone, 36% fat	249.5 g	24.95%
Sucrose	160 g	16.00%
Dextrose	26 g	2.60%
Powdered Skim Milk	50 g	5.00%
Guar Gum	1.25 g	0.125%
Locust Bean Gum	1.25 g	0.125%
Salt	1 g	0.10%
Batch Weight	1000 g	
Serving Temperature	−13.73°C	

Mix-In Ingredients	Quantity
Sponge Cake or Madeleines	50 g
Espresso Coffee, brewed	30 g
Coffee Liqueur or Rum	15 g
Miniature Chocolate Chips	15 g
Cocoa Powder, for dusting	

Component	Percent
Fats	9.99%
Sugars	18.39%
MSNF	11.56%
Other Solids	0.33%
Water	59.73%
Total Solids	40.27%
POD	18.71
PAC	27.46

Gelato al Tiramisù

Tiramisù Gelato

I developed this gelato to have the traditional flavors of tiramisù. Many versions of tiramisù do not contain liquor. Many Italians say this is the original way. Controversy surrounds many foods in Italy. These days, adding liquor to tiramisù is common. For the gelato version, I think it is essential to keep the cake from freezing into solid blocks after being moistened with espresso. The traditional cake for tiramisù is pan di Spagna (sponge cake). For small quantities of gelato, I suggest buying madeleines, which are made from a sponge cake batter.

1. In a small bowl, combine dextrose, guar gum, locust bean gum, and salt. Mix well. Reserve.
2. Combine milk and sucrose in a stainless-steel pot. Heat to 35°C (95°F), whisking occasionally.
3. Add skim milk powder and whisk to dissolve completely.
4. Continuing to heat the milk mixture, slowly sprinkle in the dextrose mixture, whisking constantly to avoid lumps and keeping the mixture below 45°C (113°F). After the dextrose mixture is incorporated, heat to 85°C (185°F), stirring constantly and scraping the bottom of the pot with a rubber spatula.
5. Add mascarpone. Use a whisk to completely incorporate the mascarpone.
6. Heat to 66°C (151°F), stirring constantly. Hold at 66°C (151°F) for 30 minutes, stirring if needed. (If the 30-minute hold is in a water bath or in a commercial pasteurizer, no stirring is needed. If the 30-minute hold is on the cooktop, you will need to stir occasionally to equalize the temperature.)
7. Chill quickly, preferably in an ice bath. Allow to mature overnight, covered and refrigerated at 4°C (39°F) or less.
8. Meanwhile, cut the sponge cake into 1 centimeter (½ inch) cubes. Spread the cubes on a baking sheet and bake at 125°C (250°F) until the cake has lost much of its moisture but is not brown or hard, about 18 to 20 minutes. When cold, refrigerate the cake.
9. In a small bowl, combine espresso and rum and refrigerate.
10. Just before freezing the gelato, add water to return the base to the calculated batch weight. Blend with an immersion blender. Taste and adjust salt, if necessary.

(continued next page)

Gelato Formulas and Recipes for Component Ingredients

11. Freeze in a batch freezer.
12. About 2 minutes before the gelato is ready to be removed from the batch freezer, sprinkle the cake with the espresso-rum mixture. (If you do this too far in advance, the cake will disintegrate.)
13. Transfer the gelato from the batch freezer to a tub, stopping periodically to sprinkle in some of the espresso- and rum-soaked cake bits and the chocolate chips.
14. When the pan is full, dust the top thickly with cocoa powder.
15. Harden in a blast freezer or deep freezer.
16. When serving, you can dust individual portions with more cocoa powder.

Ingredient	Quantity	Percent
Toasted Coconut Milk	525 g	52.50%
Heavy Cream (36% fat)	131 g	13.10%
Water	131 g	13.10%
Sucrose	153 g	15.30%
Dextrose	17 g	1.70%
Powdered Skim Milk	40 g	4.00%
Guar Gum	1.25 g	0.125%
Locust Bean Gum	1.25 g	0.125%
Salt	0.5 g	0.05%
Batch Weight	1000 g	
Serving Temperature	−14.45°C	

Component	Percent
Fats	11.85%
Sugars	17.46%
MSNF	9.36%
Other Solids	0.83%
Water	60.50%
Total Solids	39.50%
POD	20.73
PAC	28.90

Gelato al Cocco Tostato

Toasted Coconut Gelato

Toasted coconut gelato is perhaps a more typical coconut flavor for Americans than gelato made with coconut milk. Gelato made with coconut milk has a purer coconut flavor, but it is also more subtle than gelato made with toasted coconut. See the recipe for toasted coconut milk in the "Component Ingredients" section at the end of this chapter. Although the calculated serving temperature of this gelato is lower than typical, the presence of the coconut solids keeps the gelato firm at the slightly warmer standard gelato serving temperature of approximately −13°C.

1. In a small bowl, combine dextrose, 10 grams of sucrose, guar gum, locust bean gum, and salt. Mix well. Reserve.
2. Combine toasted coconut milk, water, and remaining sucrose in a stainless-steel pot. Heat to 35°C (95°F), whisking occasionally.
3. Add skim milk powder and whisk to dissolve completely.
4. Continuing to heat the milk mixture, slowly sprinkle in the dextrose mixture, whisking constantly to avoid lumps and keeping the mixture below 45°C (113°F). After the dextrose mixture is incorporated, heat to 85°C (185°F), stirring constantly and scraping the bottom of the pot with a rubber spatula.
5. Add cream. Mix well. Heat to 75°C (167°F), stirring constantly, and hold for 15 seconds.
6. Chill quickly, preferably in an ice bath. Allow to mature overnight, covered and refrigerated at 4°C (39°F) or less.
7. Just before freezing the gelato, add water to return the base to the calculated batch weight. Blend with an immersion blender. Taste and adjust salt, if necessary.
8. Freeze in a batch freezer.
9. Transfer the gelato from the batch freezer to a tub.
10. Harden in a blast freezer or deep freezer.

Gelato alla Vaniglia
Vanilla Gelato

Ingredient	Quantity	Percent
Milk, 2%	532.5 g	53.25%
Heavy Cream (36% fat)	250 g	25.00%
Sucrose	135 g	13.50%
Dextrose	20 g	2.00%
Fructose	20 g	2.00%
Powdered Skim Milk	39 g	3.90%
Guar Gum	1.25 g	0.125%
Locust Bean Gum	1.25 g	0.125%
Salt	1 g	0.10%
Batch Weight	1000 g	
Serving Temperature	−13.63°C	

Mix-In Ingredients	Quantity
Vanilla Bean, chopped	1 or 2 beans
Vanilla Extract or Paste	As needed

Component	Percent
Fats	10.07%
Sugars	17.34%
MSNF	10.08%
Other Solids	0.33%
Water	62.18%
Total Solids	37.82%
POD	18.73
PAC	27.25

When making vanilla gelato, I prefer that the vanilla not be timid. In fact, I like a profound vanilla flavor. If you're using smaller vanilla beans, I suggest using 1½ or 2. If using larger beans, 1 should be sufficient to create an intense vanilla flavor. In either case, if the gelato does not have enough vanilla taste, you can add vanilla extract or paste just before putting it into the batch freezer.

1. In a small bowl, combine dextrose, guar gum, locust bean gum, and salt. Mix well. Reserve.
2. Puree the chopped vanilla bean with some of the milk in a high-powered blender. Use the remaining milk to rinse out the blender jar.
3. Combine vanilla-infused milk, sucrose, and fructose in a stainless-steel pot. Heat to 35°C (95°F), whisking occasionally.
4. Add skim milk powder and whisk to dissolve completely.
5. Continuing to heat the milk mixture, slowly sprinkle in the dextrose mixture, whisking constantly to avoid lumps and keeping the mixture below 45°C (113°F). After the dextrose mixture is incorporated, heat to 85°C (185°F), stirring constantly and scraping the bottom of the pot with a rubber spatula.
6. Add cream. Mix well. Heat to 75°C (167°F), stirring constantly, and hold for 15 seconds.
7. Chill quickly, preferably in an ice bath. Allow to mature overnight, covered and refrigerated at 4°C (39°F) or less.
8. Just before freezing the gelato, add water to return the base to the calculated batch weight. Blend with an immersion blender. Taste and adjust salt, if necessary.
9. Freeze in a batch freezer.
10. Transfer the gelato from the batch freezer to a tub.
11. Harden in a blast freezer or deep freezer.

Gelato al Caffè Vietnamita

Vietnamese Coffee Gelato

Ingredient	Quantity	Percent
Milk, 2%	131.5 g	13.15%
Heavy Cream (36% fat)	160 g	16.00%
Condensed Milk, Eagle Brand	370 g	37.00%
Brewed Vietnamese Coffee	300 g	30.00%
Dextrose	15 g	1.50%
Powdered Skim Milk	20 g	2.00%
Guar Gum	1.25 g	0.125%
Locust Bean Gum	1.25 g	0.125%
Salt	1 g	0.10%
Batch Weight	1000 g	
Serving Temperature	−13.39°C	

Component	Percent
Fats	8.93%
Sugars	19.40%
MSNF	9.79%
Other Solids	1.21%
Water	60.67%
Total Solids	39.33%
POD	19.85
PAC	26.77

Vietnamese coffee is made with a single-serving metal drip filter. The coffee is dripped directly into the serving cup to which a dollop of condensed milk has been added. Different brands of condensed milk contain different percentages of sugar. This recipe was standardized using Eagle Brand condensed milk. If this brand is not available, check the Food Data Central website (see Appendix G, "References and Resources," for the web address) to find brands that have a similar composition. Directions for brewing Vietnamese coffee for this gelato are contained in the "Component Ingredients" section at the end of this chapter.

1. In a small bowl, combine dextrose, guar gum, locust bean gum, and salt. Mix well. Reserve.
2. Combine milk, brewed coffee, and condensed milk in a stainless-steel pot. Heat to 35°C (95°F), whisking occasionally.
3. Add skim milk powder and whisk to dissolve completely.
4. Continuing to heat the milk mixture, slowly sprinkle in the dextrose mixture, whisking constantly to avoid lumps and keeping the mixture below 45°C (113°F). After the dextrose mixture is incorporated, heat to 85°C (185°F), stirring constantly and scraping the bottom of the pot with a rubber spatula.
5. Add cream. Mix well. Heat to 75°C (167°F), stirring constantly, and hold for 15 seconds.
6. Chill quickly, preferably in an ice bath. Allow to mature overnight, covered and refrigerated at 4°C (39°F) or less.
7. Just before freezing the gelato, add water to return the base to the calculated batch weight. Blend with an immersion blender. Taste and adjust salt, if necessary.
8. Freeze in a batch freezer.
9. Transfer the gelato from the batch freezer to a tub.
10. Harden in a blast freezer or deep freezer.

Gelato all'Anguria
Watermelon Gelato

When I set out to develop this gelato, none of my gelato colleagues was hopeful. The thought was that the flavor of watermelon was too mild for gelato. Using watermelon for sorbetto was viewed as a no-brainer (sorbetto does not contain milk or cream), but using it for gelato was not so obvious. Watermelon contains a lot of, well, water, in comparison to the amount of flavorful compounds. To make a gelato that tastes like watermelon required some creativity to balance the gelato while maximizing the amount of watermelon that is included.

Ingredient	Quantity	Percent
Milk, 2%	24.5 g	2.45%
Heavy Cream (36% fat)	220 g	22.00%
Sucrose	123 g	12.30%
Dextrose	11 g	1.10%
Powdered Skim Milk	88 g	8.80%
Guar Gum	1.25 g	0.125%
Locust Bean Gum	1.25 g	0.125%
Salt	1 g	0.10%
Freshly Pureed Watermelon	530 g	53.00%
Batch Weight	1000 g	
Serving Temperature	−13.10°C	

Component	Percent
Fats	8.13%
Sugars	16.60%
MSNF	9.99%
Other Solids	1.50%
Water	63.78%
Total Solids	36.22%
POD	17.84
PAC	26.20

1. In a small bowl, combine dextrose, 10 grams of sucrose, guar gum, locust bean gum, and salt. Mix well. Reserve.
2. Combine milk, cream, and remaining sucrose in a stainless-steel pot. Heat to 35°C (95°F), whisking occasionally.
3. Add skim milk powder and whisk to dissolve completely.
4. Continuing to heat the milk mixture, slowly sprinkle in the dextrose mixture, whisking constantly to avoid lumps and keeping the mixture below 45°C (113°F). After the dextrose mixture is incorporated, heat to 85°C (185°F), stirring constantly and scraping the bottom of the pot with a rubber spatula.
5. Chill quickly, preferably in an ice bath. Allow to mature overnight, covered and refrigerated at 4°C (39°F) or less.
6. Meanwhile, cube the watermelon and remove the seeds. Refrigerate.
7. Just before freezing the gelato, puree the watermelon in a high-powered blender, food processor, or commercial immersion blender. Weigh out the correct amount and add it to the mature base.
8. Add water to return the base to the calculated batch weight. Blend with an immersion blender. Taste and adjust salt, if necessary.
9. Freeze in a batch freezer.
10. Transfer the gelato from the batch freezer to a tub.
11. Harden in a blast freezer or deep freezer.

Ingredient	Quantity	Percent
Milk, 2%	208 g	20.80%
Water	390.5 g	39.05%
Sucrose	50 g	5.00%
Dextrose	25 g	2.50%
Powdered Skim Milk	65 g	6.50%
Guar Gum	1.25 g	0.125%
Locust Bean Gum	1.25 g	0.125%
Salt	1 g	0.10%
White Chocolate	245 g	24.50%
Extra-Virgin Olive Oil	13 g	1.30%
Base Weight	1000 g	
Serving Temperature	−13.53°C	

Component	Percent
Fats	10.75%
Sugars	17.19%
MSNF	9.95%
Other Solids	3.99%
Water	58.11%
Total Solids	41.89%
POD	17.68
PAC	27.06

Gelato al Cioccolato Bianco e Olio EVO

White Chocolate Extra-Virgin Olive Oil Gelato

It is difficult to coax much flavor out of white chocolate because the most flavorful part of the cocoa pod, the cocoa solids, is not included. Nonetheless, there are devoted white chocolate fans. This is the gelato for you! It is important to use an excellent quality white chocolate, preferably one with very light (or no) vanilla added. If you use too much vanilla, the end result will taste like vanilla gelato, not white chocolate. The extra-virgin olive oil does not affect the taste but does improve the mouthfeel, as the oil is liquid at a lower temperature than the cocoa butter.

1. In a small bowl, combine dextrose, guar gum, locust bean gum, and salt. Mix well. Reserve.
2. Combine milk, water, and sucrose in a stainless-steel pot. Heat to 35°C (95°F), whisking occasionally.
3. Add the white chocolate, broken into pieces, and stir until melted, keeping the temperature below 45°C (113°F).
4. Add skim milk powder and whisk to dissolve completely.
5. Continuing to heat the milk mixture, slowly sprinkle in the dextrose mixture, whisking constantly to avoid lumps and keeping the mixture below 45°C (113°F). After the dextrose mixture is incorporated, heat to 85°C (185°F), stirring constantly and scraping the bottom of the pot with a rubber spatula.
6. Chill quickly, preferably in an ice bath. Allow to mature overnight, covered and refrigerated at 4°C (39°F) or less.
7. Just before freezing the gelato, add water to return the base to the calculated batch weight less the weight of the olive oil (987 grams for a single batch). Blend with an immersion blender. Taste and adjust salt, if necessary.
8. Freeze in a batch freezer. When the gelato is partially frozen and is mounding over the blades, add the olive oil and finish freezing.
9. Transfer the gelato from the batch freezer to a tub.
10. Harden in a blast freezer or deep freezer.

Gelato Formulas and Recipes for Component Ingredients

Ingredient	Quantity	Percent
Milk, 2%	431.5 g	43.15%
Heavy Cream (36% fat)	165 g	16.50%
Sucrose	147.5 g	14.75%
Fructose	10 g	1.00%
Powdered Skim Milk	55 g	5.50%
Egg Yolks	90 g	9.00%
Salt	1 g	0.10%
Dry Marsala	100 g	10.00%
Batch Weight	1000 g	
Serving Temperature	−18.69°C	

Component	Percent
Fats	9.20%
Sugars	16.20%
MSNF	10.16%
Other Solids	1.96%
Water	62.48%
Total Solids	37.52%
POD	17.59
PAC	37.37

Gelato allo Zabaione

Zabaione Gelato

Zabaione is a classic Italian dessert made from eggs, sugar, and marsala whisked over boiling water until thick. Because eggs feature prominently in zabaione, egg yolks are a critical flavoring ingredient for this gelato. Egg yolks have emulsifying properties and, in the quantities used here, stabilizing properties also, so no additional stabilizers are needed. Marsala comes in a range of sugar contents and alcohol percentages. I suggest using Florio Superiore Dry Marsala. If it is not available, choose another dry Marsala with 18% alcohol. Because of the alcohol, the PAC of this gelato is quite high. The serving temperature is therefore lower than is typical.

1. Beat the egg yolks and sucrose until very light colored, almost white.
2. Combine all ingredients except Marsala in a stainless-steel pot.
3. Heat to 69°C (157°F), stirring constantly with a rubber spatula. Hold at 69°C (157°F) for 30 minutes, stirring if needed. (If the 30-minute hold is in a water bath or in a commercial pasteurizer, no stirring is needed. If the 30-minute hold is on the cooktop, occasional stirring will be needed to equalize the temperature.)
4. Chill quickly, preferably in an ice bath. Allow to mature overnight, covered and refrigerated at 4°C (39°F) or less.
5. Meanwhile, weigh out the Marsala, cover tightly, and refrigerate.
6. Just before freezing the gelato, add water to return the base to the calculated batch weight less the weight of the Marsala (900 grams for a single batch). Blend with an immersion blender. Taste and adjust salt, if necessary.
7. Freeze in a batch freezer. When the gelato is partially frozen and is mounding over the blades, add the cold Marsala and finish freezing.
8. Transfer the gelato from the batch freezer to a tub.
9. Harden in a blast freezer or deep freezer.

Make Your Own Artisan Italian Gelato

Gelato alla Zuppa Inglese
Zuppa Inglese Gelato

Alkermes is a traditional liqueur used in numerous Italian sweets, including zuppa inglese. It is bright red. If it is not available, choose another liqueur or use rum. I like the effect that the color brings to the gelato so I would choose another deeply colored liqueur if I did not have Alkermes. As with tiramisù, the traditional cake for zuppa inglese is pan di Spagna (sponge cake). For small quantities of gelato, I suggest buying madeleines, which are made from a sponge cake batter. I like using dark chocolate chips in this gelato.

1. Beat the egg yolks and sucrose until very light colored, almost white.
2. Combine all ingredients except vanilla paste, sponge cake, Alkermes, and chocolate chips in a stainless-steel pot.
3. Heat to 69°C (157°F), stirring constantly with a rubber spatula. Hold at 69°C (157°F) for 30 minutes, stirring if needed. (If the 30-minute hold is in a water bath or in a commercial pasteurizer, no stirring is needed. If the 30-minute hold is on the cooktop, occasional stirring will be needed to equalize the temperature.)
4. Chill quickly, preferably in an ice bath. Allow to mature overnight, covered and refrigerated at 4°C (39°F) or less.
5. Meanwhile, cut the sponge cake into 1 centimeter (½ inch) cubes. Spread the cubes on a baking sheet and bake at 125°C (250°F) until the cake has lost much of its moisture but is not brown or hard, about 18 to 20 minutes. When cold, refrigerate the cake.
6. Just before freezing the gelato, add the vanilla paste.
7. Add water to return the base to the calculated batch weight. Blend with an immersion blender. Taste and adjust salt, if necessary.
8. Freeze in a batch freezer.
9. About 2 minutes before the gelato is ready to be removed from the batch freezer, sprinkle the cake with Alkermes liqueur to moisten. (If you do this too far in advance, the cake will disintegrate).
10. Transfer the gelato from the batch freezer to a tub, stopping periodically to sprinkle in some of the Alkermes-soaked cake bits and the chocolate chips.
11. Harden in a blast freezer or deep freezer.

Ingredient	Quantity	Percent
Milk, 2%	537 g	53.70%
Heavy Cream (36% fat)	160 g	16.00%
Egg Yolk	92 g	9.20%
Sucrose	155 g	15.50%
Dextrose	25 g	2.50%
Powdered Skim Milk	30 g	3.00%
Salt	1 g	0.10%
Batch Weight	1000 g	
Serving Temperature	−12.86°C	

Off-Balance Ingredient	Quantity
Vanilla Paste	7.50 g

Mix-In Ingredients	Quantity
Sponge Cake or Madeleines	50 g
Alkermes Liqueur	As needed
Miniature Chocolate Chips	12.5 g

Component	Percent
Fats	9.26%
Sugars	17.85%
MSNF	8.70%
Other Solids	2.00%
Water	62.20%
Total Solids	37.80%
POD	18.00
PAC	25.71

Gelato Formulas and Recipes for Component Ingredients

Component Ingredients

Some gelato flavors require the preparation of flavoring ingredients. As some of these component ingredients are used in more than one gelato, all are placed in this section for ease of use. Unless multiple sets of ingredient quantities are listed, the recipe produces enough of the component for a 1-kilogram batch of gelato.

Apple Puree

Ingredient	Quantity
Coarsely Chopped Apple	480 g
Ground Cinnamon	1.5 g
Water	30 g

1. Peel, core, and coarsely chop enough apples to make 480 grams of apple pieces.
2. In a 2-quart stainless-steel pot, combine the apple and cinnamon.
3. Weigh the pot and contents and record the weight.
4. Add 30 grams of water to the apple mixture in the pot.
5. Cover and simmer, stirring occasionally, until the apples are soft, approximately 20 to 30 minutes, depending on the apples used.
6. Weigh the pot and its contents to be sure that all the added water has been cooked off. That is, the weight of the pot and contents should be no more than the weight recorded in step 3. The cooked apples should be moist from liquid released by the apples, however.
7. Refrigerate the cooked apples, covered, in the pot.
8. When you are ready to make the gelato, weigh the cooked apples and the pot and add enough water to reach the weight recorded in step 3.
9. Thoroughly puree the apples using a high-powered blender, food processor, or commercial immersion blender.

Brown Butter

1. Use approximately twice as much butter as the amount of brown butter desired.
2. Gently melt the butter in a wide, shallow light-colored pan. A stainless-steel sauté pan is ideal. A dark pan will make it difficult to gauge the doneness of the butter.
3. Cook over moderate heat, swirling the pan often, until most of the foaming subsides.
4. Reduce the heat to low as the butter can burn quickly after it stops foaming.
5. Cook until the milk solids, which will have fallen to the bottom of the pan, are medium-brown and the butter has a nutty smell.
6. Remove the pan from the heat and immediately pour off the liquid butter, keeping the brown solids in the pan.

Candied Orange Peel

This same process works for lemon peel.

1. Wash and dry fresh, unblemished oranges. Using a sharp knife, score through the peel to the flesh below, quartering the peel. Remove the peel without breaking. If there is a large amount of white pith on the underside of the peel, use a dull knife or a spoon to scrape out some of it to create an even layer.
2. Cut the peel into strips approximately ½-centimeter (¼-inch) wide.
3. Weigh the prepared peel.
4. Juice the oranges once the pith is removed.
5. Make an approximate 66 Brix[19] syrup as follows:
   - Multiply the weight of the peel by three. Multiply the result by 0.66. That is the amount of sugar to use.
   - Multiply the weight of the peel by three. Multiply the result by 0.34. That is the amount of liquid to use.
   - For the liquid, strain the juice and add enough water to reach the desired weight.
   - Combine sugar and liquid. Bring to a boil, stirring occasionally.
6. Add prepared peel to the boiling syrup. Return to a boil and boil for 90 seconds. Remove from the heat. Cover the pot and allow the peel to cool for about 30 minutes. Remove the peel from the syrup and lay it out on a rack. Allow it to dry overnight, uncovered, at room temperature. Cover the syrup and allow it to remain at room temperature.
7. Repeat the process of bringing the syrup to a boil, boiling the peel for 90 seconds, allowing the peel to cool partially, and laying it out on a rack overnight on the second day and again on the third day.
8. On the fourth day, roll the peel in granulated sugar.
9. Store in a loosely covered container until all tackiness is gone, approximately 3 days. Cover tightly and refrigerate.

---

[19] A 66 Brix syrup is a syrup that is 66% sugar by weight. For certain applications, such as making jams and preserves, accounting for the sugar content of the juice is necessary. That degree of accuracy is not needed for this preparation, so we are simply ignoring the sugar content of the juice.

Gelato Formulas and Recipes for Component Ingredients

Ingredient	Quantity
Granulated Sugar	200 g
Light Corn Syrup	15 ml
Slivered Almonds	180 g

Croccante

1. Lightly toast the almonds as described in the recipe for Toasted Nuts.
2. Combine the sugar and corn syrup in a shallow, wide, heavy-bottomed pan. Using a metal spoon, stir until well-combined and all the sugar is moistened.
3. Over low heat allow the sugar to melt, stirring occasionally.
4. When the sugar mixture is clear and amber colored, remove from the heat and quickly stir in the toasted almonds.
5. Pour onto a buttered sheet pan and spread with a spoon.
6. Allow to cool and break into pieces.

Espresso

Ingredient	Qty	Qty	Qty	Qty	Qty
Water	900 g	450 g	300 g	225 g	150 g
Ground Espresso Coffee	120 g	60 g	40 g	30 g	20 g
After straining add water to make	600 g	300 g	200 g	150 g	100 g

As an alternative to pulling multiple shots of espresso for gelato, this method achieves the same flavor with much less work.

1. Bring water to a boil.
2. Add ground espresso coffee beans.
3. Stir and steep for 4 minutes, covered.
4. Strain through a fine mesh sieve, preferably twice using a fine sieve and a very fine sieve.
5. Strain the resulting liquid through a paper coffee filter.
6. Add enough water to the strained espresso liquid to obtain the final weight noted.

Ingredient	Qty	Qty
Water	375 g	750 g
Dried Hibiscus Flowers	60 g	120 g
Whole Cloves	0.375 g	0.75 g
Stick Cinnamon, Ceylon or Saigon	2.5 g	5 g
After straining add water to make	300 g	600 g

Hibiscus Infusion

1. Bring the water to a boil.
2. Remove from the heat. Add the hibiscus flowers and spices.
3. Cover and allow to steep until cool.
4. Strain the solids from the liquid and press lightly to extract as much liquid as possible.
5. Cover and refrigerate the hibiscus infusion.
6. Add enough water to the strained liquid to obtain the weight noted in the chart above.

Ingredient	Quantity
Sucrose (Table Sugar)	10.13 g
Dextrose	27.37 g
Water	27.5 g
Smooth, Natural Peanut Butter	75 g

Ingredient	Quantity
Raisins	100 g
Water	200 g
Dextrose	85 g
Sucrose (Table Sugar)	30 g

Ingredient	Quantity
Coarsely Chopped Strawberries	110 g
Dextrose	44 g
Sucrose (Table Sugar)	15.4 g

Ingredient	Qty	Qty
2% Milk	1050 g	525 g
Unsweetened, Flaked Coconut	263 g	131 g
After straining add water to make	1050 g	525 g

Peanut Butter Sauce

1. Bring water, sucrose, and dextrose to a simmer.
2. Stir in the peanut butter and gently boil, stirring constantly, until smooth and fully incorporated.
3. Cover and refrigerate until cold.

Raisins in Syrup

1. Combine all ingredients.
2. Simmer until sugars are dissolved.
3. Boil, uncovered, until the temperature reaches 104°C (219°F).
4. Cover and cool.
5. Rest at room temperature overnight before using.

Strawberry Sauce

1. Clean and hull the strawberries.
2. Coarsely chop 110 grams of strawberries.
3. Combine strawberries, dextrose, and sucrose in a small non-reactive pot.
4. Allow to stand briefly to begin to extract some juice from the berries.
5. Cook on low heat to dissolve the sugars.
6. Bring to a boil and boil briskly until the temperature reaches 102.5°C (217°F).
7. Remove from heat. Cover and refrigerate until cold.

Toasted Coconut Milk

1. Spread the coconut on a rimmed baking sheet.
2. Toast in the oven at 180°C (350°F) until golden, tossing the coconut every 2 to 3 minutes. The time will vary based on the moisture content of the coconut.
3. When the coconut is toasted, immediately put it onto a cool baking sheet so it does not continue to cook from the retained heat of the original baking sheet.
4. Cool the coconut and crush coarsely by hand.
5. Heat the milk to 85°C (185°F). Remove from the heat. Add the coconut and stir well. Cover and allow to steep until cool.
6. Squeeze the coconut through several layers of cheesecloth to extract as much liquid as possible.
7. Add enough water to the strained liquid to obtain the weight noted in the chart above.

Toasted Nuts

This process works for all nuts, though the cooking time will vary from one type of nut to another.

1. Preheat the oven to 180°C (350°F).
2. Spread the nuts on a baking sheet.
3. Bake for 4 minutes. Mix the nuts.
4. Repeat baking and mixing at 3-minute intervals until nuts are golden brown in places and smell fragrant. (It is best to undercook the nuts rather than to overcook them, which can create an acrid taste.)
5. When the nuts are toasted, immediately put them onto a cool baking sheet so they do not continue to cook from the retained heat of the original baking sheet.

Vietnamese Coffee

Ingredient	Qty	Qty	Qty
Water	825 g	412 g	206 g
Ground Vietnamese Coffee	100 g	50 g	25 g
After straining add water to make	600 g	300 g	150 g

Some brands of Vietnamese coffee have added flavoring. I recommend not using these. Many Vietnamese restaurants in the United States make their coffee with Café du Monde, a coffee and chicory blend from New Orleans. This is the coffee I typically use for this gelato.

1. Bring water to a boil. Remove from the heat.
2. Add ground coffee.
3. Stir and steep for 4 minutes, covered.
4. Strain through a fine mesh sieve, preferably twice, using a fine sieve and a very fine sieve.
5. Strain the resulting liquid through a paper coffee filter.
6. Add enough water to the strained coffee liquid to obtain the final weight noted in the chart above.

Chapter 129

Troubleshooting: What Happened to My Gelato?

Before discussing the most common defects that can be found in gelato, I want to remind you to use a perfectly balanced recipe — one that contains the correct proportion of components that Italian gelatieri insist on when creating gelato formulas. All the gelato recipes in this book are balanced. Minor variations exist among gelato masters in Italy regarding the appropriate ranges for each of the components of gelato, but the ranges are similar. If each of the components of a gelato recipe lands in the middle of the range recommended by any of the gelato masters, it is likely to be within the ranges recommended by the others. Only at the high and low extremes is there likely to be much of a difference.

Many gelato recipes that I find in books and on the internet are not balanced. An unbalanced gelato can lead to a myriad of problems, including being too hard, too soft, gritty, greasy, or icy. I always develop my own recipes, though I use available recipes and lists of gelato flavors from various gelato shops for inspiration. I would never use a gelato formula developed by someone else without putting it through my gelato balancing tool to confirm that it is, in fact, balanced.

Appendix A contains such a tool: a gelato balance worksheet. This worksheet is the essence of the calculations that my automated gelato balancing tool performs. The tool draws on a large database of ingredients that I have amassed over years based on personal literature and product research. Appendix B contains an abbreviated version of this database with the ingredients you are most likely to use when making gelato.

For all the potential defects listed in this chapter, the first question should be: Are you certain the formula is balanced, preferably with each ingredient near the middle of the acceptable range? If you have verified that the formula is balanced, and you have double- and triple-checked your arithmetic, only then should you consider other troubleshooting options.

The next question to consider is: Have you measured everything precisely and accurately? This is an especially important question for ingredients that are used in minute quantities (like stabilizers).

Have you followed the directions? Factors like pasteurization temperatures and times, maturing times and temperatures, and storage conditions can affect the final product.

This chapter assumes that you are using a gelato batch freezer that is designed well and functioning properly. A malfunctioning batch freezer, or one that is loaded with too much or too little product, will likely not produce good gelato.

My Gelato Is Icy

Several factors can lead to icy gelato.

Freezing took too long

Long freezing times can be a problem with domestic gelato batch freezers. One of the key jobs of the batch freezer is to cause nucleation, that is, the creation of ice. This occurs around the inside edge of the cylinder in most batch freezers. This is the coldest part of the machine. The longer it takes to freeze the gelato, the more likely it is that existing ice crystals will grow in size as unfrozen water binds to the existing ice crystals and freezes. The larger the ice crystals, the more likely it is that the gelato will feel icy. If you think this is the cause of your icy gelato, be sure the base is as cold as possible before putting it in the batch freezer. If it is possible that you have overloaded the batch freezer, try a smaller batch size. If your batch freezer needs to pre-chill before adding the gelato, be sure that step is completed before adding the gelato base.

Too much free water

Stabilizers, such as guar gum, locust bean gum, and eggs thicken the mixture. A thick, or "stabilized," mixture reduces the movement of water. A reduction in the movement of water reduces the likelihood of large ice crystals forming. The percentage of stabilizers is not addressed specifically by gelato balancing parameters. Because the quantity of stabilizers is not part of balancing gelato, it is worth considering whether insufficient stabilization is leading to an excess of free water, even if the formula is perfectly balanced. I typically use guar gum and locust bean gum in equal quantities, usually 0.125% of the total batch weight for each. If you think this is the cause of your icy gelato, gradually increase the quantity of stabilizers up to 0.25% of the total batch weight for each, if needed.

Held too long, either at storage temperature or serving temperature

Nucleation, the formation of new ice crystals, only occurs in the batch freezer. Once removed from the batch freezer, ice crystals begin the process of combining into larger crystals. The lower the temperature, the longer the gelato can be held without noticeable loss of quality, but even in a deep freeze at –18°C to –20°C (0°F to –4°F), gelato should not be held longer than about 1 month. At serving temperature, approximately –13°C (9°F), noticeable loss of quality can occur after 48 to 72 hours.

Allowed to partially melt, then refrozen

Though not really a defect in terms of the production or storage of the gelato, allowing gelato to partially soften and refreeze will quickly lead to the formation of large ice crystals.

My Gelato Is Too Hard

If you have ruled out the issues described in the overview of this chapter, the main reasons gelato can be too hard are as follows.

Too low a temperature

Most gelato is designed to be served at −13°C (9°F) plus or minus about 1°C (2°F). Most freezers used for storage, domestically or professionally, are set at −18°C (0°F) or lower. Ideally, gelato should be allowed to equilibrate in a freezer set to serving temperature before serving. If this is not practical, put the amount of gelato that you intend to use in a container in the refrigerator for about 15 minutes before serving. If you do this with more gelato than you intend to use and freeze what is left over, you are creating ideal conditions to make icy gelato.

Insufficient free water

The "Other Solids" category of all gelato balancing worksheets and apps does not differentiate between the types of solids. Some ingredients, like certain pulpy fruit, thicken the gelato base more than others, even if the percent of total solids is within range. One way to create more free water, making the gelato less thick, is to decrease the amount of these ingredients while maintaining balance. Another option is to consider adding a small amount of liquor to the mixture. In both cases, you will not be able to calculate a serving temperature accurately using the standard method of dividing the PAC by −2, so your efforts will need to be guided by trial and error.

My Gelato Is Too Soft

With a balanced recipe, it would be unusual to have gelato that is too soft. The only common exception would be if you included alcohol in the mixture and didn't account for the effect on PAC, and thus on serving temperature.

My Gelato Is Not Smooth

Different defects can cause a gelato to feel not smooth. The solution depends on its exact nature.

Large ice crystals

Ice is probably the most common reason gelato is not smooth. If the grittiness diminishes in your mouth, it is probably related to large ice crystals that are melting. See the section, "My Gelato Is Icy" earlier in this chapter.

Gritty or sandy textures

Gritty texture can be caused by lactose that has crystallized. If so, it may be due to the addition of too much nonfat milk powder. Check the balance of the recipe.

Lumpy gelato

Assuming you are using a well-balanced recipe, consider the quantity of stabilizers. Too much stabilizer, even in a mixture with the correct percent of fat, can cause too much partial coalescence (see Chapter 8, "Emulsifiers and Stabilizers") leading to the formation of fat globules that can feel lumpy.

Small curds in the gelato

As you will see in the recipes in this book, you can add quite a lot of acid to gelato and not curdle the milk if it is done properly. On the other hand, adding acidic ingredients (such as some fruit juices, sour cream, and yogurt) at the wrong time (such as when the base is being heated) can cause the milk to curdle, just as if you were making ricotta cheese. Acidic ingredients should always be added when the gelato base is mature and cold, and the mixture should be frozen immediately.

My Gelato Is Greasy

Although commonly a symptom of having too much fat in the gelato, a greasy feel likely would not be an issue if you were using a well-balanced recipe. The type of fat may be an issue, however. Not all fats react the same when churned into gelato. Fat that does not liquify quickly at body temperature can create a greasy feel in the mouth. This is often an issue with chemically altered fats and oils that, in any case, have no place in artisan Italian gelato.

As with lumpy gelato, too much stabilizer can also lead to gelato with a greasy feel. It is possible to get a gelato that feels greasy if the dairy products are not appropriately homogenized. While this is rarely a problem with commercially available dairy products, it could be an issue when making gelato from non-homogenized milk and cream.

In Summary

I can assure you, from experience, that you will have few problems to troubleshoot if you use a balanced gelato formula, measure carefully, and follow the mixing and freezing techniques in this book. If you develop your own gelato formulas, the issue you are more likely to encounter is the effect that some solids have on the texture of gelato, even if the formula is balanced. This is a rare problem that has occurred only a few times for me while making hundreds of different gelato formulations. Once you become familiar with the look and feel of gelato at different stages, from cooking the base to chilling and then freezing the gelato, you will quickly identify issues created by some ingredients and be able to make adjustments to the formula. This was exactly my approach when developing the formulas for pumpkin pie and fig gelati.

PART THREE

Pro Tips: The Science of Gelato

 138 *Make Your Own Artisan Italian Gelato*

The Texture of Gelato

Texture is one of the key defining qualities of gelato. At temperatures well below the freezing point of water, why is the gelato not just a solid block of ice? Some complex bits of physical chemistry are at play in that little tub of gelato.

States of Matter

There are three states of matter: solid, liquid, and gas. Gelato contains all three simultaneously and therein lies one of the keys to the texture of gelato.

Gelato Is an Emulsion

An emulsion is a mixture of two (or more) liquids that ordinarily are not miscible (mixable). That is, one will not dissolve in the other. Combining oil and vinegar to make salad dressing is an emulsion. It is not a stable emulsion. Within seconds of shaking, the oil and vinegar begin to separate. Mayonnaise is also an emulsion. It is a stable emulsion. In traditional mayonnaise, the stability comes from the emulsifying and stabilizing properties of egg yolk.

In gelato, the emulsion consists of fat droplets (usually from dairy products but occasionally from other products, such as nut pastes or chocolate) in water. Gelato is approximately 60% water. The water comes largely from the dairy component of gelato, but there are other sources of water, such as fruit and fruit juice, coffee, and sometimes even water itself.

Though not as stable as mayonnaise, the stability of the emulsion in gelato was provided traditionally by egg yolks. Many gelato recipes, especially those for the home cook, still contain eggs. The downside is that eggs can contribute an eggy flavor that may not be welcome in many flavors of artisan gelato. Who wants a fresh strawberry gelato to taste like egg custard?

Eggs contribute fat, which can make it more difficult to get the right proportions of fat, water, sugar, and other ingredients. However, some styles of gelato are richer. Bologna in particular is known for rich, egg-based gelato, often called *crema*.

For individuals interested in making gelato for sale, eggs are expensive, and using them when they do not contribute specifically to the flavor, texture, or richness required adds unnecessary cost.

Eggs are used in gelato more often in northern Italy than in its southern regions. Still, as a general rule, makers of artisan gelato do not use eggs unless the flavor or richness of egg is a desired characteristic of the final product.

Gelato Is a Foam

Small air bubbles are distributed throughout the gelato, making it a foam as well as an emulsion.

The air is incorporated as the gelato base is churned. Air adds softness to gelato. The percentage of air in the finished gelato in relation to the liquid gelato base is called *overrun*.

Artisan gelato usually has between 20% and 30% overrun. At 25% overrun, one liter of gelato base would freeze into 1¼ liters of gelato. This is comparable to the overrun in super-premium ice cream.

Low-quality ice cream, however, can have up to 100% overrun. Look at a container of supermarket ice cream. You will be hard-pressed to find one that has the weight listed. Usually, just the volume of the ice cream is listed. This volume includes the added air.

The amount of air incorporated into gelato is largely determined by the speed of churning. Churning at slower speeds incorporates less air. The design of the dasher also affects the amount of air that is beaten into the mixture. Consider the difference in beating egg whites with a wire whisk and a dough hook. Clearly the whisk will beat in more air than a dough hook, and doing so at high speed will beat in air faster than at a low speed.

Theoretically, you could keep beating egg whites at lower speed until you have beaten in as much air as they will hold. With gelato, the limiting factor is freezing. The slower the air is beaten into the base mixture, the less air there will be in the finished product because, unlike making a meringue, mixing stops when the base is frozen.

Gelato Is a Solid

Ice is a solid and gelato contains ice. Whereas air bubbles contribute softness, ice crystals contribute firmness. The smaller the ice crystals, the smoother the gelato.

Ice crystals are formed around the sides of the batch freezer in a process called *nucleation*. Nucleation is the formation of a new phase, in this case the formation of a solid (ice) from a liquid (water).

It takes very cold temperatures to trigger nucleation. The temperature of the cylinder of a batch freezer is usually between −20°C (−4°F) and −30°C (−22°F). As they form, the crystals are scraped off by the dasher and moved to the center of the mixture. Initially the crystals melt in the center of the mixture but serve to chill it. Eventually, the mixture is cold enough that the ice crystals do not melt and the gelato begins to solidify.

The faster the gelato base is frozen, all else being the same, the smaller the ice crystals will be. The speed of freezing the mixture is largely determined by the power of the freezing unit in the batch freezer. This is the main area where commercial batch freezers excel compared to domestic ones.

The number of ice crystals is set the moment the gelato is removed from the batch freezer. More ice crystals will not be formed because the conditions in the deep freezer or display case do not result in nucleation. The existing ice crystals can get larger as more of the liquid in the mixture is frozen. Over time, ice crystals will merge, creating fewer and larger ice crystals. When ice crystals get too large, the smoothness of the gelato suffers.

Although ice is the main solid in gelato, everything in gelato that is neither air nor liquid (almost all of which is water) is a solid. Solids are what give gelato its flavor. Solids also contribute to the consistency, texture, and appearance of gelato.

Gelato Is a Solution

Not all the water in gelato is frozen. The amount of unfrozen water varies with the temperature, but at serving temperature, the amount of unfrozen water is usually between 25% and 35%. The typical serving temperature for gelato is approximately –13°C (9°F) plus or minus 1°C (2°F). A typical deep freeze is about –18°C (0°F). A blast freezer, used to harden gelato after it is removed from the batch freezer can be even colder.

The colder the gelato, the more water will be frozen. The more frozen water, the harder the gelato. The texture of gelato, then, is crucially dependent on serving it at the correct temperature. Gelato served directly from a home freezer never has the texture of artisan gelato from a gelateria because, quite simply, it is too cold. There are ways to mitigate this situation, though, as described in Chapter 3, "The Process of Making Gelato."

Pulling It All Together

Holding gelato together is the *matrix*. This is the unfrozen solution part of the mixture. It is composed of water and whatever is dissolved in the water. This includes sugars, salts, and minerals predominantly.

Dispersed throughout the matrix is a fat-in-water emulsion consisting of fat droplets surrounded by emulsifying agents, such as milk proteins and, possibly, lecithin.

Also dispersed throughout the matrix are air bubbles, a foam. The air bubbles stay in place because much of the mixture is frozen, but also because they are surrounded by fat molecules and protein molecules that inhibit the air bubbles from traveling around in the matrix and joining together. The presence of stabilizers, which makes for a thicker consistency, also inhibits the movement of air bubbles.

Finally, dispersed throughout the mixture are solids that are not dissolved — primarily ice but there are other solids as well, such as fiber from fruit.

A Complex System

For such a simple pleasure, gelato is an incredibly complex system. All three states of matter — solid, liquid, and gas — coexist in it simultaneously. The interrelationships between these three states, moderated by temperature, largely account for the texture of gelato. Mastering this balance ensures that your creation is delicious and memorable.

Freezing Point Depression

The concept of *freezing point depression* is critical to creating gelato formulas that have the desired consistency at serving temperature. Many publications, some listed in Appendix G, "References and Resources," provide detailed scientific explanations for freezing point depression. My goal is to describe the concept and how to apply it to making artisan gelato.

At one atmosphere pressure (nominally, sea level), the freezing point of pure water is 0°C (32°F). If you dissolve salt in water, the freezing point will be lower. How much the freezing point is lowered is a function of the concentration of salt in the water. Many of us make use of this process each winter when we put salt on our sidewalks to get rid of ice. More salt means less ice at lower temperatures.

The amount the freezing point is depressed is a characteristic of the solvent,[20] which in this example is water. It is not a characteristic of what is dissolved in the solvent (the solute). This is good news because when creating gelato formulas, you just need to know the value of this number for water — the only component of gelato that actually freezes.

At the concentrations of ingredients used in making gelato, freezing point depression is constant. This is also good news. That means if the freezing point is lowered by 1°C with a given concentration of solute (sugar, for example), and you double the amount of sugar, the freezing point will be lowered by 2°C (twice as much).

To calculate the concentration of solute, you need to know the number of particles that are dissolved in the solvent. These are molecules and ions. When you dissolve sugar in water, the number of particles is equal to the number of molecules added. When you dissolve salt in water, the number of particles is equal to twice the number of molecules added. This is because salt (sodium chloride) breaks apart into sodium ions and chloride ions in water. If you evaporate all the water, the sodium and chloride ions will join together again and form salt as we know it.

But how do you know how many molecules you are adding? Scientists use a measure called a *mole*[21] (abbreviated as *mol*). This is a very, very, very large number. Remember, molecules are extremely small so it takes a lot of them to weigh very much. You can look up the weight of a mole of any solute of interest in making gelato. This is called the *molar weight*. For example, the molar weight of common sugar (sucrose) is 342.297 grams/mol. That means a

---

[20] This is referred to as a colligative property. "Colligative properties of solutions are properties that depend upon the concentration of solute molecules or ions, but not upon the identity of the solute. Colligative properties include vapor pressure lowering, boiling point elevation, freezing point depression, and osmotic pressure." [https://www.chem.fsu.edu/chemlab/chm1046course/colligative.html. Accessed December 21, 2021.]

[21] A mole is $6.02214076 \times 10^{23}$ that is, 602,214,076,000,000,000,000,000.

mole of sugar, that is 602,214,076,000,000,000,000,000 sugar molecules, weighs less than half a kilogram![22]

The molar weight of dextrose is 180.156 grams/mol. That means that a given weight of dextrose will have almost twice as many molecules (particles) as an equivalent weight of sucrose. Gram for gram, dextrose has almost twice the freezing point depression as an equal weight of sucrose because it contains almost twice as many molecules in a given weight.

Just how much is that freezing point depression? For water, it is 1.853°C for every mole of a solute per kilogram of water.

In practical terms, only three categories of solutes are of concern when calculating the freezing point depression of a gelato base:

1. Sugars
2. (Added) salt
3. Alcohol (ethanol)

While it is true that every molecule of every substance dissolved in the base contributes to freezing point depression, you can ignore some of them because they contribute so little to the final calculation. Milk protein is one of these substances. Proteins are large molecules, and the number of these molecules compared to the number of sugar molecules is very small.

Milk also contains various salts, but again very little, so you typically can ignore this contribution to freezing point depression. When creating gelato formulas, the amount of milk in a gelato base should be confined to a narrow range so that the contribution to freezing point depression from milk proteins and salts will be relatively constant from one gelato to the next.

Most gelato does not contain alcohol, but when it does, you need to consider its profound effect on freezing point depression. Most of my gelato formulas contain a small amount of added salt because it improves the flavor. Though the effect is modest, I always include it in the calculation of freezing point depression. When including salt, remember that each molecule separates into two ions in solution, so its effect on freezing point depression is twice what would be suggested from its molar weight.

In addition to the sugars used in gelato, such as sucrose, glucose, and fructose, milk contains lactose. In Italy, the contribution of lactose to freezing point depression is included in the calculation. This is usually not the case in the United States and the United Kingdom when the same concept is applied to ice cream. I always include lactose in my calculation of freezing point depression.

---

[22] Throughout this book I use the metric system exclusively for ingredient quantities. I do this because gelato ingredients must be weighed for precision, which means no cups and tablespoons, and because scaling a formula up and down is much easier with the metric system.

Far and away, the ingredients of most concern in calculating freezing point depression are sugars because they are present in the largest quantity in gelato.

Calculating Freezing Point Depression

The change in freezing point of a gelato base can be calculated using the following formula:

$$\Delta T_F = -(K_F \cdot m \cdot i)$$

where:

ΔT_F is the change in freezing temperature in degrees Celsius.

K_F is the cryoscopic constant (the amount the freezing temperature of the solvent changes when a solute is added). For water it is $1.853\,°C \cdot kg/mol$.

m is the molality of the solute, that is, the number of particles of solute per kilogram of solvent given as mol/kg.

i is the van 't Hoff constant. The van 't Hoff constant refers to the number of particles that are formed from each molecule of solute. For sugars and ethanol it is 1. For sodium chloride it is 2.

If more than one solute is contributing to the freezing point depression, as is almost always the case with gelato, you calculate the effect of each solute separately and add them together, resulting in a formula that looks like this:

$$\Delta T_F = -[(K_F \cdot m_\alpha \cdot i_\alpha) + (K_F \cdot m_\beta \cdot i_\beta) + (K_F \cdot m_\gamma \cdot i_\gamma) + \ldots]$$

The ellipsis (…) indicates that these same calculations are repeated, as needed, for each solute of importance in the mixture.

This can be simplified to:

$$\Delta T_F = -K_F \cdot [(m_\alpha \cdot i_\alpha) + (m_\beta \cdot i_\beta) + (m_\gamma \cdot i_\gamma) + \ldots]$$

The concept of freezing point depression is important for creating gelato formulas, or for verifying that somebody else's formula will work as intended. Fortunately you will not have to do these complex calculations! This is because of the concept of PAC.

PAC

PAC is an acronym for *potere anticongelante,* which in English means anti-freezing power. The concept of PAC enables you to simplify the calculation of freezing point depression considerably, making the resulting calculation particularly useful to creating gelato formulas.

Freezing Point Depression

PAC uses sucrose (common table sugar) as the reference point. One PAC unit refers to the anti-freezing power of a 1% solution of sucrose in water, that is 1 gram sucrose per 100 grams of solution. In this system, the PAC of sucrose is assigned a value of 100. Thus:

100 [the PAC of sucrose] × 1% [the concentration of sucrose in the mix] = 1

A gelato that contains 190 grams of sucrose per kilogram would have a PAC of 19 because 190 grams per 1000 grams is a 19% solution, the equivalent of 19 PAC units. Alternatively:

100 [the PAC of sucrose] × 19% [the concentration of sucrose in the mix] = 19

Using the formula for calculating freezing point depression given above, you could calculate the freezing point of a 19% solution of sucrose, but with PAC, you do not need to do that. Knowing the PAC of a gelato provides a good indication of the approximate serving temperature.

To use PAC, you need to know the PAC contributed by each of the ingredients that you wish to include in the calculation. A PAC Table is included in Appendix C of this book. Consider these two sugars as an example: lactose and dextrose.

Remember that freezing point depression is related to the concentration of particles (molecules or ions) dissolved in the solvent. Lactose has the same molecular weight as sucrose, so a 1% solution of lactose has as many molecules as a 1% solution of sucrose. That means the effect on the freezing point is identical. Thus, the PAC of lactose is 100, just like sucrose.

The molecular weight of dextrose is 180.156. The molecular weight of sucrose is 342.297. Because a molecule of dextrose weighs less than a molecule of sucrose, any given weight of dextrose will have more molecules than the same weight of sucrose. Specifically, the proportional difference will be 342.297 ÷ 180.156 = 1.9. So, the effect on freezing point depression will be 1.9 times as much for dextrose as for an equivalent weight of sucrose. That means the PAC of dextrose is 190 (1.9 times the PAC of sucrose).

Two other solutes to be aware of are alcohol (ethanol) and salt (sodium chloride). The molecular weight of ethanol is 46.07 and that of sodium chloride is 58.44.

The PAC of ethanol is 7.43 times the PAC of sucrose (342.297 ÷ 46.07 = 7.43) or 743.

The PAC of sodium chloride is 11.71 times the PAC of sucrose (342.297 ÷ 58.44) × 2 = 11.71) or 1171. Remember, each molecule of sodium chloride separates into one sodium ion and one chloride ion in solution so it contains twice as many particles. That is why after dividing the molecular weight of sucrose by the molecular weight of salt, you need to multiply by 2.

The PAC numbers for salt and ethanol are quite large compared to sugars. Luckily, very little salt is added to gelato. The high PAC for alcohol indicates why only small amounts of spirits can be added to gelato to get the right texture at serving temperature.

If you want to know the PAC of any solute and you do not have a PAC table handy, or the table does not include the solute that you are interested in, just look up the molecular weight (the internet will make quick work of this) and divide the molecular weight of sucrose (342.297) by the molecular weight of the solute, just as we did for dextrose, and multiply by 100. Do not forget, however, that if the solute separates into ions as do most salt molecules, multiply the result by the number of ions that each molecule of solute separates into to get an accurate PAC.

> The term, "freezing point depression factor" or FPDF is often used in the United States and the United Kingdom rather than PAC. They mean the same thing with one exception. In Italy, when calculating PAC, the lactose in milk is included. In the United States and United Kingdom, the lactose is usually ignored when calculating the FPDF for ice cream. For example, the PAC of our fiordilatte gelato is 26.42 but the FPDF (calculated the same way as PAC but excluding the lactose) is 23.08.

Percent of Frozen Water

Not all the water in gelato is frozen. As the water in the gelato base begins to freeze, the frozen water molecules (ice crystals) are removed from the solution. The solutes are now dissolved in slightly less liquid water. Because the solution is more concentrated, the freezing point becomes a little lower than it was at the beginning. As more and more water freezes, the remaining solution becomes more and more concentrated until it reaches the point at which the freezing point of the remaining solution is below the temperature of the freezer. Some of the water in the gelato base remains unfrozen as a thick syrup, typically around 25% to 35%. This unfrozen syrup is the *matrix*.

In Summary

The dissolved solids (solutes) in gelato, mostly sugars, are responsible for lowering the freezing point of the mixture. You can calculate the freezing point depression from the concentrations of each of the solutes in degrees Celsius. Fortunately, rather than doing this using a complicated formula, you can use a simplified calculation. Because the effect on freezing point depression is related to molecular weight, this simplified process relies on comparing the molecular weights of each of the solutes to that of sucrose. I discuss these calculations in detail in Chapter 11, "Creating Gelato Formulas," and Chapter 12, "Adjusting PAC and POD." For now, the important point is to recognize that all dissolved solids lower the freezing point of a gelato base, making it important that you calculate their effect in order to create gelato that is soft and creamy at the usual serving temperature.

Emulsifiers and Stabilizers

Although they can have a bad reputation, emulsifiers and stabilizers are not inherently bad. To be sure, they can be overused, and even used to replace more tasty and expensive ingredients, but without some emulsifiers and stabilizers, gelato as we know it just would not be possible.

Emulsifiers

Fat molecules are *non-polar*. That means the electrons are distributed equally across the molecule.

Water molecules are *polar*. One side of the molecule is slightly positively charged and one side is slightly negatively charged.

Polar and non-polar molecules do not form stable mixtures. Consider a vinegar-and-oil salad dressing. Shaking the mixture vigorously creates an emulsion, but a very unstable one. The oil separates from the vinegar within moments of shaking.

If you add a dollop of mustard to that dressing, the emulsion will not separate for hours to days depending on the type of mustard added.[23] Now consider mayonnaise. For all practical purposes mayonnaise does not separate.

Oil-and-vinegar salad dressing and mayonnaise are examples of water-in-oil emulsions. The oil is present in larger quantity and constitutes what is called the continuous phase. Water (such as that contained in vinegar, egg white, and egg yolk) is the discontinuous phase.

The salad dressing, with mustard, and the mayonnaise, made with egg yolks, are stable emulsions because of added emulsifiers. Mustard seeds contain proteins and polysaccharides and egg yolks contain lecithin. Each of these is an emulsifier. Emulsifiers have a hydrophilic[24] end and a hydrophobic[25] end. Once the discontinuous phase is broken into small droplets, emulsifiers surround the droplets with the hydrophilic end pointing toward the water and the hydrophobic end pointing toward the fat. This coating prevents the droplets from coalescing, or readily joining together.

Gelato is an oil-in-water emulsion, unlike mayonnaise, which is a water-in-oil emulsion. Gelato is around 60% to 65% water by weight, making water the continuous phase and fat the discontinuous phase. In artisan gelato, milk proteins are the primary emulsifiers. Milk proteins have a polar end and a non-polar end. The non-polar end mixes well with fat, which is non-polar, while the polar end mixes well with water, which is polar.

---

[23] Cook's Illustrated (n.d.).
[24] Having a strong affinity for water.
[25] Having little or no affinity for water.

You want the fat to stay dispersed throughout the water phase of the gelato base. That is, you do not want it to all coalesce. However, you want some degree of *partial* coalescence as the gelato is being frozen. This is because the fat molecules trap air bubbles. If they do not partially coalesce, insufficient air will be trapped in the gelato as it is being frozen. Remember that air provides softness to gelato. Without enough trapped air, the gelato will be hard.

Milk proteins are almost too good at being emulsifiers. They can actually inhibit partial coalescence because they can thickly coat the fat globules if they are present in too high a proportion. If another emulsifier is included in the base, some of the milk proteins will be displaced from the fat globules and replaced by the other emulsifier. Depending on the characteristics of this other emulsifier, it can be easier for partial coalescence to occur.

Before the advent of powdered nonfat milk, gelato makers did not have many options for increasing the amount of milk protein in gelato. Egg yolks were commonly added to gelato as emulsifiers. The lecithin in egg yolks is a good emulsifier. It displaces some of the milk proteins around the fat globules, thereby improving partial coalescence.

Egg yolks, however, can add an eggy taste to gelato, more so as the percentage increases. Unless you are making a gelato where egg is an inherent part of the flavor profile, the taste of egg may be undesirable. A fresh fruit gelato generally does not benefit from the taste of eggs.

Egg yolks also add fat. The extra fat can be a problem in a gelato that is already pushing the limit on fat content with nut pastes or chocolate, even though the eggy taste would likely not be very noticeable in these gelati.

Artisan gelato is frequently made without the addition of egg yolks and with nothing more than milk protein as an emulsifier, albeit added milk protein from nonfat milk powder, proving that emulsifiers other than milk protein are not necessary to create luscious gelato.

Whey proteins make up about 20% of the protein in milk. The other 80% is casein. Whey proteins are less heat stable than casein. When heated, whey proteins begin to denature, that is, they change shape and expose parts of their molecular structures that were not previously exposed. These newly exposed parts are both hydrophilic and hydrophobic, improving their emulsifying capabilities. The extent of denaturation of whey proteins is a complex function of temperature and time, beginning at about 60°C (140°F) and reaching full denaturation at about 90°C (194°F). However, at around 90°C (194°F), it is possible that some insoluble aggregates will be formed that can negatively affect the texture of the gelato.

All the ingredients used in artisan Italian gelato should be natural. Ingredients derived by chemical extraction or manufacture do not qualify. There are a number of ways to extract lecithin, usually from plants such as soybeans or sunflower seeds, that could qualify as natural. While I do not advocate the universal use of lecithin in artisan Italian gelato, I think you could make a case that the ingredient would be permissible depending on how it is derived.

If you want to experiment with lecithin, start with approximately 0.05% to 0.1% of the gelato base by weight. That is, multiply the weight of the gelato base in grams by 0.0005 at the low end to 0.001 at the high end. One kilogram of base would have 0.5 to 1 gram of lecithin added. You could get approximately the same amount of lecithin from 10 to 20 grams of egg yolk.[26]

Buttermilk has a greater number of phospholipids with emulsifying properties than does milk.[27] In theory, buttermilk could be used as an emulsifier, especially powdered or condensed buttermilk. In practice, however, I have not seen buttermilk used in artisan Italian gelato. The resulting product would likely have a noticeable buttermilk flavor, as well.

There really are no other emulsifiers that would be acceptable for use in artisan Italian gelato because they do not qualify as natural products. These include emulsifiers that are commonly used in ice cream and in non-artisan gelato, including Polysorbate-80 and mono- and diglycerides.

Stabilizers

Stabilizers are thickeners. Basically, they thicken the water phase of the gelato. Thickening water increases viscosity, which limits the movement of water molecules in the mixture. Thickeners have several beneficial effects on gelato.

The amount of frozen water in gelato is determined by freezing point depression (see Chapter 7, "Freezing Point Depression"). The number of ice crystals, however, is determined by many factors including the speed at which the gelato is frozen. For a given quantity of frozen water (determined by freezing point depression and the temperature of the mix), having more ice crystals means the ice crystals are smaller. Smaller ice crystals result in smoother gelato. Although speed of freezing the mixture is a major determinant of ice crystal size, stabilizers also help to reduce the size of ice crystals.

Once frozen, stabilizers retard the development of larger ice crystals. Thawing and refreezing gelato, such as what may occur when a display case or storage freezer is opened and closed, results in larger ice crystals. The formation of new ice crystals happens only in the batch freezer because the super-cold temperature of the cylinder wall allows for nucleation (the formation of new ice crystals) to occur. In a display case or freezer, once any amount of the gelato melts, it attaches to existing ice crystals when it refreezes. It does not form new ice crystals. Thus, the number of ice crystals decreases and their size increases. Ultimately, the larger ice crystals will result in a gritty gelato.

Smaller air bubbles result in softer, smoother gelato. A mixture that is more viscous produces smaller air bubbles. Try whipping milk. You get a bunch of very large air bubbles

---

[26] An egg yolk weighs about 15 grams.
[27] Underbelly (2016a).

that disappear in moments. If you whip a cooked custard, which is more viscous, you get lots of smaller air bubbles. A stabilized mixture, that is, a more viscous mixture, produces more and smaller air bubbles than a non-stabilized mixture.

As with ice crystals, air bubbles only decrease in number and increase in size in storage after the gelato is frozen in the batch freezer. Air bubbles grow by two processes: disproportionation and coalescence. In disproportionation, some air transfers from smaller to larger bubbles. In coalescence, two bubbles join to become one larger one. The increased viscosity of a stabilized mixture inhibits both disproportionation and coalescence.

Stabilizers also slow melting. Gelato with smaller air bubbles melts more slowly than gelato with larger air bubbles. In addition, regardless of air bubbles, mixtures that are more viscous melt more slowly than mixtures that are less viscous. Using stabilizers results in a more viscous mixture.

To be most effective, stabilizers need to be fully hydrated, that is, fully combined with water. Hydration is usually a product of time and temperature, with different parameters for different stabilizers.

Although numerous stabilizers are used in the production of ice cream, only a few of them are commonly used in artisan Italian gelato:

1. Locust bean gum (E410)[28]
2. Guar gum (E412)
3. Egg yolks
4. Cornstarch
5. Gelatin (E441)

Of these, locust bean gum and guar gum are the most commonly used stabilizers for artisan Italian gelato and are often used in combination. Locust bean gum excels at suppressing ice crystal formation. Guar gum is a better thickener than locust bean gum. Used together, they have excellent stabilizing properties.

Locust bean gum is derived from seeds of the carob tree *(Ceratonia siliqua)*, which is native to the Mediterranean region. It has been used as a thickener since at least 79 CE.[29] Portugal, Italy, Spain, and Morocco were responsible for nearly 75% of the world's production in 2016.[30] Locust bean gum should be heated to 85°C (185°F) to ensure that it is fully hydrated, though there is some variability in the required temperature based on the published literature.

---

[28] E numbers are codes used in Europe for food additives, unlike in the United States where scientific or common names are used to list food additives. The E stands for *Europe*. The additives can be natural or synthetic.
[29] Underbelly (2016b).
[30] Wikipedia (2021a).

Guar gum is derived by milling the large endosperm of the guar bean *(Cyamopsis tetragonoloba)*.[31] India produces about 65% of the world's production of guar beans. Guar gum fully hydrates without being heated.

In addition to their emulsifying properties, egg yolks can be used for their stabilizing properties but at a much higher percentage. Although common in homemade gelato, in artisan Italian gelato, egg yolks are usually reserved for making crema or for flavors of gelato that require the flavor of egg.

Cornstarch is used in a style of Sicilian gelato, but otherwise it is not common. Cornstarch is produced by steeping corn. After grinding, the starch is removed by washing and centrifuging and then drying.[32] Tapioca and arrowroot can be used in a manner similar to cornstarch.

Gelatin is translucent and nearly colorless and flavorless. Although it is an excellent stabilizer and is easy to use, gelatin is rarely employed in the production of artisan Italian gelato. It is relatively expensive and is typically derived from animal collagen (mostly pigs and cattle,[33] though it can be derived from poultry and fish as well), which can lead to religious objections and make it unacceptable to vegetarians.

Stabilizers not typically used in artisan Italian gelato include: xanthan gum (E415), carrageenans (E407), sodium alginate (E401), carboxymethylcellulose (E466), and pectin (E440). None of these products qualifies under a strict interpretation of the requirements for artisan Italian gelato because the methods of producing or extracting them render them not natural.

In Summary

Stabilizers and emulsifiers are essential to the production of artisan Italian gelato. The most common emulsifier is milk protein, usually added in the form of nonfat powdered milk. Egg yolk is also an emulsifier, but its use is usually reserved for styles and/or flavors of gelato that require or benefit from egg. Stabilizers make the mixture more viscous, contributing to smaller ice crystals and enhanced trapping of air for improved texture. Locust bean gum and guar gum are two commonly used stabilizers. Egg yolk can be used as a stabilizer, but at a much higher percentage of the mixture than is needed for its emulsifying property. In all instances, the tenets of artisan Italian gelato require that stabilizers and emulsifiers be natural, not synthetic or chemically derived.

---

[31] Wikipedia (2021b).
[32] Wikipedia (2021c).
[33] Wikipedia (2021d).

Sweetening Power

The concept of sweetening power, called *potere dolcificante* (POD) in Italian, is simple. Not all sugars have the same degree of sweetness per unit of weight. Establishing the relative sweetness of each sugar enables a gelatician to tweak a formula to achieve desired results.

Suppose a gelato has the right degree of sweetness but its "scoopability" is not acceptable at serving temperature. One can swap out a portion of sucrose for another sugar that affects PAC differently (see Chapter 7, "Freezing Point Depression").

For example, if the gelato is too hard at serving temperature, the *potere anticongelante* (PAC) needs to be increased. Remember that increasing the PAC decreases the approximate serving temperature so that at any given temperature, the gelato will be less frozen, therefore less hard, than before the PAC was increased. To increase PAC, you can substitute dextrose for some of the sucrose. Remember, the PAC of dextrose is 190 compared to the PAC of sucrose, which is 100. Substituting an equivalent weight of dextrose for some of the sucrose will increase the PAC. However, dextrose is less sweet than sucrose so it would not be a gram-for-gram swap if you want to maintain the same degree of sweetness. Gram for gram, more dextrose would need to be added than sucrose removed to keep the sweetness the same.

As with PAC, POD is evaluated in comparison to sucrose, which is assigned a value of 100. Determining relative sweetness, however, is not as straightforward as determining PAC. The latter is a physicochemical property that can be directly measured. Relative sweetness can be assessed only by tasting. Because not everyone's taste is the same, POD is inherently variable. As you can see in Table 9-1, different authorities come up with different relative sweetness measures for the same sugar.

Table 9-1. Relative sweetness of selected sweeteners[34]

Sweetener	Source						
	Wikipedia (2022)	O'Brien-Nabors (2012)	Dream Scoops (2018b)	Pancoast and Junk (1980)	Hull (2010)	Jiménez-Flores, et al. (2006)	Nickerson (1974)
Sucrose	100		100	100	100	100	100
Dextrose			74	70–80	80	75	56
Fructose	117–175		173	150–160	170	115	125
Galactose	65						
Honey			130				
Invert Sugar			125				
Karo Light Corn Syrup			33				
Lactose	16		16	40		20	30
Maltodextrin			20				
Maltose	33–35						
Trehalose		15–45[35]					
42DE Corn Syrup				40–45	50		

Note: Sucrose is the reference and is always assigned a value of 100.

If you use commercially available gelato software to develop your formulas, it will likely have default values for POD built in. You should be able to change these if you wish. When calculating POD, I use the values listed in Table 9-2.

Table 9-2. Relative sweetness used when developing gelato formulas

Sugar	POD
Sucrose	100
Dextrose	75
Fructose	150
Lactose	16
Maltose	30
Galactose	65

Differences in sweetness are not the only differences between sugars. Fructose, for example, creates the perception of sweetness sooner than sucrose but it also fades faster.[36] The sweetness of trehalose, on the other hand, is more persistent.[37] The perceived sweetness of a sugar can change with the concentration. For example, see trehalose in Table 9-1, which has the largest range of sweetening power related to concentration of any sugar used in making gelato.

---

[34] Adapted from Mullan (2012) and other sources.
[35] At concentrations from 2.3% to 22.2% (w/w).
[36] Mullan (2012).
[37] O'Brien-Nabors (2012).

156   *Make Your Own Artisan Italian Gelato*

Other ingredients can affect sweetness. For example, inclusion of acids like lemon juice will reduce the perceived sweetness, while vanilla can often increase the perception of sweetness even when the concentration of sugar is the same in both samples.

Finding the right sweetness for a gelato is a matter of trial and error. You can improve the process by looking at the POD values of a gelato that is close in characteristics to the variation you are trying to develop. For example, when I developed my peanut butter gelato formula, I looked at my established formulas for almond gelato and pistachio gelato when setting an initial quantity of sucrose and dextrose for my first attempt. Peanuts and pistachios have slightly more sugar than almonds, on average. In the end, the formula for pistachio gelato worked well for peanut butter gelato to my taste. Though my almond gelato contains slightly more added sugar, the result is slightly less sweet than my peanut butter and pistachio gelati.

In Summary

In the end, sweetness is a matter of taste. Gelato masters in Italy generally agree that gelato in northern Italy is less sweet than gelato in southern Italy. This difference, they say, is based on the preferences of their customers.

When developing a new gelato formula, POD can provide a general guideline, but it must be tempered by judgment and trial and error. That is because the taste of the gelato is influenced by other ingredients. For example, at the same POD, a cantaloupe gelato will taste sweeter than a lime gelato, whereas a lime gelato could be mouth-puckering at a POD that makes a perfect mango gelato.

Once you get the desired degree of sweetness in a particular gelato, you can use the concept of POD to adjust formulas to maintain it while modifying the serving temperature or body of a gelato if needed. Combinations of sweeteners can interact in ways that produce a perception of sweetness that is different from the theoretical calculation. What might seem to be the perfect ratio of different sweeteners to achieve a desired degree of sweetness and serving temperature could turn out to be slightly off-target when tested. Successive batches often require incremental changes to the sweeteners and potentially other ingredients.

Scoopability

Italians expect every gelato in the display case of a gelateria to have the same degree of "scoopability" — not too hard, not too soft. I do not think the same thing can be said of how people from the United States or United Kingdom regard ice cream.

Gelato is a simple everyday treat in Italy, but that simplicity does not mean Italians are casual about its sensory qualities. In fact, they are very serious about how gelato "feels" on the tongue. Gelato is expected to be cold but not too cold, creamy, dense, soft, almost chewy, and very flavorful.

Making every gelato in the display case have the same degree of scoopability is a serious endeavor for the artisan gelato maker.

The main factors affecting scoopability are:

1. The percent of water in the gelato
2. The anti-freezing power of the mixture (PAC)
3. Serving temperature
4. Amount of air in the gelato (overrun)
5. Suspended solids

These factors work in combination to affect the scoopability of gelato.

Percentage of Water

The most significant determinant of the hardness of gelato is the amount of frozen water. The amount of frozen water is determined by three factors: the PAC (anti-freezing power) of the mixture, the serving temperature, and the percentage of water in the mixture.

The PAC of the mixture and the serving temperature of the gelato work in tandem to determine what percentage of the water is frozen. Many authorities say that something in the range of 65% to 75% frozen water is ideal for gelato. Determining how much water is actually frozen is complicated stuff and not generally attempted by artisan Italian gelato makers. That type of assessment is usually left to the corporate players who, in any case, are not making artisan Italian gelato if one adheres to the definition of gelato from the Gelatieri per il Gelato (see the Introduction).

Even without knowing the actual amount of frozen water, you can get a sense of how frozen water affects the texture of the gelato. As an example, suppose a gelato contains 58% water and 75% of that water is frozen. That means that 43.5% (58% × 75%) of the gelato consists of frozen water, that is, ice crystals. Ice is hard. Now, if the gelato contains 75% water (which it should not), 56.25% (75% × 75%) of the gelato would be ice if 75% of the water is frozen. The higher the percentage of water in the mixture, and the greater the percentage of frozen water, the harder the gelato will be.

This is why the PAC of the mixture and the serving temperature of the gelato are so important. As noted in Chapter 7, "Freezing Point Depression," the amount of dissolved solids in the gelato mixture determines the anti-freezing power of the mixture, with sugars responsible for the majority of that effect.

I endeavor to have between 58% and 68% water in my gelato mixture, aiming to stay near the bottom half of that range. Remember, the greater the percentage of water in the mixture, the more ice will be present for a given percentage of frozen water.

Serving Temperature

A simple formula used by gelatieri to determine approximate serving temperature in degrees Celsius is dividing the PAC of the mixture by –2. For example, if PAC is 26, the approximate serving temperature is 26 ÷ (–2) = –13°C. The approximate typical temperature of a gelato display case is –13°C (9°F), plus or minus 1°C (2°F). As a starting point, in developing gelato formulas, I try to achieve a PAC of 26 to 27.

You can use this formula to your advantage in some circumstances. I once created a gelato based on the flavor of a bourbon old fashioned. This was intended for a dinner party of adults, so I wanted a considerable amount of alcohol in the gelato, not just a light flavor of bourbon. Adding alcohol increases the PAC — that is, it lowers the serving temperature — far more than sugar. Because I was serving this gelato at a private home, I did not have a display case, and that worked in my favor. I simply created a gelato that had a serving temperature close to that of a typical home freezer, which is about –18°C (0°F). That means the PAC was about 36.

A gelato with a PAC of 36 would be mostly melted in a gelato display case, just as a traditional gelato would be too hard to serve out of a home freezer.

As discussed previously, air contributes softness to gelato, thereby affecting its scoopability. Although industrial continuous ice cream freezers can create overruns of 100% or more, gelato batch freezers are designed to incorporate a modest amount of air, somewhere around 20% to 30%.

Though there are more rigorous ways of determining the overrun of gelato, you can use the following method to get a reasonable idea of the overrun of any given gelato:

1. Put some gelato (perhaps 1000 milliliters, carefully measured just as the gelato is coming out of the batch freezer) into a measuring container, making sure there are no pockets of trapped air and that you do not overly compress the gelato as you fill the container.

2. Allow the gelato to melt. Measure the volume of the melted gelato. The difference between the two measurements, divided by the volume of the melted gelato, is the overrun. For example, if 1000 milliliters of gelato is 800 milliliters after melting, the amount of overrun is:

$$1000 \text{ ml} - 800 \text{ ml} = 200 \text{ ml}$$

$$200 \text{ ml} \div 800 \text{ ml} = 0.25 = 25\%$$

Remember, overrun is the amount of air incorporated into the gelato as a proportion of the volume of the mixture *before* freezing. The volume of the gelato, after melting, if measurements are done carefully, should match the volume of mixture before the gelato was frozen.

For all practical purposes, there is nothing you can to do modify the amount of air your gelato batch freezer churns into the gelato. Nor, for the most part, would you want to make dramatic changes as a modest amount of overrun is a hallmark of artisan Italian gelato. Judiciously using ingredients with emulsifying and stabilizing properties will allow you to capture the air that is churned into the gelato and hold it in the form of a foam in the frozen product.

Suspended Solids

While dissolved solids, such as sugars, affect freezing point depression, suspended solids do not. Suspended solids, however, contribute firmness to gelato. All else being equal, a gelato made with nut pastes or cocoa powder, each of which contribute a lot of suspended solids, will be firmer than one without. To get a gelato with a lot of suspended solids to have the same mouthfeel as one without these solids, adjustments in PAC may be necessary. Increasing the PAC to achieve a lower serving temperature, meaning that at standard serving temperature there will be slightly less frozen water, will make for a slightly softer gelato, compensating for the firmness contributed by the suspended solids.

In Summary

Italians, and by extension anyone who endeavors to make artisan Italian gelato, expect every gelato in a display case to have a similar texture. Using a balanced formula that has an appropriate PAC and serving the gelato at the correct temperature will get you most of the way to the goal. As needed, adjustments can be made to modify scoopability based on trial and error after the initial formula has been established.

Creating Gelato Formulas

Artisan Italian gelato consists of very few ingredients: dairy (milk, cream, nonfat powdered milk), sugars, flavor from natural ingredients (such as fruit, nuts, chocolate, coffee), and stabilizers (either egg yolk or vegetable-based products). This chapter provides guidance for creating your own formulas using these ingredients.

Balancing Gelato

The composition of *all* ingredients used in making gelato is categorized into the following components:

1. Fat
2. Sugar
3. Nonfat milk solids
4. Other solids
5. Water

For example, the composition of 2% milk, using this system, is shown in Table 11-1.

Table 11-1. Composition of 2% milk

Component	Percent
Fat	1.90%
Sugar	0.00%
Nonfat milk solids	9.00%
Other solids	0.00%
Water	89.10%
Total	**100.00%**

The total of these categories should equal 100%, which it does.

Note that even though milk contains the sugar lactose, by convention when defining the composition of dairy products, lactose is included as part of the nonfat milk solids.

The composition of bananas is shown in Table 11-2.

Table 11-2. Composition of bananas

Component	Percent
Fat	0.29%
Sugar	15.80%
Nonfat milk solids	0.00%
Other solids	8.61%
Water	75.30%
Total	**100.00%**

The composition represents average values. Different types of bananas have slightly different compositions, as does the same type of banana grown at different times and in different locations. Unless these differences are large, which can happen with certain ingredients, they are not likely to affect the final product.

Defining the composition of each ingredient used in gelato production according to this five-component categorization is of fundamental importance. In addition to these five components, which are mutually exclusive, you must also calculate the *total solids* in the mixture.

Total solids represent everything that is not water, and the value is simply the sum of the four non-water components. For 2% milk, total solids account for 10.9%. For bananas, total solids are 24.7%.

There are established ranges for each of the six components (fat, sugars, nonfat milk solids, other solids, and water, plus the calculated category of total solids). The best results are obtained when each individual component is within its established range. The process of developing a formula for which each component is within range is called "balancing" the gelato. Such a gelato is referred to as "balanced."

Some gelato masters go so far as to say that if a formula is not balanced, it is not gelato. I do not agree with this extreme position in the absolute. That is, one component can be slightly out of range and the final product can still be gelato. Getting too many components out of range, or even one of them too far out of range, could well mean that the resulting product is not gelato. I always try to balance my gelato formulas. Occasionally, but rarely, to get a desired characteristic, such as sweetness or serving temperature, it might be necessary to have a component be slightly out of range.

The amount a component is out of range should be very small and generally within the margin of error for calculating the composition of the ingredients themselves. I rarely allow a component to vary outside the established range by more than about 0.2 percentage points.

Established ranges for balancing a gelato formula are shown in Table 11-3, though there can be minor differences between the ranges used by different gelato masters.

Table 11-3. Desired percentages of each component in gelato

Component	Percent
Fat	6–12%
Sugar	16–22%
Nonfat milk solids	8–12%
Other solids	0–?%
Water	58–68%
Total solids	**32–42%**

Although some experts say the upper limit for other solids is in the range of 4% or 5%, this is not the case based on my experience. As long as the percent of *total* solids in the mixture is within range, the percentage of other solids is not a significant factor. For example, if fat, sugar, and nonfat milk solids were each at the bottom end of the range, they would total 6% + 16% + 8% = 30%. Because total solids can go as high as 42%, it would be possible to incorporate up to 12% other solids and still have a balanced gelato. Nut gelati, in particular, have relatively large amounts of other solids and can push an arbitrary 4% or 5% limit on other solids, at least if enough nut paste is used to produce a flavorful gelato.

In general, I aim to have each category close to the middle of the established range, but sometimes it is necessary to do otherwise. For example, I once developed a gelato formula using chestnut flour as the flavoring agent to mimic a northern Italian dessert made from that flour. Because chestnut flour constitutes "other solids," I needed to maximize the amount I could put in the gelato to get the desired flavor. That meant pushing all the other ingredients toward the bottom of their respective ranges.

To show how balancing works, consider this formula for fiordilatte gelato, the simplest gelato there is (but arguably one of the most important), shown in Table 11-4.

Table 11-4. Fiordilatte gelato formula

Desired percentages			6–12%	16–22%	8–12%	0–?%	58–68%	32–42%
Ingredient	Quantity*	Percent	Fats*	Sugars*	NF Milk Solids*	Other Solids*	Water*	Total Solids*
Milk, 2%	525.00	52.50%						
Heavy Cream (36% fat)	263.00	26.30%						
Sucrose	135.00	13.50%						
Dextrose	20.00	2.00%						
Fructose	20.00	2.00%						
Powdered Skim Milk	34.00	3.40%						
Guar Gum	1.25	0.125%						
Locust Bean Gum	1.25	0.125%						
Salt	0.50	0.05%						
Base Weight	**1000.00**	100.00%						
Final Percentages								

* All quantities in grams

Starting with the 2% milk, you know from Table 11-1 that 2% milk contains 1.9% fat. You know from our gelato formula that fiordilatte gelato contains 525 grams of 2% milk. Multiplying 1.9% fat by 525 grams of milk yields 9.975 grams of fat from 2% milk.

Similarly, 2% milk contains 9% nonfat milk solids. Multiplying this by 525 grams of milk yields 47.25 grams of nonfat milk solids.

The calculation for water is 89.1% water × 525 grams milk = 467.775 grams water.

Total solids is the sum of all solids in the milk: 9.975 grams fat + 47.25 grams nonfat milk solids = 57.225 grams total solids.

As a check of the calculations, the sum of water and total solids should be 525 grams: 467.775 grams water + 57.225 grams solids = 525 grams of 2% milk.

The results, with rounding, are listed in Table 11-5.

Table 11-5. Fiordilatte gelato showing contribution from 2% milk

Desired percentages			6–12%	16–22%	8–12%	0–?%	58–68%	32–42%
Ingredient	Quantity*	Percent	Fats*	Sugars*	NF Milk Solids*	Other Solids*	Water*	Total Solids*
Milk, 2%	525.00	52.50%	9.98	0.00	47.25	0.00	467.78	57.23
Heavy Cream (36% fat)	263.00	26.30%						
Sucrose	135.00	13.50%						
Dextrose	20.00	2.00%						
Fructose	20.00	2.00%						
Powdered Skim Milk	34.00	3.40%						
Guar Gum	1.25	0.125%						
Locust Bean Gum	1.25	0.125%						
Salt	0.50	0.05%						
Base Weight	525.00	52.50%						
Final Percentages								

* All quantities in grams

Referring to Appendix B, "Ingredient Composition," enables you to complete the rest of the table. The quantity of each ingredient is multiplied by the percentage of each component (fats, sugars, and so on) to arrive at the total amount of that component for that ingredient, as shown in Table 11-6.

Table 11-6. Fiordilatte gelato fully balanced

Desired percentages			6–12%	16–22%	8–12%	0–?%	58–68%	32–42%
Ingredient	Quantity*	Percent	Fats*	Sugars*	NF Milk Solids*	Other Solids*	Water*	Total Solids*
Milk, 2%	525.00	52.50%	9.98	0.00	47.25	0.00	467.78	57.23
Heavy Cream (36% fat)	263.00	26.30%	94.94	0.00	16.54	0.00	151.51	111.49
Sucrose	135.00	13.50%	0.00	135.00	0.00	0.00	0.00	135.00
Dextrose	20.00	2.00%	0.00	18.40	0.00	0.00	1.60	18.40
Fructose	20.00	2.00%	0.00	20.00	0.00	0.00	0.00	20.00
Powdered Skim Milk	34.00	3.40%	0.24	0.00	32.40	0.00	1.36	32.64
Guar Gum	1.25	0.125%	0.00	0.00	0.00	1.25	0.00	1.25
Locust Bean Gum	1.25	0.125%	0.01	0.00	0.00	1.24	0.00	1.25
Salt	0.50	0.05%	0.00	0.00	0.00	0.50	0.00	0.50
Base Weight	525.00	52.50%	105.17	173.64	96.19	2.80	622.44	377.56
Final Percentages			**10.52%**	**17.34%**	**9.62%**	**0.28%**	**62.24%**	**37.76%**

* All quantities in grams

To recap, total solids is the sum of all solids in the mixture. In this example, it is 10.52% fats + 17.34% sugars + 9.62% nonfat milk solids + 0.28% other solids = 37.76% total solids.

As a check of the calculations, the sum of water plus total solids should be 100%, which it is: 62.24% water + 37.76% other solids = 100%.

To perform these calculations, you need a database that includes the percentage of each of the components (fat, sugar, nonfat milk solids, other solids, and water) of each ingredient. Although you can purchase software that comes preloaded with a database of ingredients, you should check the accuracy of the entries by researching each ingredient to see if you agree with the pre-loaded information. Most software comes from Europe and is loaded with information about European (mostly Italian) ingredients. Even though all software programs that I am aware of enable you to add ingredients and their compositions, you may want to consider developing your own spreadsheet and database.

Building in Flavor

Balancing a gelato is important, but so is building in flavor.

As I note elsewhere in this book, gelato is served at a warmer temperature than ice cream, and it often has less fat. For these reasons, gelato can have more intense flavor than ice cream. Fat and cold both dull taste. In my experience, the best gelato tastes more like its namesake flavor (for example, cherry, pistachio, coffee, and so on) than the best ice cream.

To maximize the ability of gelato to deliver flavor, you should take the critical step of optimizing the amount of the flavor ingredients in your gelato formula. Optimizing a flavor ingredient often means maximizing the amount of that ingredient, though not always. Let me explain further.

When developing a fruit gelato, unless the fruit is either particularly intense or mild, I start developing my formula by factoring 40% fruit into the mixture. From that starting point, I then balance the other ingredients. It may be necessary to modify the percentage of fruit to get the other ingredients to balance. After making a batch, I adjust the amount of fruit, if necessary, based on the taste of the final product.

Before committing to freezing a batch, you can do a taste test by mixing a small amount of the base, say 50 grams or 100 grams, leaving out ingredients like stabilizers, and tasting it. Remember that the flavor will be slightly muted at the serving temperature of –13°C (9°F).

Even the most flavorful watermelon is mild-tasting. To get the most flavor possible, my watermelon gelato is 53% fruit. Watermelon is mostly water, which creates a challenge with incorporating enough milk, as milk is also mostly water. To maximize the amount of watermelon and still have enough nonfat milk solids, I minimized the amount of liquid milk and increased the amount of powdered nonfat milk.

Lime juice is quite tart. Making a lime gelato with 40% lime juice would be too tart for most people. My lime gelato has less than 15% lime juice. Also, because citrus zest has loads of flavor, I steep lime zest in the milk before mixing the base for a depth of flavor that I cannot get from juice alone.

Sometimes there are other limiting factors. For example, nut pastes contain a considerable amount of solids. To keep total solids within the desired range while balancing the other ingredients in the gelato, it is difficult to work in more than about 13% nut paste by weight.

I encourage you to study the gelato formulas in Part Two of this book, paying particular attention to the percentages of the flavor ingredients in each gelato. This should provide a good starting point when developing your own flavors.

In thinking about flavor ingredients, consider which of the components of your gelato are likely to be most impacted by them and what is, therefore, likely to be the component that limits the amount of the flavor ingredient you can use. Nut pastes are high in fats and other solids. Fruit is often high in sugar and, as with watermelon, sometimes in water. Chocolate is high in fats. Each of these components influences how much of the flavor ingredient can be added while still producing a balanced gelato.

Researching Ingredient Composition

If you are creating your own database of gelato ingredients, adding an ingredient to an existing database, or confirming the accuracy of entries in gelato software you purchased, you need a method to research ingredients and their composition.

For ingredients available in the United States, I usually start with the United States Department of Agriculture's (USDA's) FoodData Central website: https://fdc.nal.usda.gov/index.html.

My go-to Italian site is the Ministero delle Politiche Agricole, Alimentari e Forestali's CREA website: https://www.crea.gov.it/-/tabella-di-composizione-degli-alimenti. Also useful are:

Valori Nutrizionali degli Alimenti: https://www.valori-alimenti.com

Zanichelli Online per la Scuola: https://online.scuola.zanichelli.it/cappellivannucchi/files/2012/11/Tabelle_Cappelli_Vanucchi_5959.pdf

If those websites do not provide the information I need, I search the National Institute of Health's PubMed website (https://pubmed.ncbi.nlm.nih.gov) or Research Gate (https://www.researchgate.net). These sites turn up scholarly articles that take a bit more reading than the neatly prepared tables found in the other sites. Finally, if necessary, I do a general internet search using a search engine.

Much of the information about food ingredients contains more detail than you need for making gelato. Once you obtain information on fat, sugar, nonfat milk solids, and water, everything else is considered other solids. Refer to Table 11-7, which shows part of the USDA's Food Data Central website entry for blueberries, for a useful example.

Recall that you are trying to determine the percentages of the following components:

1. Fat
2. Sugar
3. Nonfat milk solids
4. Other solids
5. Water

The quantities given are the amounts (in grams) per 100 grams of blueberries.

According to this reference, blueberries contain 0.33 grams of fat (yellow highlighting) per 100 grams of berries, or 0.33%. Though this is a negligible amount, the information is readily available so I include it in my database.

The total amount of sugar (blue highlighting) is 9.96 grams per 100 grams or 9.96%. At this point you are only concerned about total sugar content, but note also that the amounts of different sugars are included (sucrose, glucose, fructose, lactose, maltose, and galactose). You will use these percentages at a later stage when calculating PAC and POD.

Because blueberries are not a dairy product, they do not contain any milk solids.

Water (green highlighting) equals 84.2 grams per 100 grams of berries, or 84.2%.

Table 11-7. USDA FoodData Central entry for blueberries (highlighting added)

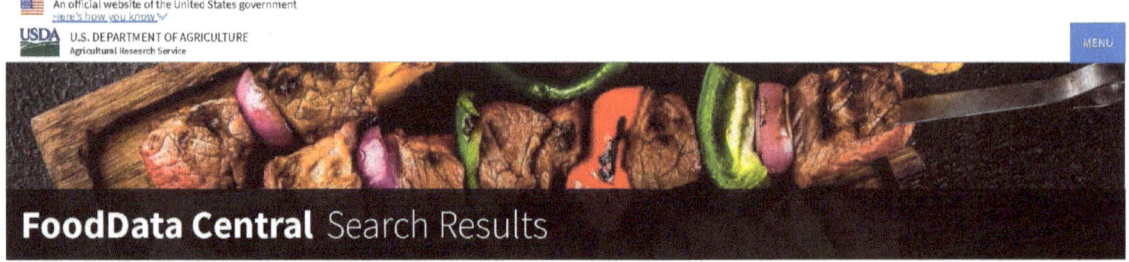

ARS HOME · FOODDATA CENTRAL · FOOD SEARCH · BLUEBERRIES, RAW (SR LEGACY, 171711)

Blueberries, raw

SR Legacy, released in April 2018, is the final release of this data type and will not be updated. For more recent data, users should search other data types in FoodData Central.

Data Type: SR Legacy
Food Category: Fruits and Fruit Juices
FDC ID: 171711
NDB Number: 9050
FDC Published: 4/1/2019

Nutrients   **Measures**   **Other Information**

Portion:

100g

Name	Amount	Unit	Deriv. By	n	Samples	Min	Max	Median	Footnote	Last Updated
Water	84.2	g	Analytical	12		80.7	86.8			9/1/2002
Energy	57	kcal	Calculated							6/1/2010
Energy	240	kJ	Calculated							6/1/2010
Protein	0.74	g	Analytical	12		0.6	0.97			9/1/2002
Total lipid (fat)	0.33	g	Analytical	12		0.2	0.5			9/1/2002
Ash	0.24	g	Analytical	12		0.19	0.3			9/1/2002
Carbohydrate, by difference	14.5	g	Calculated							6/1/2010
Fiber, total dietary	2.4	g	Analytical	4		2.3	2.8			9/1/2002
Sugars, total including NLEA	9.96	g	Analytical	8		7.67	12.3			9/1/2002
Sucrose	0.11	g	Analytical	8		0.07	0.14			9/1/2002
Glucose (dextrose)	4.88	g	Analytical	8		3.74	6			9/1/2002
Fructose	4.97	g	Analytical	8		3.86	6.26			9/1/2002
Lactose	0	g	Analytical	8		0	0			9/1/2002
Maltose	0	g	Analytical	8		0	0			9/1/2002
Galactose	0	g	Analytical	8		0	0			9/1/2002
Starch	0.03	g	Analytical	4		0	0.11			9/1/2002

https://fdc.nal.usda.gov/fdc-app.html#/food-details/171711/nutrients

The sum of fat + sugar + nonfat milk solids + water = 0.33% + 9.96% + 0% + 84.2% = 94.49%. The balance, 5.51%, by definition, constitutes other solids.

Note that the categories are not mutually exclusive. For example, carbohydrate includes fiber, sugar, and starch. Even then, the total of fiber, sugar, and starch does not equal the 14.5 grams attributed to carbohydrate. Also note, though, that the amount of carbohydrate is a calculated value while the others are the result of actual analysis, which should be more accurate.

Ash includes everything that is left if the substance is burned. Basically, this amounts to minerals and salts, which are listed on the other ten pages of this entry (not reproduced here). Ash is part of total solids.

Sometimes, the quantities of the individual sugars do not sum exactly to the amount of total sugar. Usually, this difference is quite minimal and probably derives from rounding errors. When this occurs, I allocate the difference to each of the sugars in proportion to their percentage of total sugar.

Stabilizers

All gelato requires stabilizers, whether egg yolks, vegetable gums, starch such as cornstarch, or gelatin. The reasons for this are explained in Chapter 8, "Emulsifiers and Stabilizers." But what quantities should you use?

My standard stabilizer combination is equal parts locust bean gum and guar gum. My starting concentration is 0.125% of each, or 1.25 grams per kilogram of gelato base. These proportions can vary based on experience and taste testing. For example, cream cheese contains locust bean gum and some other stabilizers as well. I either reduce or eliminate locust bean gum in gelato that contains cream cheese depending on the percentage of cream cheese in the mixture. I usually reduce, but do not eliminate, the guar gum as well.

Some fruits contain solids that act as stabilizers, enabling you to reduce or eliminate the added stabilizers. This is true with dried figs. Notice that the fig gelato formula in this book does not contain any stabilizers. The mixture is too thick when stabilizers are added.

When using egg yolks to stabilize gelato, my starting assumption is 9% egg yolk, or 90 grams per kilogram of gelato base.

I do not use cornstarch, gelatin, or other stabilizers. Remember, each stabilizer counts as an ingredient and must be accounted for when balancing the gelato.

Additional Pointers

Professional gelato formulas are always based on weight. That is, you weigh liquids as well as solids. Nothing is measured by volume. Gelato batches are always expressed in terms of weight.

I suggest you have a standard batch weight for all gelato formulas you develop. Not all gelaticians do this. In fact, I was not taught to do this when I first learned to make gelato. I created balanced gelato formulas that were approximately 1 kilogram because that is the batch size that worked best in the batch freezer I had originally. Now I create all my gelato formulas to be exactly 1 kilogram and I suggest you do the same. My current home batch freezer works well with a 2-kilogram batch, but when I am in Italy teaching, 3 to 4 kilograms is better for the machine I use there. The gelato workbook that I developed contains a function that allows me to upsize (or, theoretically, downsize) the gelato to any given quantity. The quantities of all the ingredients are recalculated instantaneously.

One of the advantages of a standard batch size is that you can plug in the quantities of guar gum, locust bean gum, and salt at the very beginning of formula development, knowing that the percentages will be correct because the final weight of the batch is known before you begin. Because my starting assumption is that I will use 0.125% guar gum, 0.125% locust bean gum, and 0.1% salt, and my nominal batch size will be 1000 grams, I enter 1.25 grams guar gum, 1.25 grams locust bean gum, and 1 gram salt at the very start. These quantities might get adjusted based on taste testing or experience, but I have a standard starting point that makes formula development easier.

If you are not familiar with the metric system, now is the time to start. It makes developing gelato formulas, and upsizing and downsizing them, easier than any other alternative. If you do not believe me, take the formula for fiordilatte gelato listed in Table 11-4 and calculate the quantities of each ingredient based on the percentages, assuming a batch size of 2 pounds. In addition, because Americans usually use volume measures for everything, not weight, the next step would be to convert all the pounds and ounces to cups, tablespoons, and teaspoons. I do not recommend measuring gelato ingredients this way because volume measures are less precise than weight measures, but just thinking about it shows the complexity of not using the metric system.

I have read my share of books, articles, and government regulations related to dairy science. I am always eager to recalculate in metric some of the requirements described in American measures. Almost always the result is an elegantly simple relationship that is completely obscured by using pounds, ounces, gallons, and fluid ounces.

One last observation, if you are still not keen on the idea of using the metric system. Whenever I teach artisan Italian gelato in Italy, about half the class is American and the other half is from everywhere else in the world. We only use the metric system in class. By the end of the week, the Americans are always comfortable using metric. I promise you, once you start using the metric system, you will become comfortable quickly and you will never look back.

Direct and Indirect Gelato Formulas

All the gelato formulas in this book are direct formulas. That is, each gelato is created from the ground up to achieve the best balance and serving temperature.

A gelateria may choose to use indirect formulas, especially if gelato is being made by staff other than the gelatiere. For an indirect gelato, flavors that have similar composition, such as peach, mango, nectarine, and melon are grouped together. The average amounts of each of the main ingredients (milk, cream, sucrose, dextrose, locust bean gum, guar gum, and salt) across all the related gelato formulas are calculated. These quantities are then mixed into a base. When it is time to make the gelato, the fruit puree is added to the base and the gelato can be put in the batch freezer.

If some of these gelati contain dextrose and others contain fructose, the base can be made without these sugars. These additional sugars can be added along with the fruit puree.

There is less likelihood of error with this system. Production can go faster, too, because large quantities of base can be made and pasteurized in slightly more time than would be required to make the base for an individual flavor using the direct method. The trade-off, however, is that each individual gelato is not as ideally balanced as it would be if the direct method were used. The serving temperature may not be ideal either.

In Summary

Developing gelato flavors is truly a fun part of the gelato experience. Creating a gelato formula is much easier than developing a cake recipe. Gelato is like an open-book exam. Before starting, you know where you want to end up with each of the main components. Your major task is to maximize flavor while tweaking the amounts of the other ingredients to get the right percentages. You can even start by just swapping out one fruit for another fruit of similar composition, creating a whole new flavor in the process.

Adjusting PAC and POD

Balancing a gelato, as demonstrated in the previous chapter, is only part of the calculations you need to do to create a gelato formula. It is a very big part, but a part, nonetheless. Even a completely balanced gelato will not necessarily have the desired serving temperature or sweetness. Different sugars affect freezing point depression and sweetness differently. Within the acceptable range for sugars, you can use different sugars to fine-tune PAC and POD to get serving temperature and sweetness right.

Getting PAC Right

As noted earlier in the book, PAC is the abbreviation for *potere anticongelante,* which means "anti-freezing power" in Italian. In Chapter 11, I explained how to balance a formula for fiordilatte gelato, but I did not take PAC into account. Here's how you do it.

Remember from Chapter 7, "Freezing Point Depression," that only three types of solutes are of practical significance in calculating PAC:

1. Sugars
2. Salts
3. Alcohol

The first step is to calculate the contribution of 2% milk to the PAC of the fiordilatte gelato.

The fiordilatte gelato base contains 52.5% of 2% milk calculated as:

525 grams of 2% milk ÷ 1000 grams of gelato base = 52.5% milk in gelato base

The only solute in milk that is of concern when calculating PAC is lactose. You can see from Appendix B, "Ingredient Composition," that 2% milk contains 4.89% lactose.[38]

Because our fiordilatte gelato contains 52.5% of 2% milk, and 2% milk contains 4.89% lactose, the percentage of lactose in the gelato base contributed by the milk can be determined as follows:

52.5% × 4.89% = 2.567% lactose from milk in gelato base

The PAC of lactose is the same as the PAC of sucrose as both have the same molecular weight. Thus a 2.567% solution of lactose has the same PAC as a 2.567% solution of sucrose.

---

[38] Remember that the lactose in dairy products is included in the category of nonfat milk solids, not sugars, when balancing gelato. However, lactose is included as a sugar when calculating PAC and POD. See Chapter 11, "Creating Gelato Formulas," for more information.

Remember that 1 PAC unit is equal to the anti-freezing power of a 1% solution of sucrose (common table sugar). Therefore, the PAC of a 2.567% solution of lactose is 2.567.

Now calculate the contribution to PAC from heavy (36%) cream. The fiordilatte gelato base contains 26.30% heavy cream calculated as:

$$263 \text{ grams of heavy cream} \div 1000 \text{ grams of gelato base} = 26.30\%$$
$$\text{heavy cream in gelato base}$$

As with milk, the only solute in cream that is of concern when calculating PAC is lactose. We see from Appendix B, "Ingredient Composition" that heavy cream contains 2.92% lactose.

Because our fiordilatte gelato contains 26.3% heavy cream, and heavy cream contains 2.92% lactose, the percentage of lactose in our gelato base contributed by the heavy cream is:

$$26.30\% \times 2.92\% = 0.768\%$$

Because lactose and sucrose have the same PAC, a 0.768% solution of lactose contributes 0.768 to the PAC of our gelato base.

Notice in Table 11-4 that the spreadsheet I use to balance gelato formulas includes the percentage of every ingredient used in making the gelato base. For the subsequent calculations, you will start with the percentages shown in that table.

Our fiordilatte gelato base contains 13.50% sucrose. The percentage of sucrose in sucrose is 100%. Thus, our gelato base really contains 13.50% sucrose:

13.50% sucrose in gelato base × 100% sucrose in sucrose = 13.50% sucrose in gelato base

The PAC of a 13.50% solution of sucrose is:

$$13.50\% \text{ sucrose} \times 100 = 13.50$$

Our gelato base contains 2.00% fructose. From Appendix C, "PAC Table," you see that the PAC of fructose is 190. The contribution to PAC of 2.00% fructose is:

$$2.00\% \text{ fructose} \times 190 = 3.80$$

The situation with dextrose is different.

Our gelato base contains 2.00% of the ingredient dextrose. But the ingredient dextrose contains 8% water (see Appendix B, "Ingredient Composition"), meaning that there is only 92% pure dextrose in dextrose. Thus, our gelato base contains 1.84% pure dextrose, calculated as:

2.00% dextrose (ingredient) in gelato base × 92% (pure) dextrose
in dextrose (ingredient) = 1.84% pure dextrose in gelato base

From the data in Appendix C you can determine that the PAC of dextrose is 190. The contribution to PAC is:

$$1.84\% \text{ dextrose} \times 190 = 3.496$$

To calculate the contribution from powdered skim milk, you first calculate the percentage of lactose contributed to the gelato base:

3.40% powdered skim milk in gelato base × 50% lactose (in powdered skim milk) = 1.7% lactose in gelato base

The PAC of lactose is 100 (Appendix C). The contribution to PAC of powdered skim milk is thus:

$$1.70\% \text{ lactose} \times 100 = 1.70.$$

Guar gum and locust bean gum do not contribute to PAC. This leaves only the contribution from salt to calculate. The PAC of salt is 1171. The contribution to PAC of salt in fiordilatte gelato is:

$$0.05\% \text{ salt in gelato base} \times 1171 = 0.586 \text{ PAC}$$

You can then sum the individual contributions to PAC to determine the PAC of our fiordilatte gelato, as shown in Table 12-1.

Table 12-1. PAC of fiordilatte gelato

Ingredient	PAC
Milk, 2%	2.567
Heavy Cream (36% fat)	0.768
Sucrose	13.500
Dextrose	3.496
Fructose	3.800
Powdered Skim Milk	1.700
Guar Gum	0.000
Locust Bean Gum	0.000
Salt	0.586
Total	**26.417**

The relationship between PAC and serving temperature is quite simple. Dividing PAC by −2 gives the approximate serving temperature in °C. For our fiordilatte gelato:

$$26.42 \div -2 = -13.2°C \ (8.2°F)$$

The temperature of most gelato showcases is kept at −13°C, plus or minus 1°C, so a calculated serving temperature of −13.2°C is on target. Remember, though, that this is an approximation and other factors affect scoopability besides PAC. A gelato with total solids

Adjusting PAC and POD

on the high end of the range feels firmer than a gelato with total solids on the low end, even if both are calculated to have the same serving temperature based on PAC. Ultimately, tasting the gelato at serving temperature determines if the texture is appropriate.

Because the gelato is balanced and you have the PAC right, you would be ready to make the first test batch of this gelato. When testing the gelato, you would be particularly concerned about flavor, sweetness, texture, and creaminess at serving temperature. In terms of flavor, there is not much you can do except use high-quality dairy ingredients because fiordilatte does not have any other flavoring ingredients. You have much more room to adjust sweetness, texture, and creaminess. You would do this by adjusting the sugars in the mixture, which will affect sweetness as well as serving temperature.

For example, if your display case typically maintained a temperature of −14°C, this gelato might be too firm, as the recommended serving temperature is around −13°C. You could add more sugar to increase the PAC of the base, thereby decreasing the serving temperature. Which sugar you add would be partially dependent on whether or not you were concerned about affecting the sweetness of the gelato.

This is where the concept of POD comes in.

Calculating POD

As noted earlier in this book, POD is the abbreviation for *potere dolcificante,* which means "sweetening power" in Italian. Remember from Chapter 9, "Sweetening Power," that POD, as with PAC, is calculated as sweetness in relation to sucrose. Unlike PAC, however, which is solidly grounded in physical chemistry (molar concentration, cryoscopic constant, van 't Hoff constant), POD is based on taste. There is no way to measure sweetness directly. It is subjective and dependent on the assessment of the taster.

Different researchers have derived different values of POD for the same sugar (see Table 9-1). Part of this is due to difference in methods. The perception of sweetness is not necessarily linear,[39] that is, a 10% solution of a specific sugar is not necessarily twice as sweet as a 5% solution. The POD of trehalose goes from 0.15 to 0.45 as the concentration goes from 2.3% to 22.2%. Therefore, the perception of sweetness is partially dependent on how the sugars are tasted (for example, the concentration of a solution).

Calculating POD follows the same model as calculating PAC. Sucrose is assigned a value of 100. All other sugars are assigned a value in relation to sucrose, ranging from 16 for lactose to 150 for fructose. Appendix C, "POD Tables," contains the POD values I use.

Although the following calculations can all be done by hand, it is helpful to have a spreadsheet or gelato program that does the calculations instantaneously. This allows you to model many options with little effort other than a few keystrokes.

---

[39] Mullan (2012).

Copying the results from the calculations completed for determining the PAC of our fiordilatte gelato, you will see that the base contains the following percentages of sugars:

Ingredient	Lactose (%)	Sucrose (%)	Dextrose (%)	Fructose (%)
Milk, 2%	2.567			
Heavy Cream (36% fat)	0.768			
Sucrose		13.50		
Dextrose			1.84	
Fructose				2.00
Powdered Skim Milk	1.70			
Total	5.035	13.50	1.84	2.00

You can calculate the POD of our fiordilatte gelato as follows:

$$POD = (\% \text{ Sugar \#1} \times POD \text{ Sugar \#1}) + (\% \text{ Sugar \#2} \times POD \text{ Sugar \#2}) + (\% \text{ Sugar \#3} \times POD \text{ Sugar \#3}) + (\% \text{ Sugar \#4} \times POD \text{ Sugar \#4})$$

$$POD = (\% \text{ Lactose} \times POD \text{ Lactose}) + (\% \text{ Sucrose} \times POD \text{ Sucrose}) + (\% \text{ Dextrose} \times POD \text{ Dextrose}) + (\% \text{ Fructose} \times POD \text{ Fructose})$$

$$POD = (0.05035 \times 16) + (0.1350 \times 100) + (0.0184 \times 75) + (0.0200 \times 150)$$

$$POD = 0.806 + 13.50 + 1.38 + 3.00$$

$$POD = 18.686 = 18.69$$

Adjusting POD

The perception of sweetness is affected by other ingredients. For example, the perception of sweetness is enhanced by vanillin.[40] Acidity, a food's color, and interactions with other sweeteners can all affect the perception of sweetness.[41]

For all the foregoing reasons, I rarely make major changes in a gelato formula based on the calculated POD without first tasting it. That does not mean, though, that I do not make some estimates of the desired POD when developing gelato formulas. When developing my formula for raspberry gelato, I looked at the POD values for my formulas for blueberry, blackberry, and strawberry gelati. Of these three, blueberry has the lowest POD, blackberry is next, and strawberry has the highest. I find blackberries and strawberries to be more tart than blueberries, so even though the POD values are higher, the blackberry and strawberry gelati do not taste sweeter than the blueberry gelato. I find raspberries to be more tart than strawberries, so I designed my initial formula with a POD that was even higher.

---

[40] Clarke (2004), 130.
[41] Mullan (2012).

If you look through the gelato formulas in the first part of this book, you will see that they range in POD from approximately 16 to approximately 20, with most clustering in the 17 to 19 range. This is a natural outcome of balancing a gelato to have 16% to 22% sugar, mostly sucrose, with other sugars used to correct the PAC.

After tasting a gelato, you are in a position to decide if it should be more sweet or less sweet and if the texture and consistency are on target at the usual serving temperature. This is where the concept of POD, as subjective as it is, comes in. Even though the data underlying POD are less scientific than those for PAC, the concept is useful in helping you adjust gelato formulas to achieve desired goals.

For example, if your gelato is too hard, you know you need to increase the PAC, but do you simultaneously need to adjust sweetness?

If you need to increase both PAC and POD (in other words, the gelato is too hard at serving temperature as well as not being sweet enough), you could start by adding more sucrose. Sucrose is typically the least expensive sweetener and the usual first choice. You may be in a situation where you are reaching the limit on the percent of total solids in your gelato base so simply adding more sucrose may not be an option. In such a case, you could substitute fructose for a portion of the sucrose. Fructose has both a higher PAC and a higher POD than sucrose, so you could increase both without adding to total solids by doing a partial substitution.

If you need to maintain PAC but decrease POD (in other words, the scoopability of the gelato is correct at serving temperature but it is too sweet) you could substitute dextrose for a portion of the sucrose. You could also consider using lactose and trehalose, as they have the same PAC as sucrose but a lower POD.

If you need to maintain PAC but increase POD, you have fewer options. Remembering that the POD of lactose is quite low but its PAC is the same as sucrose, you could decrease the powdered skim milk, and thus the lactose it contributes. This would enable you to add another sugar to increase POD while maintaining PAC. You need to be certain that nonfat milk solids are still within range, but you can get some mileage out of this approach.

In Summary

Adjusting the sugar composition of gelato to modify PAC and POD to create the desired serving temperature and sweetness is the final step in creating a gelato formula. These last two chapters have addressed balancing and then PAC and POD in sequence. If using gelato software, or a spreadsheet and database that you develop, these three calculations happen simultaneously. If you adjust sugar to improve balance, the PAC and POD immediately recalculate. If you are only occasionally going to develop gelato formulas, you can do the calculations manually, but if you plan on developing many formulas, a basic spreadsheet is a welcome tool.

Appendices

Appendix A: Gelato Worksheets

Balance Worksheet

Flavor _____ Author _____ Date _____

Ingredient	Weight (g)	%	Component Quantity in grams					
			Fats	Sugars	MSNF	Other Solids	Water	Total Solids
TOTAL (grams)								
PERCENT								
TARGET RANGE	1000 g	100%	6-12%	16-22%	8-12%	0-5%	58-68%	32-42%

Off Balance Ingredients	

Mix In Ingredients	

PAC _____

Estimated Serving Temperature in °C* _____

POD _____

*Estimated serving temperature = PAC / -2

184   *Make Your Own Artisan Italian Gelato*

Instructions for Balance Worksheet

1. Enter ingredients in far-left column followed by weight in grams and percent of the total mixture assuming a target of 1000 grams for the mixture.
2. Enter the weight, in grams, of each component (fats, sugars, MSNF, other solids, and water) by multiplying the weight of the ingredient by the percentage of the component using the data in Appendix B.
3. Calculate Total Solids by summing the fats, sugars, MSNF, and other solids across each row.
4. Check the entries by summing the water and total solids for each row. The result should equal the ingredient weight (second column). If the ingredient contains ethanol, add it to the water for this step.
5. Enter the total weight of each component by summing the columns.
6. Calculate the percent of each component by dividing the total weight of each component by the total weight of the mixture.
7. Confirm that the percentages are within the target ranges. Aim to be as close to the center of each range as possible.
8. Proceed to the POD and PAC Worksheet.

PAC and POD Worksheet

Flavor _____ Author _____ Date _____

Ingredient	%	Sucrose	Dextrose	Fructose	Lactose	Maltose	Galactose	Ethanol	Salt	
TOTAL PERCENTAGE										SUM
CONTRIBUTION TO PAC										
CONTRIBUTION TO POD										

Instructions for the PAC and POD Worksheet

1. Copy each ingredient and its percentage of the mixture from the Balance Worksheet.
2. Sum the percent column to confirm that it equals 100% as a check on accuracy of the entries.
3. Using the information in Appendix B, complete the entries for each row by multiplying the percent of each type of sugar plus the ethanol and salt by the percent of the ingredient. Enter a 0 in any cell where the ingredient does not contain the specified sugar, ethanol, or salt.
4. Calculate the Total Percentage of each sugar and of the ethanol and salt by summing down each column.
5. For each column, calculate the contribution to PAC by multiplying the total percentage of the specified sugar plus the ethanol and salt by the values found in Appendix C.
6. For each column, calculate the contribution to POD by multiplying the total percentage of the specified sugar by the values found in Appendix D. Ethanol and salt do not contribute to POD.
7. Enter the PAC and POD by summing the last two rows and entering the information in the two bottom right cells.

Appendix B: Ingredient Composition

Ingredient	Fats	Sugars	Milk Solids	Other Solids	Water	Total Solids	Sucrose	Dextrose	Fructose	Lactose	Maltose	Galactose	Ethanol
Almond Butter (American)	55.50%	4.43%	0.00%	40.07%	0.00%	100.00%	4.34%	0.02%	0.00%	0.00%	0.07%	0.00%	0.00%
Almond Extract	5.00%	0.00%	0.00%	0.00%	45.00%	5.00%	0.00%	0.00%	0.00%	0.00%	0.00%	0.00%	50.00%
Almond Paste	55.00%	4.43%	0.00%	40.57%	0.00%	100.00%	4.34%	0.02%	0.00%	0.00%	0.07%	0.00%	0.00%
Amaretto (DiSaronno)	0.00%	10.00%	0.00%	0.00%	62.00%	10.00%	10.00%	0.00%	0.00%	0.00%	0.00%	0.00%	28.00%
Apple, Raw	0.13%	10.10%	0.00%	3.07%	86.70%	13.30%	0.82%	3.25%	6.03%	0.00%	0.00%	0.00%	0.00%
Apricot	0.39%	9.24%	0.00%	3.97%	86.40%	13.60%	5.87%	2.37%	0.94%	0.00%	0.06%	0.00%	0.00%
Banana	0.29%	15.80%	0.00%	8.61%	75.30%	24.70%	4.18%	5.55%	6.09%	0.00%	0.00%	0.00%	0.00%
Blackberry	0.49%	4.88%	0.00%	6.43%	88.20%	11.80%	0.07%	2.31%	2.40%	0.00%	0.07%	0.03%	0.00%
Blueberry	0.33%	9.96%	0.00%	5.51%	84.20%	15.80%	0.11%	4.88%	4.97%	0.00%	0.00%	0.00%	0.00%
Bourbon, 80 Proof	0.00%	0.00%	0.00%	0.01%	66.60%	0.01%	0.00%	0.00%	0.00%	0.00%	0.00%	0.00%	33.39%
Butter	84.00%	0.00%	0.00%	0.00%	16.00%	84.00%	0.00%	0.00%	0.00%	0.00%	0.00%	0.00%	0.00%
Butter, Brown	100.00%	0.00%	0.00%	0.00%	0.00%	100.00%	0.00%	0.00%	0.00%	0.00%	0.00%	0.00%	0.00%
Cantaloupe	0.18%	7.88%	0.00%	1.74%	90.20%	9.80%	3.32%	2.08%	2.40%	0.00%	0.02%	0.06%	0.00%
Carrots	0.24%	4.74%	0.00%	6.72%	88.30%	11.70%	3.60%	0.59%	0.55%	0.00%	0.00%	0.00%	0.00%
Cherry, Sour	0.30%	8.49%	0.00%	5.11%	86.10%	13.90%	0.80%	4.18%	3.51%	0.00%	0.00%	0.00%	0.00%
Cherry, Sweet	0.20%	12.82%	0.00%	4.78%	82.20%	17.80%	0.15%	6.59%	5.37%	0.00%	0.12%	0.59%	0.00%
Chocolate, 72% Cacao	38.70%	25.80%	0.00%	35.50%	0.00%	100.00%	38.70%	0.00%	0.00%	0.00%	0.00%	0.00%	0.00%
Chocolate, White (Green & Black's Organic)	36.76%	40.38%	7.70%	14.95%	0.21%	99.79%	40.38%	0.00%	0.00%	9.62%	0.00%	0.00%	0.00%
Cinnamon	0.00%	0.00%	0.00%	100.00%	0.00%	100.00%	0.00%	0.00%	0.00%	0.00%	0.00%	0.00%	0.00%

Ingredient	Fats	Sugars	Milk Solids	Other Solids	Water	Total Solids	Sucrose	Dextrose	Fructose	Lactose	Maltose	Galactose	Ethanol
Cocoa Mass	53.33%	0.00%	0.00%	46.67%	0.00%	100.00%	0.00%	0.00%	0.00%	0.00%	0.00%	0.00%	0.00%
Cocoa Powder, 10–12% Fat	11.00%	0.00%	0.00%	84.00%	5.00%	95.00%	0.00%	0.00%	0.00%	0.00%	0.00%	0.00%	0.00%
Cocoa Powder, 22–24% Fat	23.00%	0.00%	0.00%	75.00%	2.00%	98.00%	0.00%	0.00%	0.00%	0.00%	0.00%	0.00%	0.00%
Coconut Cream (Aroy-D)	21.00%	0.04%	0.00%	0.01%	78.95%	21.05%	0.01%	0.02%	0.02%	0.00%	0.00%	0.00%	0.00%
Coconut Cream (Kara)	23.30%	0.40%	0.00%	0.01%	76.29%	23.71%	0.01%	0.02%	0.02%	0.00%	0.00%	0.00%	0.00%
Coconut, Dry	27.99%	36.75%	0.00%	19.80%	15.46%	84.54%	15.60%	12.24%	8.89%	0.00%	0.00%	0.00%	0.00%
Coffee, Espresso, Brewed	0.18%	0.00%	0.00%	2.02%	97.80%	2.20%	0.00%	0.00%	0.00%	0.00%	0.00%	0.00%	0.00%
Coffee, Vietnamese, Brewed	0.15%	0.00%	0.00%	1.68%	98.17%	1.83%	0.00%	0.00%	0.00%	0.00%	0.00%	0.00%	0.00%
Coffee, Ground Roasted	14.00%	0.00%	0.00%	86.00%	0.00%	100.00%	0.00%	0.00%	0.00%	0.00%	0.00%	0.00%	0.00%
Cream Cheese (Philadelphia)	35.70%	0.00%	9.91%	1.79%	52.60%	47.40%	0.00%	0.00%	0.00%	3.76%	0.00%	0.00%	0.00%
Cream, 36% Fat	36.10%	0.00%	6.29%	0.00%	57.61%	42.39%	0.00%	0.00%	0.00%	2.92%	0.00%	0.00%	0.00%
Dates, Deglet Noor	0.39%	63.40%	0.00%	15.71%	20.50%	79.50%	23.80%	19.90%	19.60%	0.00%	0.12%	0.00%	0.00%
Dates, Medjool	0.15%	66.50%	0.00%	12.05%	21.30%	78.70%	0.53%	33.70%	32.00%	0.00%	0.30%	0.00%	0.00%
Dextrose	0.00%	92.00%	0.00%	0.00%	8.00%	92.00%	0.00%	92.00%	0.00%	0.00%	0.00%	0.00%	0.00%
Dulce de Leche (La Lechera)	7.69%	46.15%	11.76%	5.70%	28.70%	71.30%	37.76%	1.70%	0.32%	5.34%	0.00%	1.03%	0.00%
Egg Yolk	26.50%	0.56%	0.00%	20.64%	52.30%	47.70%	0.08%	0.18%	0.08%	0.08%	0.08%	0.08%	0.00%
Fig, Dried	0.92%	47.90%	0.00%	21.18%	30.00%	70.00%	0.07%	24.80%	22.90%	0.00%	0.00%	0.13%	0.00%
Fructose	0.00%	100.00%	0.00%	0.00%	0.00%	100.00%	0.00%	0.00%	100.00%	0.00%	0.00%	0.00%	0.00%
Grapes, Red, Seedless	0.00%	17.34%	0.00%	4.46%	78.20%	21.80%	0.00%	8.17%	9.17%	0.00%	0.00%	0.00%	0.00%
Guar Gum	0.50%	0.00%	0.00%	84.50%	15.00%	85.00%	0.00%	0.00%	0.00%	0.00%	0.00%	0.00%	0.00%

Ingredient	Fats	Sugars	Milk Solids	Other Solids	Water	Total Solids	Sucrose	Dextrose	Fructose	Lactose	Maltose	Galactose	Ethanol
Guava, Common, Raw	0.98%	8.92%	0.00%	9.30%	80.80%	19.20%	0.05%	3.90%	3.97%	0.00%	1.01%	0.00%	0.00%
Guava Extract (Amoretti)	0.00%	90.00%	0.00%	0.00%	10.00%	90.00%	90.00%	0.00%	0.00%	0.00%	0.00%	0.00%	0.00%
Hazelnut Paste	65.00%	6.14%	0.00%	23.86%	5.00%	95.00%	2.91%	1.52%	0.80%	0.00%	0.91%	0.00%	0.00%
Honey	0.00%	82.10%	0.00%	0.80%	17.10%	82.90%	0.89%	35.80%	40.90%	0.00%	1.44%	3.10%	0.00%
Kumquat	0.86%	9.36%	0.00%	8.98%	80.80%	19.20%	0.00%	4.68%	4.68%	0.00%	0.00%	0.00%	0.00%
Lactose	0.00%	100.00%	0.00%	0.00%	0.00%	100.00%	0.00%	0.00%	0.00%	100.00%	0.00%	0.00%	0.00%
Lemon Juice	0.24%	2.52%	0.00%	4.94%	92.30%	7.70%	0.43%	0.99%	1.10%	0.00%	0.00%	0.00%	0.00%
Licorice Root, Ground	0.00%	0.00%	0.00%	100.00%	0.00%	100.00%	0.00%	0.00%	0.00%	0.00%	0.00%	0.00%	0.00%
Lime Juice	0.07%	1.69%	0.00%	7.44%	90.80%	9.20%	0.48%	0.60%	0.61%	0.00%	0.00%	0.00%	0.00%
Locust Bean Gum	0.50%	0.00%	0.00%	99.50%	0.00%	100.00%	0.00%	0.00%	0.00%	0.00%	0.00%	0.00%	0.00%
Maltose	0.00%	0.00%	0.00%	100.00%	0.00%	100.00%	0.00%	0.00%	0.00%	0.00%	100.00%	0.00%	0.00%
Mango	0.38%	13.70%	0.00%	2.42%	83.50%	16.50%	6.97%	2.01%	4.68%	0.00%	0.00%	0.00%	0.00%
Maple Syrup	0.06%	60.50%	0.00%	7.04%	32.40%	67.60%	58.30%	1.60%	0.52%	0.00%	0.00%	0.00%	0.00%
Marsala, Dry (Florio Superiore)	0.00%	4.00%	0.00%	0.00%	78.00%	4.00%	0.00%	2.00%	2.00%	0.00%	0.00%	0.00%	18.00%
Mascarpone (Auricchio)	36.67%	0.00%	10.00%	3.33%	50.00%	50.00%	0.00%	0.00%	0.00%	3.33%	0.00%	0.00%	0.00%
Mascarpone (BelGioioso)	50.00%	0.00%	7.00%	0.00%	43.00%	57.00%	0.00%	0.00%	0.00%	2.10%	0.00%	0.00%	0.00%
Mascarpone (Ciresa)	36.00%	0.00%	8.80%	0.00%	55.20%	44.80%	0.00%	0.00%	0.00%	3.00%	0.00%	0.00%	0.00%
Mascarpone, Murray's	42.86%	0.00%	8.21%	3.57%	45.36%	54.64%	0.00%	0.00%	0.00%	4.64%	0.00%	0.00%	0.00%
Milk, 1% (American)	0.95%	0.00%	9.35%	0.00%	89.70%	10.30%	0.00%	0.00%	0.00%	4.96%	0.00%	0.00%	0.00%
Milk, 2% (American)	1.90%	0.00%	9.00%	0.00%	89.10%	10.90%	0.00%	0.00%	0.00%	4.89%	0.00%	0.00%	0.00%

Ingredient	Fats	Sugars	Milk Solids	Other Solids	Water	Total Solids	Sucrose	Dextrose	Fructose	Lactose	Maltose	Galactose	Ethanol
Milk, Condensed Whole (Eagle)	7.69%	48.71%	15.38%	1.02%	27.20%	72.80%	48.71%	0.00%	0.00%	7.69%	0.00%	0.00%	0.00%
Milk, Skim (American)	0.08%	0.00%	9.12%	0.00%	90.80%	9.20%	0.00%	0.00%	0.00%	5.05%	0.00%	0.00%	0.00%
Milk, Whole (American)	3.20%	0.00%	8.70%	0.00%	88.10%	11.90%	0.00%	0.00%	0.00%	4.81%	0.00%	0.00%	0.00%
Nectarine	0.28%	7.89%	0.00%	2.83%	89.00%	11.00%	4.83%	1.67%	1.39%	0.00%	0.00%	0.00%	0.00%
Nutmeg	0.00%	0.00%	0.00%	100.00%	0.00%	100.00%	0.00%	0.00%	0.00%	0.00%	0.00%	0.00%	0.00%
Olive Oil, Extra-Virgin	100.00%	0.00%	0.00%	0.00%	0.00%	100.00%	0.00%	0.00%	0.00%	0.00%	0.00%	0.00%	0.00%
Orange Juice, Homemade	0.00%	8.35%	0.00%	3.35%	88.30%	11.70%	4.61%	1.77%	1.97%	0.00%	0.00%	0.00%	0.00%
Peach	0.27%	8.39%	0.00%	3.04%	88.30%	11.70%	4.76%	1.95%	1.53%	0.00%	0.08%	0.06%	0.00%
Peanut Butter	50.00%	6.25%	0.00%	43.75%	0.00%	100.00%	6.13%	0.06%	0.06%	0.00%	0.00%	0.00%	0.00%
Peanuts, Oil Roasted, Salted	52.50%	4.18%	0.00%	41.87%	1.45%	98.55%	4.03%	0.08%	0.08%	0.00%	0.00%	0.00%	0.00%
Pear, Bartlett	0.16%	9.69%	0.00%	6.05%	84.10%	15.90%	0.43%	2.50%	6.76%	0.00%	0.00%	0.00%	0.00%
Persimmon, Japanese	0.19%	12.54%	0.00%	6.97%	80.30%	19.70%	1.54%	5.44%	5.56%	0.00%	0.00%	0.00%	0.00%
Pineapple, Canned in Juice, Drained	0.10%	14.30%	0.00%	2.10%	83.50%	16.50%	8.70%	2.51%	3.08%	0.00%	0.00%	0.00%	0.00%
Pistachio Paste	55.00%	9.70%	0.00%	35.30%	0.00%	100.00%	3.35%	2.89%	2.73%	0.00%	0.73%	0.00%	0.00%
Pomegranate Juice	0.29%	12.60%	0.00%	1.11%	86.00%	14.00%	0.00%	6.28%	6.37%	0.00%	0.00%	0.00%	0.00%
Pumpkin, Canned (Libby's)	0.41%	4.10%	0.00%	5.49%	90.00%	10.00%	0.00%	2.05%	2.05%	0.00%	0.00%	0.00%	0.00%
Raspberry	0.19%	2.68%	0.00%	11.53%	85.60%	14.40%	0.01%	0.99%	1.68%	0.00%	0.00%	0.00%	0.00%
Rice, Arborio, Uncooked	0.40%	0.00%	0.00%	87.60%	12.00%	88.00%	0.00%	0.00%	0.00%	0.00%	0.00%	0.00%	0.00%
Ricotta, Whole Milk	11.00%	0.00%	11.44%	0.00%	77.56%	22.44%	0.00%	0.00%	0.00%	3.63%	0.00%	0.00%	0.00%
Rosewater	0.00%	0.00%	0.00%	0.00%	100.00%	0.00%	0.00%	0.00%	0.00%	0.00%	0.00%	0.00%	0.00%

Ingredient	Fats	Sugars	Milk Solids	Other Solids	Water	Total Solids	Sucrose	Dextrose	Fructose	Lactose	Maltose	Galactose	Ethanol
Rum, 80 Proof	0.00%	0.00%	0.00%	0.01%	66.60%	0.01%	0.00%	0.00%	0.00%	0.00%	0.00%	0.00%	33.39%
Saffron, Powdered	5.85%	0.00%	0.00%	82.25%	11.90%	100.00%	0.00%	0.00%	0.00%	0.00%	0.00%	0.00%	0.00%
Salt (Sodium Chloride)	0.00%	0.00%	0.00%	100.00%	0.00%	100.00%	0.00%	0.00%	0.00%	0.00%	0.00%	0.00%	0.00%
Sherry, Cream	0.00%	13.00%	0.00%	0.00%	69.00%	13.00%	0.00%	0.00%	13.00%	0.00%	0.00%	0.00%	18.00%
Sour Cream	19.40%	0.00%	5.85%	1.65%	73.10%	26.90%	0.00%	0.00%	0.00%	3.41%	0.00%	0.00%	0.00%
Strawberry	0.22%	5.34%	0.00%	3.34%	91.10%	8.90%	0.11%	2.39%	2.84%	0.00%	0.00%	0.00%	0.00%
Sugar (Sucrose)	0.00%	100.00%	0.00%	0.00%	0.00%	100.00%	100.00%	0.00%	0.00%	0.00%	0.00%	0.00%	0.00%
Sugar, Turbinado	0.00%	99.20%	0.00%	0.77%	0.03%	99.97%	99.20%	0.00%	0.00%	0.00%	0.00%	0.00%	0.00%
Tamarind	0.60%	38.80%	0.00%	29.20%	31.40%	68.60%	0.37%	18.18%	18.54%	0.00%	1.71%	0.00%	0.00%
Tamarind Puree (Goya, 22%)	0.13%	8.54%	0.00%	6.42%	84.91%	15.09%	0.08%	4.00%	4.08%	0.00%	0.38%	0.00%	0.00%
Vanilla Extract	0.06%	12.60%	0.00%	0.34%	52.60%	13.00%	12.60%	0.00%	0.00%	0.00%	0.00%	0.00%	34.40%
Water	0.00%	0.00%	0.00%	0.00%	100.00%	0.00%	0.00%	0.00%	0.00%	0.00%	0.00%	0.00%	0.00%
Watermelon	0.15%	6.20%	0.00%	2.20%	91.45%	8.55%	1.21%	1.58%	3.36%	0.00%	0.06%	0.00%	0.00%
Whiskey, Irish 80 Proof	0.00%	0.00%	0.00%	0.01%	66.60%	0.01%	0.00%	0.00%	0.00%	0.00%	0.00%	0.00%	33.39%
Zucchero di Canna	0.00%	99.20%	0.00%	0.77%	0.03%	99.97%	99.20%	0.00%	0.00%	0.00%	0.00%	0.00%	0.00%

Appendix C: PAC Table

PAC (*potere anticongelante*) is a measure of the relative anti-freezing power of a gelato ingredient. Of primary concern are sugars, salt, and ethanol. No other ingredients are present in sufficient quantity to have a major impact on the freezing point of the gelato.

PAC is calculated in relation to sucrose. One PAC unit is the anti-freezing power of a 1% solution of sucrose.

To calculate the PAC of any ingredient, divide the molecular weight of sucrose (342.297) by the molecular weight of the ingredient, multiply by 100, and then multiply by the van 't Hoff constant for the ingredient. Except for salt (sodium chloride), the van 't Hoff constant is 1 for all ingredients of interest in making gelato. For salt, the van 't Hoff constant is 2 because salt separates into two ions in solution.

Ingredient	Molecular Weight	van 't Hoff Constant	PAC
Sucrose	342.297	1	100
Dextrose	180.156	1	190
Ethanol	46.07	1	743
Fructose	180.156	1	190
Galactose	180.156	1	190
Lactose	342.297	1	100
Maltose	342.30	1	100
Salt	58.44	2	1171

Appendix D: POD Tables

These are the values for POD (*potere dolcificante*), also referred to as sweetening power or relative sweetness, that I use when developing gelato formulas:

Sugar	POD
Sucrose	100
Dextrose	75
Fructose	150
Galactose	65
Lactose	16
Maltose	30

Unlike PAC (*potere anticongelante*), also referred to as anti-freezing power or freezing point depression, POD is determined by panels of tasters making the results inherently variable. This table gives POD values from several different sources.[42] Note: Sucrose is the reference and is always assigned a value of 100.

	Source						
	Wikipedia (2022)	O'Brien-Nabors (2012)	Dream Scoops (2018b)	Pancoast and Junk (1980)	Hull (2010)	Jiménez-Flores, *et al.* (2006)	Nickerson (1974)
Sweetener							
Sucrose	100		100	100	100	100	100
Dextrose			74	70–80	80	75	56
Fructose	117–175		173	150–160	170	115	125
Galactose	65						
Honey			130				
Invert Sugar			125				
Karo Light Corn Syrup			33				
Lactose	16		16	40		20	30
Maltodextrin			20				
Maltose	33–35						
Trehalose		15–45[43]					
42DE Corn Syrup				40–45	50		

---

[42] Adapted from Mullan (2012) and other sources.
[43] At concentrations from 2.3% to 22.2% (w/w).

Appendix E: Pasteurization Tables

These tables are adapted from the *Grade A Pasteurized Milk Ordinance, 2019 Revision,* published by the U.S. Department of Health and Human Services, Public Health Service, Food and Drug Administration. These are provided for reference only. Appropriate pasteurization parameters must be determined based on your own jurisdictional law and regulation.

For Gelato That Does Not Contain Eggs

Temperature[44]	Time	Type
66°C	30 minutes	Vat Pasteurization
75°C	15 seconds	High Temperature, Short Time

For Gelato That Contains Eggs

Temperature	Time	Type
69°C	30 minutes	Vat Pasteurization

---

[44] These temperatures reflect the fact that gelato contains added sweeteners, which therefore requires that the temperatures be three degrees Celsius higher than would otherwise be needed.

Appendix F: Glossary

Balancing	The foundation of developing a gelato formula that creates the characteristic gelato experience of consistency, texture, temperature, appearance, and intensity of flavor. Balancing requires that each component of the gelato base (fats, sugars, nonfat milk solids, other solids, water, and total solids) be present within established percentages.
Batch Freezer	A machine that produces gelato, sorbetto, and other frozen desserts by chilling the base (also called the mixture) and blending it through the action of the dasher. A batch freezer is so named because it freezes batches of base, unlike a continuous freezer that has a constant input of base and output of frozen product.
Blast Freezer	A freezer unit that is designed to rapidly bring down the temperature of whatever is put in it, often by blowing very cold air. The faster gelato is hardened after being removed from the batch freezer, the smaller the ice crystals, making for a smoother product. A blast freezer is essential for the commercial production of artisan gelato. For small-scale production, a well-maintained deep freezer is adequate as batch after batch of gelato will not be added within a short period of time.
Casein	The predominant protein in cow's milk, comprising approximately 80% of the protein. Casein is poorly soluble in water and is typically suspended in milk as casein micelles.
Coalescence	The process of smaller droplets merging to form larger droplets. When applied to gelato, fat droplets that are in suspension can coalesce. Air that is present as a foam (bubbles), can coalesce with other air bubbles. Partial coalescence of fat occurs as the gelato base is being mixed and frozen in the batch freezer. It contributes to the texture of gelato.
Colligative Property	A property of a solution that is dependent on the ratio of solute particles to solvent particles. Colligative properties are not dependent on the nature of the solute, but only on the solvent. The colligative property of importance in making gelato is freezing point depression. Solutes, such as sugar molecules, lower the freezing point of water, the solvent which is the major component of gelato.
Colloid	A mixture in which very small particles of one substance are dispersed throughout another substance in which the first substance is not soluble. Gelatin and jelly are both colloids.

Continuous Phase	In an emulsion, the continuous phase is the substance present in larger quantity in which the second, non-miscible (non-mixable), substance is distributed. The substance present in smaller quantity is the discontinuous phase.
Denaturation	As applied to proteins, denaturation is the process of breaking many weak bonds within the molecule, producing a structure that is looser and more random than the highly ordered structure of a protein in its original state. Denaturation can be caused by heat or chemical means.
Dextrose Equivalent	The amount of reducing sugars present in a product compared to pure dextrose on a dry basis. Related to gelato, the dextrose equivalent (DE) of a syrup indicates the extent to which starch has been converted to sugar. The degree of conversion of a starch, such as cornstarch, to sugars, such as are present in corn syrup, can vary. The DE is a measure of the degree of conversion. Because the sugars produced in the conversion are not all dextrose, and the exact composition of sugars produced varies with the method of conversion, DE is not a measure of the sweetness of the product. In addition, DE does not correlate directly with anti-freezing power. A reputable supplier should be able to provide you with the relative sweetness of the syrup from which you can estimate its effect on POD and the average molecular weight of the syrup from which you can calculate PAC.
Disaccharide	A sugar that contains two monosaccharide molecules (simple sugars) joined together. Sucrose (table sugar) and lactose are both disaccharides.
Discontinuous Phase	In an emulsion, the discontinuous phase is the substance present in smaller quantity. It is dispersed in the substance present in larger quantity, which is referred to as the continuous phase. The substances forming the continuous and discontinuous phases are not miscible (mixable).
Disproportionation	When speaking of gelato, disproportionation is the process whereby some of the air in a smaller air bubble within the gelato transfers to a larger air bubble.
Emulsifier	A substance that helps two non-miscible (non-mixable) liquids mix together. Emulsifiers have a hydrophilic end and a hydrophobic end. The hydrophilic end extends into the water and the hydrophobic end extends into the oil. Egg yolks, predominantly because of the lecithin they contain, are emulsifiers. Casein, the predominant protein found in milk, is an emulsifier.
Emulsion	A mixture of two (or more) liquids which are not miscible (mixable or soluble). Emulsions are typically categorized as oil-in-water emulsions or water-in-oil emulsions. Milk is an oil-in-water emulsion whereas mayonnaise is a water-in-oil emulsion.
Endosperm	The tissue in a plant seed that surrounds and acts as a food store for the developing plant embryo.

Freezing Point Depression	One of the colligative properties of a solvent. When solute molecules or ions are introduced into a solvent, the freezing point of that solution is lower than the freezing point of the pure solvent. The amount of the freezing point depression is proportional to the ratio of solute to solvent, usually expressed as molality.
Gelataio	An individual who makes and/or sells gelato (Italian).
Gelatician	An individual who makes gelato (English).
Gelatiere	Though there is some difference of opinion, the word *gelatiere* refers to an individual who makes gelato, like a gelataio, but who is more of an artist in that the individual also develops formulas for gelato. The plural (which you will also see in this book) is *gelatieri*. [The feminine forms are *gelatiera* and *gelatiere* for singular and plural, but they can be confusing because gelatiera is more commonly used to refer to the machine that freezes gelato.]
Hydration	In very general terms, hydration is the process of water absorption by a substance.
Hydrophilic	Having an affinity for water. The term comes from the Greek words for "water-loving."
Hydrophobic	Repelling or not mixing with water. The term comes from the Greek words for "water-fearing."
Molality	A measure of the concentration of a solution. It is expressed as the number of moles of a solute per kilogram of solvent.
Mole	In chemistry, a mole (or mol) is a count of the number of atoms or molecules. One mole is equal to 602,214,076,000,000,000,000,000 atoms or molecules.
Monosaccharide	A simple sugar that cannot be divided into simpler sugars.
MSNF	An abbreviation for *milk solids nonfat*. It refers to all the serum solids (that is, water-soluble solids) in milk that are comprised of protein, sugar, and minerals.
Nucleation	As applied to gelato, nucleation is the formation of ice crystals in the gelato base. Nucleation occurs on the cold walls of the drum of the batch freezer where small numbers of water molecules become arranged in the crystalline (solid) form of ice. After nucleation, additional water molecules are deposited on these crystals causing the ice crystals to grow.
Overrun	The amount of air incorporated into gelato as it is being frozen. Overrun is expressed as the volume of air incorporated as a percentage of the original volume of the liquid gelato base. At 25% overrun, 1 liter of gelato base would have 250 milliliters of air incorporated for a total volume of 1.25 liters.

PAC	An acronym that stands for the Italian term, *potere anticongelante* (anti-freezing power). PAC is a user-friendly way to apply the concepts of freezing point depression to gelato. One PAC unit is defined as the freezing point depression power of a 1% solution of sucrose. The approximate serving temperature of a gelato in degrees Celsius is equal to its PAC divided by -2. Thus, a gelato with a PAC of 26 has a freezing point depression power equivalent to a 26% solution of sucrose and an approximate serving temperature of $-13°C$
Partial Coalescence	See *Coalescence*.
POD	An acronym that stands for the Italian term, *potere dolcificante* (sweetening power). Similar to PAC, sucrose is used as the standard. One POD unit is defined as the sweetness of a 1% solution of sucrose. Unlike freezing point depression which can be measured precisely, sweetening power can only be determined by taste testing. Because of this, the published POD values for different sugars can vary.
Polysaccharide	A carbohydrate consisting of three or more monosaccharides joined together.
Reducing Sugar	A sugar that is able to donate an electron in a chemical reaction. All monosaccharides are reducing sugars but not all disaccharides and polysaccharides are. The amount of reducing sugar present is referred to as the dextrose equivalent (DE). The DE of dextrose is 100, but the DE of sucrose, a sweeter sugar that is a disaccharide, is 0. The chemical structure of sucrose makes it unable to donate an electron.
Scoopability	A term that refers to the hardness of gelato. A gelato that is too hard, typically from too much frozen water or too much solid matter in the gelato, is not easily scoopable.
Solute	The substance, present in the smaller quantity, that is dissolved in another substance (the solvent) to form a solution. A solute can be solid, liquid, or gas.
Solution	A homogeneous mixture of one or more substances (the solutes) dissolved in another, usually liquid, substance (the solvent).
Solvent	The substance, present in the larger quantity, in which another substance (the solute) is dissolved to form a solution. A solvent is usually a liquid.
Stabilizer	When referring to gelato, a stabilizer is a substance that binds water molecules and thickens the mixture, making it more viscous. Heating a mixture of cornstarch and water makes the water more viscous. In this instance, cornstarch is a stabilizer.
Suspension	A heterogeneous mixture in which solids are distributed throughout another substance, usually liquid, without being dissolved. Muddy water is an example of a suspension.

van 't Hoff Constant	A measure of the extent to which molecules of a solute separate in solution. A molecule of sucrose remains a molecule of sucrose in solution so the van 't Hoff constant is 1. A molecule of sodium chloride (salt) separates into sodium ions and chloride ions in solution so the van 't Hoff constant is 2. The number of particles, such as molecules and ions, in solution affects the colligative properties of a solution. For gelato, the colligative property of importance is freezing point depression, which is related to the hardness or softness of the gelato at a specific temperature.
Whey Protein	A group of proteins found in milk. Whey protein comprises approximately 20% of the protein found in cow's milk. Whey protein denatures at high temperature.

Appendix G: References and Resources

References

Clarke, Chris (2004). *The Science of Ice Cream*. Cambridge, England: The Royal Society of Chemistry.

Cook's Illustrated (n.d.) "What Kind of Mustard Should Be Used in a Vinaigrette?" Accessed January 3, 2022. https://www.americastestkitchen.com/cooksillustrated/how_tos/6627-what-kind-of-mustard-should-be-used-in-a-vinaigrette.

Dream Scoops (2018a). "Ice Cream Science." Accessed November 1, 2021. https://www.dreamscoops.com/ice-cream-science.

Dream Scoops (2018b). "The Importance of Sugar in Ice Cream." Accessed July 18, 2022. https://www.dreamscoops.com/ice-cream-science/sugar-in-ice-cream.

Food and Drug Administration (2019). *Grade "A" Pasteurized Milk Ordinance*. U.S. Department of Health and Human Services. Accessed May 29, 2022. https://www.fda.gov/media/140394/download.

Food Safety and Inspection Service (2017). "Danger Zone." U.S. Department of Agriculture. Accessed August 5, 2022. https://www.fsis.usda.gov/food-safety/safe-food-handling-and-preparation/food-safety-basics/danger-zone-40f-140f.

Gelatieri per il Gelato (2012). *Definizione di Gelato Artigianale di Tradizione Italiana*. Accessed January 8, 2022. http://marcodd.it/gelatieriperilgelato.com/wp-content/uploads/2018/04/definizione-del-gelato-artigianale-di-tradizione-italiana.pdf.

Hull, Peter (2010). *Glucose Syrups: Technology and Applications*. Chichester, England: Wiley-Blackwell.

Jiménez-Flores, Rafael, Norman J. Klipfel, and Joseph Tobias (2006). "Ice Cream and Frozen Desserts." In *Dairy Science and Technology Handbook, Volume 2: Product Manufacturing*, edited by Y. H. Hui. Hoboken, NJ: John Wiley & Sons.

Mullan, W.M.A. (2012). "How Do You Get the Sweetness of Ice Cream or Gelato Just Right?" Accessed October 21, 2021. https://www.dairyscience.info/index.php/ice-cream/220-ice-cream-sweetness.html. Updated May 2013. Updated February 2014. Updated April 2017.

Mullan, W.M.A. (2013). "Perfect Ice Cream or Gelato. Getting the Hardness or 'Scoopability' Just Right." Accessed August 9. 2021. https://www.dairyscience.info/index.php/ice-cream/228-ice-cream-hardness.html. First posted 13 May 2013. Modified: February 2014; August 2015; January 2017; January 2018; April 2018.

Nickerson, T.A. (1974). "Lactose." In *Fundamentals of Dairy Chemistry*, 2nd Edition, edited by B.H. Webb, A.H. Johnson, and J.A. Alford. Westport, CT: AVI Publishing.

O'Brien-Nabors, Lyn, ed. (2012). *Alternative Sweeteners*, 4th Edition. Boca Raton, FL: CRC Press, 444–445.

Pancoast, Harry M., and W. Ray Junk (1980). *Handbook of Sugars*. Westport, CT: AVI Pub. Co.

Underbelly (2016a). "Ice Cream Emulsifiers." Accessed December 28, 2021. https://under-belly.org/ice-cream-emulsifiers.

Underbelly (2016b). "Ice Cream Stabilizers." Accessed 4 January 2022. https://under-belly.org/ice-cream-stabilizers.

Wikipedia (2021a). "Locust Bean Gum." Accessed January 3, 2022. https://en.wikipedia.org/wiki/Locust_bean_gum.

Wikipedia (2021b). "Guar Gum." Accessed January 3, 2022. https://en.wikipedia.org/wiki/Guar_gum.

Wikipedia (2021c). "Corn Starch." Accessed January 3, 2022. https://en.wikipedia.org/wiki/Corn_starch.

Wikipedia (2021d). "Gelatin." Accessed January 3, 2022. https://en.wikipedia.org/wiki/Gelatin.

Wikipedia (2022). "Sweetness." Accessed July 18, 2022. https://en.wikipedia.org/wiki/Sweetness.

Websites

Dairy Science Food Technology: www.dairyscience.info

Dream Scoops: www.dreamscoops.com

Underbelly: https://under-belly.org

Books

Corvitto, Angelo. *I Segreti del Gelato: Il Gelato Senza Segreti.* Barcelona: Vilbo Ediciones y Publicidad, 2005.

Kopfer, Torrance. *Making Artisan Gelato: 45 Recipes and Techniques for Crafting Flavor-Infused Gelato and Sorbet at Home.* Beverly, MA: Quarry Books, 2009.

Tubby, Linda. *Gelato, Ice Creams, and Sorbets.* London: Pavilion Books, 2015.

Weir, Caroline, and Robin Weir. *Ice Creams, Sorbets, & Gelati: The Definitive Guide.* London: Grub Street, 2010.

Index

A

air bubbles, 140, 151–152, 160–161
alcohol
    adding, 36
    Amaretto Gelato, 49
    Bourbon Old Fashioned Gelato, 56
    Irish Coffee Gelato, 80
    Maple Rum Raisin Gelato, 88
    overview of, 11
    PAC and, 146, 160
    Piña Colada Gelato, 101
    Rum Raisin Gelato, 109
    Tiramisù Gelato, 115–116
    Zabaione Gelato, 122
    Zuppa Inglese Gelato, 123
Almond Brittle Gelato, 46
Almond Gelato, 47
Amarena cherries
    Amarena Cherry Gelato, 48
    overview of, 12
Amaretto Gelato, 49
Apple Cinnamon Gelato, 50
Apple Puree
    Apple Cinnamon Gelato, 50
    recipe, 124
Apricot Gelato, 51

B

baked goods
    Cannoli Gelato, 58
    Carrot Cake Gelato, 60
    overview of, 13
    Tiramisù Gelato, 115–116
    Zuppa Inglese Gelato, 123
Banana Gelato, 52
Banoffi Gelato, 53
base
    cooking, 24–26
    cooling, 26–27
    maturing, 27–28
batch freezers, 29–31, 44–45
Blackberry Gelato, 54
blast freezers, 30–31
Blueberry Gelato, 55
Bourbon Old Fashioned Gelato, 56
Brown Butter
    Brown Butter Pecan Gelato, 57
    recipe, 124
buttermilk, 151

C

cacao (cocoa) products
    adding, 35
    Chocolate Gelato #1, 63
    Chocolate Gelato #2, 64
    Chocolate Peanut Butter Gelato, 65
    Dark Chocolate & Candied Orange Peel Gelato, 68
    Hazelnut Chocolate Gelato, 76
    Milk Chocolate Gelato, 91
    Milk Chocolate Peanut Butter Ripple Gelato, 92
    Mocha Gelato, 95
    overview of, 9–10
    Stracciatella Gelato, 112
    Tiramisù Gelato, 115–116
    White Chocolate Extra-Virgin Olive Oil Gelato, 121
    Zuppa Inglese Gelato, 123
cacao butter, 10
cacao liquor, 9
cacao mass, 9
cacao nibs, 9
cacao powder, 10
candied citrus peel (canditi), 12
Candied Orange Peel
    Dark Chocolate & Candied Orange Peel Gelato, 68
    recipe, 125
canned products, overview of, 13–14
Cannoli Gelato, 58
Cantaloupe Gelato, 59
Carrot Cake Gelato, 60
casein, 27, 150
Cheesecake Gelato, 61
Cherry Gelato, 62
chocolate. see cacao (cocoa) products
Chocolate Gelato #1, 63
Chocolate Gelato #2, 64
Chocolate Peanut Butter Gelato, 65
citrus
    candied citrus peel (canditi), 12
    Candied Orange Peel, 125

Dark Chocolate & Candied Orange Peel Gelato, 68
Lemon Gelato, 82–83
Lime Gelato, 85
Orange Cream Gelato, 96

coconut cream
Coconut Gelato, 66
overview of, 13–14
Piña Colada Gelato, 101

Coconut Gelato, 66
Coconut Gelato, Toasted, 117

coconut milk
overview of, 13–14
Toasted Coconut Gelato, 117
Toasted Coconut Milk, 127

Coconut Milk, Toasted, 127

coffee
Banoffi Gelato, 53
Coffee Gelato, 67
Irish Coffee Gelato, 80
Mocha Gelato, 95
overview of, 11
Tiramisù Gelato, 115–116
Vietnamese Coffee Gelato, 119, 128

component ingredients, 124–128
confectionary, overview of, 12
cornstarch, 9, 153
cream, overview of, 4

cream cheese
Carrot Cake Gelato, 60
Cheesecake Gelato, 61
overview of, 5
pasteurization and, 25, 26

Croccante
Almond Brittle Gelato, 46
recipe, 126

D

dairy products, overview of, 3–5
"danger zone," 26–27
Dark Chocolate & Candied Orange Peel Gelato, 68
dashers, 29–30

dates
Deglet Noor Date Gelato, 69
Medjool Date Gelato, 90

Deglet Noor Date Gelato, 69
dextrose, overview of, 5, 6, 7
dextrose equivalent (DE), 7
Dulce de Leche Gelato, 70

E

eggs
Egg Cream Gelato, 71
emulsions and, 139, 150
large-scale process with, 39
overview of, 8–9
pasteurization and, 25, 26
small-scale production with, 36
stabilizers and, 153
Zabaione Gelato, 122
Zuppa Inglese Gelato, 123

emulsifiers, 8–9, 149–151
emulsions, 139, 141

equipment
for commercial artisan production, 19–20
for small-scale artisan production, 17–19

Espresso
Coffee Gelato, 67
Irish Coffee Gelato, 80
Mocha Gelato, 95
recipe, 126
Tiramisù Gelato, 115–116
see also coffee

evaporated milk, overview of, 5
extracts and flavorings, overview of, 11–12

F

Fig Gelato, 72
Fiordilatte Gelato, 73

flowers
Hibiscus Gelato, 78
Hibiscus Infusion, 126
Lavender Gelato, 81
overview of, 12
Saffron and Rosewater Gelato, 110

foams, 140, 141

formulas
balancing, 43
batch size for, 44–45
creating, 163–173
direct versus indirect, 172–173
introduction to, 43–45
recipes versus, xiv
see also individual formulas

freezing, 29–30, 140–141
freezing point depression, 143–147
fructose, overview of, 5, 6
fruits

adding, 36
Amarena Cherry Gelato, 48
Apple Cinnamon Gelato, 50
Apple Puree, 124
Apricot Gelato, 51
balancing formulas and, 168
Banana Gelato, 52
Blackberry Gelato, 54
Blueberry Gelato, 55
Candied Orange Peel, 125
Cantaloupe Gelato, 59
Cherry Gelato, 62
Coconut Gelato, 66
Deglet Noor Date Gelato, 69
Fig Gelato, 72
Grape Gelato, 74
Guava Gelato, 75
heat treatment for, 37
Lemon Gelato, 82–83
Lime Gelato, 85
Mango Gelato, 86
Medjool Date Gelato, 90
Mixed Berry Gelato, 94
Orange Cream Gelato, 96
overview of, 11
Peach Gelato, 97
Peanut Butter and Jelly Gelato, 98
Persimmon Gelato, 100
Piña Colada Gelato, 101
Pineapple Gelato, 102
Pomegranate Gelato, 104
Pumpkin Pie Gelato, 105
Raspberry Gelato, 106
Strawberry Gelato, 113
Strawberry Sauce, 127
Tamarind Gelato, 114
Watermelon Gelato, 120

G

gelatin, 9, 153
gelato
    balancing, 163–167
    batch size for, 44, 171–172
    building in flavor, 167–168
    definition of, xii–xiv
    equipment for, 17–20
    greasy, 134
    hard, 133
    ice cream versus, xi–xiii
    icy, 132
    introduction to, xi–xv
    not smooth, 133–134
    process of making, 23–39, 45
    soft, 133
    texture of, 139–141
    troubleshooting, 131–134
    see also individual formulas
glucose and glucose syrup, overview of, 6–7
Grape Gelato, 74
guar gum, 8, 153
Guava Gelato, 75

H

hardening, 30–32
Hazelnut Chocolate Gelato, 76
Hazelnut Gelato, 77
herbs, overview of, 12
Hibiscus Gelato, 78
Hibiscus Infusion, 126
honey
    Honey Gelato, 79
    overview of, 8

I

ingredients
    adding flavoring, 35–36
    alcohol, 11
    baked goods, 13
    cacao (cocoa) products, 9–10
    canned products, 13–14
    coffee, 11
    component, 124–128
    composition of, 188–192
    confectionary, 12
    dairy products, 3–5
    extracts and flavorings, 11–12
    fruits, 11
    last-minute, 28
    mixing, 24
    nuts and nut-based products, 10
    researching composition of, 168–171
    stabilizers and emulsifiers, 8–9
    sugars and sweeteners, 5–8
    variation in, 43–44
    water, 8
    weighing, 23–24
Irish Coffee Gelato, 80

J

jam and fruit preserves, overview of, 12

L

Lavender Gelato, 81
lecithin, 9, 151
Lemon Gelato, 82–83
Licorice Gelato, 84
Lime Gelato, 85
locust bean gum, 8, 37, 152

M

Mango Gelato, 86
Maple Pecan Gelato, 87
Maple Rum Raisin Gelato, 88
maple syrup
    Maple Pecan Gelato, 87
    Maple Rum Raisin Gelato, 88
    overview of, 8
mascarpone
    Chocolate Gelato #1, 63
    Chocolate Gelato #2, 64
    Mascarpone Gelato, 89
    overview of, 5
    pasteurization and, 25, 26
    Tiramisù Gelato, 115–116
matrix, 141
maturation, 27–28
Medjool Date Gelato, 90
metric system, 172
milk, overview of, 3–4
Milk Chocolate Gelato, 91
Milk Chocolate Peanut Butter Ripple Gelato, 92
Mint Gelato, 93
Mixed Berry Gelato, 94
Mocha Gelato, 95
molar weight, 143–144

N

nonfat powdered milk, overview of, 4
nucleation, 140–141
nuts and nut-based products
    adding, 35–36
    Almond Brittle Gelato, 46
    Almond Gelato, 47
    Amaretto Gelato, 49
    Brown Butter Pecan Gelato, 57
    Chocolate Peanut Butter Gelato, 65
    Croccante, 126
    Hazelnut Chocolate Gelato, 76
    Hazelnut Gelato, 77
    Maple Pecan Gelato, 87
    Milk Chocolate Peanut Butter Ripple Gelato, 92
    overview of, 10
    Peanut Butter and Jelly Gelato, 98
    Peanut Butter Gelato, 99
    Pistachio Gelato, 103
    Salted Peanut Gelato, 111
    Toasted Nuts, 128

O

Orange Cream Gelato, 96
overrun, 140, 160–161

P

PAC
    adjusting, 175–178
    calculating, 145–147
    definition of, 43
    table for, 193
    worksheet for, 186–187
partial coalescence, 30, 150
pasteurization, 24–26, 37, 195
Peach Gelato, 97
peanut butter
    Chocolate Peanut Butter Gelato, 65
    Milk Chocolate Peanut Butter Ripple Gelato, 92
    Peanut Butter and Jelly Gelato, 98
    Peanut Butter Gelato, 99
    Peanut Butter Sauce, 127
Persimmon Gelato, 100
Piña Colada Gelato, 101
pineapple
    enzymatic activity of, 37
    overview of, 14
    Pineapple Gelato, 102
Pistachio Gelato, 103
POD
    adjusting, 179–180
    calculating, 178–179
    definition of, 43
    table for, 194
    worksheet for, 186–187
Pomegranate Gelato, 104
pumpkin
    overview of, 13
    Pumpkin Pie Gelato, 105

R

raisins
    Maple Rum Raisin Gelato, 88
    Raisins in Syrup, 127
    Rum Raisin Gelato, 109
Raspberry Gelato, 106
Rice Pudding Gelato, 107–108
ricotta
    Cannoli Gelato, 58
    overview of, 5
Rum Raisin Gelato, 109

S

Saffron and Rosewater Gelato, 110
salt, adjusting, 28
Salted Peanut Gelato, 111
scoopability, 159–161
serving/serving temperature, 31–32, 44, 160–161
solid, gelato as, 140–141
solution, gelato as, 141
sour cream
    adding, 36, 37
    overview of, 5
spices
    Apple Cinnamon Gelato, 50
    overview of, 12
    Pumpkin Pie Gelato, 105
    Saffron and Rosewater Gelato, 110
stabilizers, 8–9, 151–153, 171
Stracciatella Gelato, 112
straining, 26
Strawberry Gelato, 113
Strawberry Sauce
    Peanut Butter and Jelly Gelato, 98
    recipe, 127
sucrose, overview of, 5–6
sugars and sweeteners
    overview of, 5–8
    PAC and, 146
    POD and, 155–157, 178–180
    reducing, 7
sweetening power, 155–157

T

Tamarind Gelato, 114
Tiramisù Gelato, 115–116
Toasted Coconut Gelato, 117
Toasted Coconut Milk, 127
Toasted Nuts, 128

trehalose, overview of, 5, 7
troubleshooting, 131–134

V

vanilla
    overview of, 11–12
    Vanilla Gelato, 118
Vietnamese Coffee, 128
Vietnamese Coffee Gelato, 119

W

water, overview of, 8
Watermelon Gelato, 120
whey proteins, 150
White Chocolate Extra-Virgin Olive Oil Gelato, 121

Y

yogurt
    adding, 36, 37
    overview of, 5

Z

Zabaione Gelato, 122
Zuppa Inglese Gelato, 123

www.ingramcontent.com/pod-product-compliance
Lightning Source LLC
Chambersburg PA
CBHW041236240426
43661CB00066B/2906